IN FIFTY YEARS WE'LL ALL BE CHICKS

. . . AND OTHER
COMPLAINTS
FROM AN ANGRY
MIDDLE-AGED
WHITE GUY

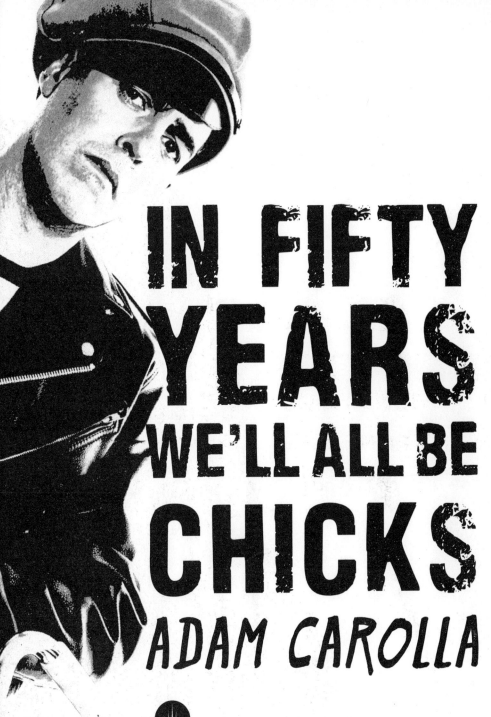

IN FIFTY YEARS WE'LL ALL BE CHICKS

ADAM CAROLLA

CROWN
ARCHETYPE

NEW YORK

Copyright © 2010 by Lotzi, Inc.

Published in the United States by Crown Archetype, an imprint of
the Crown Publishing Group, a division of Random House, Inc., New York.
www.crownpublishing.com

Crown Archetype with colophon is a trademark of Random House, Inc.

Library of Congress Cataloging-in-Publication Data is available upon request.

ISBN 978-0-307-71737-5

Printed in the United States of America

Design by Maria Elias

10 9 8 7 6 5 4 3 2 1

First Edition

This is dedicated to everyone who paid retail for this book.

CONTENTS

GET
IT
ON

For far too long I've stood idly by and watched a problem in this country get worse and worse. I'm talking about the pussification of America. We've become self-entitled, thin-skinned, hyperallergic, gender-neutral, *View*-viewing little girls. What we used to settle with common sense or a fist we now settle with hand sanitizer and lawyers.

Masculinity by any definition is disappearing. My fear is that in fifty years we'll all be chicks. I've written this in hopes of a course correction. If just one person reads this book and demands a salad *with* a hard-boiled egg and *without* goat cheese; if just one person reads this book and decides to change his own oil; if just one person reads this book, slips in a supermarket, and *doesn't* call an attorney, then I've done a horrible job and my family is going to starve. I need to sell a shitload of these things.

A LITTLE BIT ABOUT THE AUTHOR

I grew up in Los Angeles's San Fernando Valley in the seventies. I was a product of separation. I would have been a product of divorce, but divorce involves filling out paperwork and paying a county clerk sixty bucks to file it. And since there were no assets to divide, and no dog to argue over, that just left me and my sister. And the chances of my parents having a custody battle over us are about the same as two vegetarians having a custody battle over a pork chop.

The reason it took so long to write this book is that in an earlier part of my life I was a jock and a builder that lived a very blue-collar existence, not the kind that would inspire a book. I was always funny and had interesting ideas, but between the Los Angeles Unified School District and the un-unified Carolla family, I never heard the words "That's funny, you should write that down." In class my jokes and wisecracks just earned me the label of "disruptive," and at home my jokes fell on depressed, distracted ears.

My only salvation was football. I finally found something I was good at. I started playing at age seven. Football for me was an island of camaraderie and discipline in a world of depression and chaos.

My family was a devastating combination of cheap and poor. When you're cheap, poor is a great excuse. It's like if a guy is really lazy and in a wheelchair. He wouldn't have helped you move even if he was able-bodied. I was splitting time between the dilapidated shack that my mom was squatting in (it was her mother's second house, which she bought for ten thousand dollars in 1951) and my dad's one-bedroom apartment in a crappier part of North Hollywood. We were on food stamps and welfare. My mother was severely depressed and unable to keep up the house. Thus it was always a source of embarrassment for me. I slept in a converted service porch that was a little smaller than a prison cell and that housed the water heater, the washing machine (no dryer), and the electric meter. We were the only house in the Valley where the meter reader did his job from inside the house. It was very *Green Acres*. The house was a hundred years old with one bathroom, no air-conditioning, a lawn that was dead, and a roof that was sliding off. The final insult came in '71 when the earthquake took the chimney down into the neighbor's yard and never was replaced. The house didn't even have a garage to hide my mom's pile-of-shit car.

To compound my embarrassment, I couldn't read or write. As a child of the seventies, I spent first through fourth grade attending an "alternative" school. It offered a practical alternative to learning. It was pretty much one long ceramics class with a little acoustic guitar and some face painting mixed in. By the time I entered the L.A. Unified School system, even though I was entering the fifth grade, my reading level was at zygote. This was a great source of shame for me. It was a secret I kept like a survivor of incest. Except I was raped by a potter's wheel. Happily, my dirty little secret dovetailed nicely with L.A. Unified's "don't ask, don't tell" policy. My only salvation was sports and a sense of humor.

By my senior year at North Hollywood High, I'd managed to make the All Valley football team and was offered a number of scholarships to midsize colleges.

Why didn't I just take the SATs, fill out the paperwork, and take the free ride to a good university? As I mentioned above, reading and

California State Polytechnic University, Pomona

DEPARTMENT OF INTERCOLLEGIATE ATHLETICS

3801 West Temple Avenue, Pomona, California 91768 (714) 598-4611

Dear Adam,

We at California State Polytechnic University, Pomona are very interested in you as a prospective student-athlete. Your football potential is most impressive and we would like you to know that we consider you as one of our prospective "blue-chip" recruits for this coming season.

Our goal is to build a football program that can compete favorably on the national level. We feel we are progressing steadily with our head coach and former National Football League star quarterback Roman Gabriel at the helm. Your talent could assist us in making this goal a reality.

We are putting together a championship program at Cal Poly Pomona and we urge you to consider attending our university. Cal Poly University is committed to academic excellence as well as athletic success and you may rest assured we will make every effort to help you attain a quality education and a degree from one of the great universities in the West.

We welcome student-athletes who are dedicated to excellence in academics and athletics.

Cordially,

Dr. Howard Hohman
Director of Athletics

Cal Poly Pomona no longer has a football program.

writing was not my strong suit and to be fair to my parents, I'm not sure if they knew about the scholarship offers.

The next five years were a montage of carpet cleaning, crappy apartments, and ditch digging. One night, sometime in my early twenties, I decided to honestly assess myself. I came to the conclusion that I was good with my hands and had a good sense of humor.

Since I was working with my hands at the time and miserable, I decided to pursue the latter. I decided I'd give myself until my thirtieth birthday to make something happen.

The first time I tried stand-up comedy was at an open-mic night at the Comedy Store. I won't tell you how it went, I'll just tell you the story of what happened a couple hours after my first time onstage. After the show, I went back to my friend Jaynee's house, and before we headed out again she said she wanted to check her messages. It was the old-school message machine that would keep recording when somebody picked up. I stood next to her while she checked her messages, and one of them was from her friend Kim. It started with "Hey Jaynee, it's Kim. How was Adam's show?" Then I heard Jaynee's sister picking up the phone: "Jaynee's not home yet, but I was at the show." Kim said, "How did it go?" At that point Jaynee reached for the pause button, but I told her to let it go. And then I heard an honest, long, horrible evaluation of my stand-up potential. Imagine a seasoned hooker describing a roll in the sack with a fourteen-year-old virgin, and you get the idea. I was demoralized. I learned two important lessons that night. Just because all the guys are laughing on the job site doesn't mean you can walk onstage and achieve the same result, and Jaynee's sister is a bitch.

You have to understand, this is the mid-eighties: There was no Comedy Central, no FX, no YouTube. The only outlets for comedy were stand-up, *Saturday Night Live,* and that stupid sitcom with Cousin Balki.

A friend of mine's mom suggested I take improv classes at the Groundlings. That came easier to me, and I enjoyed the collaborations. When I was done with the basic class, they said, "You're funny but you're raw. And the only way we'll let you move up to the next level is if you take an acting class," which I did. I enjoyed doing group improv immensely. It combined the camaraderie I missed from football with comedy, and for the first time I was exposed to smart, funny, articulate, educated people. It was quite a pleasant culture shock going from the poverty, addiction, and illiteracy of the job site. Although it

5

always made for funny conversation with the other idiots I was swinging a hammer with.

"You're doing comedy at the Improv?"

"No, I'm doing improv comedy."

"With the groundhogs?"

"No, they're called the Groundlings. They're named after the guys who couldn't get good seats to a play in the 1600s."

"That's gay. How much do they pay you?"

"Actually, I pay them."

"Now that's gay and retarded. Mike, get over here, you gotta hear this!"

I swung a hammer by day and took improv classes by night. After four years, it was finally time for my advanced class. The class consisted of two performances over the course of three months, and twenty-four hours after the second performance they would tell you whether you made the Sunday company or if it was time to turn in your whoopee cushion. I, as luck would have it, had a great first show and a horrible second show. They're supposed to weigh them evenly, but the good show was a month and a half before and the shitty show was only twelve hours earlier. Even so, I kept my fingers crossed. When the word came that I didn't make the Sunday company, I was devastated. It felt much the same as when I stopped playing football. I had invested so much time and money and made so many friends, and it was all over. To make matters worse, by this time I was living in a no-bedroom apartment. I know they call it a studio, but if a two-bedroom apartment is called a two-bedroom and a one-bedroom apartment is called a one-bedroom, you get the idea. So living with my stripper girlfriend in a crappy part of Hollywood, I was five years away from my thirtieth birthday and a million miles away from a career in comedy. One day my girlfriend was reading through the free ads in the *Drama-Logue* and came across one entitled FORMING AN IMPROV TROUPE. So I showed up the first night. There are pros and cons to being one of the first people in an improv troupe. The bad news is there are only eight of you, and at least five of you suck. The good news is you just made the main company. The theater was directly across the street from the Italian restaurant where Robert Blake didn't shoot his wife. Me and the director, Mark Sweeney, used to stand in front of the restaurant on Saturday nights and hand out flyers only to watch people fold them in half and pick their teeth with them on the way to the car. The average attendance at a Saturday-night show was four and a half people, and one night we did a show where the only people in the audience were my grandparents. We decided to call ourselves the Acme Theatre because we knew the *LA Weekly* did their theater reviews alphabetically and we wanted to be at the top. Plus the *Weekly* would run the same review every week and we would only do two productions a year, so it was important to be front and center. The first review we ever got in the *LA Weekly* featured this line, "Mark Sweeney's bloodless conception is dead on arrival."

This review ran for eight months. Still, we kept moving forward. I even built our new theater in my hometown of North Hollywood. Logically it made no sense to continue, but instinctively I knew that all the writing, improvising, and performing would pay off one day. Even if it was just for my grandparents.

I was basically flatlining. Even though I was one of the founding members and had built the theater, I realized it was time to quit Acme. My thirtieth birthday was just around the corner—the imaginary line in the sand for my career. (Next life I'll make it nineteen.) I quit the Acme Theatre, I was still living in the house with no heat, I was making twenty bucks a pop teaching the 6:30 A.M. boxing class at Bodies in Motion, and I was doing freelance carpentry jobs. One day I was driving over Laurel Canyon into Hollywood to deliver an entertainment unit I'd built. I was listening to newly employed Jimmy Kimmel doing sports on a local morning show, *Kevin and Bean*. He told the story about Bobby McFerrin breaking his leg on the ski slopes and then said, "What's a brother doing skiing anyway?" Michael the Maintenance Man, a brother who was less interested in

HOW ARE WE DRIVING? CALL TWO-ROADS According to their press release, the Two Road Players' director M.D. Sweeney was aiming for something different from the improv-group staple of "hip, irreverent" comedy. He got it. This 11-sketch/eight-improv debut revue is neither hip nor particularly irreverent. For a comedic form that has traditionally set its sights on satirically skewering cultural excesses and pretensions, Sweeney's bloodless conception is dead on arrival. Part of the problem goes by the name of Warren Sorich, credited with writing four of the evening's more egregious misfires but *not* one of the performers on stage. Scripted improv clicks only when sketch ideas and characters evolve from material honed in the workshop — not at a typewriter. The show is not without its moments, usually those written and performed by Adam Carolla or John McCann. Carolla's "Coming Attraction" takes a nice swipe at the DMV via the horror-movie trailer; McCann's "Skipper Heem" does the Neptune Society one better by offering sports fishing along with sea burials. The evening's finest moment is McCann and Carolla together as beer-swilling good ol' boys, Monday-morning quarterbacking everything from last night's game to the finer points of high finance. The worst is Sweeney's failure to pull the plug on a final, tortuously interminable improv in which audience-suggested moods are incorporated in a sketch that then reruns and reruns and reruns. Two Roads Theater, 4348 Tujunga Ave., Studio City; Sat., 8 & 10 p.m.; indef. (818) 766-9381. (Bill Raden)

ADAM CAROLLA

Just to the left of this review was a large picture of a theater owner who'd lost his battle with AIDS.

skiing than he was in fighting, charged into the studio and started an argument with Jimmy. The next thing you knew, the fight was on. They put a call out for boxing trainers. I thought this could be my chance to see the inside of a radio studio. I'm not into feng shui or karma, but while sitting in my truck-ma, I felt something come over me. A cosmic mandate that said I had to be a part of this fight. But not to train Jimmy the Sports Guy. He was new, didn't seem to be well liked, and let's face it, white. I was really hoping to train Michael the Maintenance Man.

That week I called the radio station constantly, but I couldn't get through. So one morning before class I showed up in person. Unfortunately, I couldn't get into the building. Somebody told me they opened it at seven A.M. So I stood there by the elevators until somebody with a key card headed toward the back door. I flagged the guy down and asked if he could tell the people inside that there was a boxing instructor waiting by the elevators. Twenty minutes later, Jimmy came out. Our exchange was short since he was still working. I said, "I'm a boxing instructor." He said, "Fine, when do you want to start?" I said, "How about today?" He said, "Fine." I gave him directions to the gym and he said, "I'll see you at noon." He pulled up in a piece-of-shit RX-7 that had two different-colored fenders.

The fight was in just two weeks. That meant I had fourteen days to teach Jimmy to box and to convince him I was funny. I didn't come on too strong with the comedy at the beginning because I didn't want him to think I was some nut job just trying to get on the radio. But our daily boxing workouts quickly turned into twenty minutes of punching the heavy bag followed by two hours of drinking Snapples and talking about Howard Stern. Before I knew it, it was fight night. (Actually, the fight took place at seven forty-five in the morning, but "fight night" sounds better.) Here are the things I remember from the fight. The judges were Adam Sandler, Pat O'Brien, and John Wayne Bobbitt. Jimmy lost the fight, although it was close and I sent him out for the second round with no mouthpiece. I also remember telling Jimmy's then-wife before the fight, "Don't worry, they're wearing sixteen-ounce gloves and headgear. He won't get hurt." And she looked me in the eye and said, "I hope the guy beats the shit out of him."

I was interviewed on the radio a couple of times during the course of training Jimmy. I was extremely nervous. I remember the first joke I ever told on the radio. I was asked about Jimmy's boxing nickname. I said, "Originally we were going to call him the Brooklyn Assassin because he was born in Brooklyn, then I thought the Sand Man would be good, but after seeing him box we just settled on Jim."

Now the fight was over and so was my super-short radio career unless me and the Brooklyn Assassin could figure out a way to get me on the air. The fight was on a Friday and I was on the phone with Jimmy over that weekend and he said, "I want to get you on the air, but I don't know what you do." I said, "I'm an improvisational comedian, I'm best working off the cuff and shooting the shit with the guys." Jimmy, who only pulls his punches in the ring, said, "You better come up with a character and call in Monday morning." I knew two things: one, if I didn't hit a home run Monday morning on the *Kevin and Bean* show, there'd be no second chances, and two, I was horrible at characters.

I fell back on my Groundlings and Acme Theatre training and thought about what kind of character would feel unique yet familiar, funny and not fucked-out. I remembered some advice I'd like to say my dad gave me but that I'd read off a T-shirt (it was the name of a Pat Travers album), *Go for What You Know,* and that was the day Mr. Birchum, the woodshop teacher, was born.

Mr. Birchum taught remedial wood at Louis Pasteur Middle School in Monrovia, California. He hated kids and loved tools and his dog Sawbuck. Mr. Birchum immediately turned into an overnight sensation. Within months I was signed by the William Morris Agency. A few months after that *Loveline* radio, and then the TV show, fell into my lap.

Then came *The Man Show.* Jimmy and I had been dying to work together outside of radio. The problem was, nobody else was dying for us to work together. You have to understand that nobody in this town has a sense of humor or any imagination, and we were just a couple of schlubs from local radio. One afternoon when Jimmy was driving home after yet another failed attempt to hook up with a blonde and do some sort of he-said-she-said *Good Morning Burbank* show, he called me and said, "They keep trying to pair me up with these crazy blondes and tell me women need to like me. My own wife doesn't like me. I say we do our own show. Just me and you, our opinions, our voices. We hire our friends, one big frat house called *The Man Show*." I said, "That's an awesome idea. But first we should build a time machine so we can go back and kill Hitler's mom." (It sounded more feasible at the time.) Thank God I was wrong.

So there you have it. We're ready to get this book on the road now that you've had a peek behind my curtain to see how this monster was created, the sausage was made, and the fudge was packed.

The plaque said "best all around offensive and defensive player." It was all downhill after that.

KIDS THESE DAYS

I have two kids, twins, a boy and a girl. My girl I don't worry about; I'm sure she'll have six-pack abs, be well trained in mixed martial arts and will at least be bilingual, hopefully not bi-curious. My son I worry about. I'm pretty sure he's gonna be gay. At this point I'm just hoping he's not a bottom. Sorry to sound closed-minded and uptight, but let's face it, no dad wants his son to go gay. Not only do you get no grandkids, but I'm sure high school is no picnic for a fifteen-year-old gay boy. On the other hand, maybe I'm just viewing this through the bifocals of an old heterosexual dude. The way things are going, my son will probably get his ass kicked for *not* being gay. "Carolla thinks he's too good to suck cock. Come on, boys, let's get him."

Never mind gay. At the rate we're moving in a couple of years you won't be able to tell the difference between chicks and dudes. Sound extreme? Think about this. In every movie where advanced time-traveling beings come to our planet there's one constant: no junk. The crotch is always smooth—you can't tell the dude aliens from the chick aliens. It's not like in *Signs* Mel Gibson said, "Commander Zorback is cool, but his old lady is such a cunt." You can't tell them apart!

We can all look forward to a future of superlong fingers and no cock. I can't wait.

But that's the future. Kids today are soft, fat, and self-entitled. People ask why. Is it junk food? No. Junk food has been around for fifty years. As a matter of fact, back then it was worse. There were no salads or green apple slices in a McDonald's. If I went into a McDonald's when I was nine and someone handed me an apple, I would have kicked him in the nuts. Is it video games? Nope. Video games have been around for thirty years. None of the kids playing them back in the day were morbidly obese. We're all scratching our heads trying to figure out what we've introduced to society to ruin our kids. But it's not anything we've *added* that's ruined our kids, it's stuff we've gotten rid of.

First thing was the gym rope. Remember that thing that stretched from the floor to the ceiling in your gym class that you could never climb? That constant reminder that you were inferior? It's the only apparatus I'm aware of that makes it possible for you to be ridiculed while people stare at your nuts. Most of the kids couldn't make it to the top. But that wasn't the point; the point was you had to try while some middle-aged guy in a windbreaker who couldn't make it up a flight of stairs yelled at you. At some point somebody decided the ropes needed to be removed. Sparing the kids the rod is a good thing, sparing them the rope is a horrible idea. We should have put Lardo on that rope, given him a three-Mississippi head start, and then sent a subway rat scurrying after him. But we didn't want to shame the boy, so we took them all down, gave everyone a participation trophy and a pamphlet on secondhand smoke, and sent them to a cultural-diversity seminar. Taking down the rope would be a capital idea if there were no ropes in life. But they're everywhere. You just can't see them. They're in the workplace, they're in relationships, they're in every goal unrealized and expectation not met. The point everyone missed about the rope is you weren't supposed to make it to the top. It was there to create a fire that burned in the oversize belly of every

13

kid who couldn't shimmy up it. A fire that has now been forever extinguished with stuffed-crust pizza and Mountain Dew.

The next thing we removed was peanuts. Now, I know a lot of you assholes have a friend who works with someone who once was date-raped by a guy whose stepson was in Cub Scouts with a kid whose half brother is allergic to peanuts. I feel sorry for that kid, but that doesn't mean the other two thousand kids in his school should be denied the simple pleasure of the peanut-butter-and-jelly sandwich. Once again we have put the individual ahead of the group. How many of these kids truly have a nut allergy? I'm not saying there's no such thing as a kid who would go into anaphylactic shock if he keis-tered a PayDay. I'm saying our paranoia has turned a rare occurrence into a full-blown epidemic.

My kid's preschool adopted a no-nuts policy. I'm happy to report that last year when they asked me to emcee their charity bake sale, I explained to them that I also have a no-nuts policy. I don't emcee bake sales for paranoid nut jobs.

How is it I managed to be warehoused at one of the largest junior highs in the country with nary a kid allergic to peanuts, and now every third kid on my block has to carry a fucking syringe full of epinephrine? Have we changed physiologically in that short a period of time? Or is it, as I suspect, an emotional change? Whenever Whitey runs out of problems, these things rear their ugly heads. Remember black mold a few years back? Same group.

I saw an episode of *60 Minutes* a couple years ago where a team of doctors came up with a paste to feed the malnourished children of . . . are you sitting down? . . . Africa. The paste consisted of powdered sugar, powdered milk, and peanut butter. It was called Plumpynut and was so effective that it brought entire villages from the brink of death up to the health standards of America—colonial America. During the interview when the doctor was boasting about this amaz-ing achievement, Anderson Cooper asked, "But what about the peanut allergies?" The doctor explained it's not a problem there. So why is it that kids who are severely malnourished and basically have the immune system of a rat at an AIDS hospice aren't allergic to peanuts? I contend it's because they have real problems. We've run out of real problems so now we manufacture invisible ones.

So what's the big deal about getting rid of the peanut-butter sandwich? I'll give you two reasons, one practical and one symbolic. First, practical. No sandwich travels better than peanut butter and jelly. The time between when it's made at six forty-five in the morning to when the lunch bell rings are five of the toughest hours on a sandwich. Sliding around the floor of a school bus in a brown bag, sitting on a bench exposed to the elements, and being mashed into a dank locker will bring an egg salad or a bologna with mayo to its knees. But not the resilient PB&J. Peanut butter and jelly is the only sandwich that actually gets better with time. Like a fine cabernet that sticks to the roof of your mouth. How many other sandwiches can boast that sitting in the sun makes them taste better? Thus it's the perfect sandwich for the sack lunch. Also, no sandwich goes better with milk. But this point will be moot in a few months when the school becomes a lactose-free zone.

Now for the symbolic. If there's a kid in your class whose heart will explode if somebody whispers the name George Washington Carver, by all means ban peanut butter and jelly. My problem is that kid isn't in my kid's class. We now live in a society where everything's an emergency and we won't acknowledge a difference between the people who get hives from peanuts and the ones whose windpipes will swell shut. So who shall we blame? I blame us because we caved to the hypochondriac, *Redbook*-reading, Oprah-watching, crystal-rubbing, Whole Foods–shopping survivor-of-incest moms and their pussy-whipped attorney husbands.

I know these problems are all in our heads. And this next made-up problem is *on* my son's head. When my son was five months old, my wife told me the pediatrician suggested he had some asymmetry in his skull and that he should see a specialist. Of course the problem wasn't my son's head, it was in my wife's head, and it would eventually end up in my wallet. But we went to see the specialist anyway. I knew instinctually that since no one I ever knew growing up needed an orthopedic hockey helmet, the chances of my son actually needing one were slim. But that doesn't mean we weren't going to be sold one. Why? Because we're paranoid and we can afford it. So off to the specialist we went. He was going to run a series of tests to decide whether Sonny needed him to mold a dollar eighty-nine's worth of plastic into four thousand dollars' worth of orthopedic helmet. I already knew the outcome before the results of the test. And it's not because I know anything about medicine—keep in mind I failed biology, and driver's ed, in the tenth grade. (By the way, Mr. Deliberte and Mr. Gregory—fuck you, look who's writing a book.)

Now, I don't know anything about human anatomy, but I know everything about human nature. No termite guy is going to come to your house for a free inspection and come up with nothing. That fleet of vans with the giant fiberglass termites on the roofs didn't pay for themselves. And when's the last time you took your car to the corner garage for the free brake inspection and the guy said, "They look brand-new. Come back after you circle the globe a few times"? If this guy doesn't find anything wrong with my son's head, he's not going to be able to afford the new tits he promised his wife. Obviously he's going to find something wrong. That fleet of vans with the giant fiberglass kids' skulls on their tops didn't pay for themselves.

Anyway, I'm sure you know how this story ends. The tests suggested that if we didn't buy the four-thousand-dollar PVC yarmulke, my son was going to look like Rocky from *Mask*. So after a plaster mold was made of his head, which was about as easy as stuffing a raccoon into a garbage disposal, four to six weeks later we received the final product. The instructions were to wear the helmet twenty-three hours out of the day, every day, for three months. He lasted less than forty-five seconds. He pitched such a fit and was so miserable that we had to pry the helmet off almost immediately. Then my wife and I did that thing all parents do at some point or another. We gave each other the knowing "fuck it" nod. For those single folks reading the book, it's approximately the same look a cop gives when he's accepting a bribe. And today my son is four with a head prettier than Yul Brynner's.

Please indulge me for a moment on the off chance that the "expert" who prescribed the helmet is reading this.

Dear Fuckwad:

Obviously you don't know shit about your field. You said if my son didn't wear the helmet that his sunglasses wouldn't sit right on his head. Well, your four-thousand-dollar helmet became a four-thousand-dollar doorstop, and three years later my son's head is perfect. Which means you're either A) horrible at what you do or B) a liar preying on the guilt of moms who drive expensive SUVs. Perhaps it's a combination of incompetence and greed. Either way, you should focus full-time on your true calling— gay porn.

Thank you.

We've built our entire society around children. Even Vegas. I guess we should have seen it coming when they started putting up bouncy castles instead of real fake castles, the tasteful stucco ones where a man could get a shrimp cocktail and a whore. Can you imagine that stuff flying in the sixties with the Rat Pack there? "Hey, Frank Sinatra and Dean Martin, we want to make this town kid-friendly." "Are you fucking high? How am I gonna nail cocktail waitresses with my wife and kid out here? I'm gonna clock you in the head with this bottle of Cutty Sark and bury your ass out in the desert if you don't shut up. Now Dean, help me think of another racially insensitive joke I can use onstage when Sammy comes out."

Shortly after my twins arrived home from the hospital, I had to pay a guy a thousand bucks to go through my house and make sure I couldn't open any of my drawers or use any of my outlets. It's insane. Three years in and I still attempt to fling open my bathroom drawer only to have it get grabbed by a nylon hook. I essentially gave somebody a thousand dollars to fuck with me. It'd be like if you paid a guy to fart in your car every morning before you went to work. Think about every bottle of aspirin you've ever tried to open when you were hungover or any disposable lighter, the kind that take three hands and a bench vise to get a spark out of, or how many times you've been woken up from a nap by the backup beeper on a garbage truck—all in the name of child safety. I can't take my kid for a drive to the mailbox in a car that has eleven airbags and five crumple zones without the little shit being belted in like Buzz Aldrin. Yet can you think of the one vehicle built after 1959 that doesn't have seat belts? Cement mixer? Beer truck? A backhoe? No. They're all required to have seat belts. It's the school bus. "Hey, I've got a great idea. Let's put our kids in an unwieldy metal cigar tube piloted by a sixty-three-year-old with cataracts who has recently managed to string together nine months of sobriety." If I drove my kid to school and the kid wasn't wearing a Nomex fire suit and a six-way harness, I'd be arrested. Does anyone else see the insanity in this? I bet even prison buses have seat belts.

The other great irony in child safety is choking. Kids will put anything in their mouths, and any new parent will tell you it's a constant struggle between "eat that celery stick" and "get that pencil out of your mouth." That's why I was shocked to see that the toy set my sister bought my kids for their second birthday was plastic food. Hot dogs, carrots, strawberries, broccoli, et cetera. If you go to any preschool around the country, you'll find a bucket of fake plastic food. All made in China and all dipped in melamine before being loaded onto a filthy container ship. Of course the first thing my kids did was put the toxic plastic food in their mouths. Then I had to yell, "Get that out of your mouth, that's not for eating." And my son gave me a look that said, "What the fuck, old man? Ten minutes ago when we were sitting at the table, you were begging me to eat this carrot. Now you're slapping it out of my hand?" Who was the maniac who decided the plastic shit they could choke on should be the same shape and color as the real shit they need to put in their mouths and chew, and why is this monster still alive?

Here's a story that's a little off topic but it sort of involves my kids, so this seems like as good a chapter as any to shoehorn it in. I had walked over to Jimmy Kimmel's a couple of football seasons ago on a Sunday to watch the games. Somewhere around the second quarter of the late game somebody killed my seven-beer buzz by telling me Molly was missing. Molly's my blond Lab. She got out of Jimmy's yard, which is great for her and better for Kimmel since he's allergic to her, but horrible for me. I don't say my wife likes the dog better than me—it's probably a tie. If Molly paid the lease on her Jag, though, the pendulum would definitely swing in her direction. Either way, I had two choices—come home with Molly or don't come home at all. So I immediately took off on foot yelling Molly's name and running through the neighborhood.

Luckily, I was wearing my eating outfit. Knowing that I was gonna consume at least Molly's weight in smoked meats, I wore elastic sweatpants, an oversize T-shirt, and New Balance running shoes. As I was frantically running up and down Jimmy's street, I passed a guy watering his lawn, and he smiled and gave me the thumbs-up. It's at that point I realized in my drunken haste that I had forgotten to set down my Miller Lite. He must have been thinking, That *Man Show* guy is the real deal. I found Molly, but in the process I passed a half dozen more people, some walking their dogs, others driving their cars, never having the time to explain why I was out for a jog with a beer.

The following weekend, I was once again getting ready to head over to Kimmel's for a long afternoon of drinking, eating, and pigskin. This time I thought maybe Molly should stay at home; instead I'd bring my son, who was probably a year and a half old at the time. So I loaded him into his side of the twins' stroller and then thought, "Why should I carry over this twelve-pack of Miller Lite? Why not slide it into the bottom of the stroller where the diapers go, and save my back?" Unfortunately, that area could only accommodate a six-pack, so I had to throw the twelve-pack the only place it would fit, which of course was next to my son, on the side normally inhabited by my daughter. So off I went.

You probably know where this story is going so I'll just fast-forward to the part where the same neighbor was watering the same lawn and this time, instead of a jog with a beer, I was taking a Sunday-morning stroll with my son and a twelve-pack. Our eyes met momentarily and he had a look that I would call "confusted"—part confused, part disgusted. I'm sure he was thinking to himself, "God-damn, does this Carolla have a problem with booze or what? He can't go for a jog without a cold one, and he can't even take his son for a lap around the neighborhood without his precious medicine. He should just keep walking and drop that kid off at the nearest fire station—better to be raised in foster care than by Foster Brooks."

Dr. Drew, his wife, and all the other paranoid Caucasians I spend time with are constantly telling us we have to get on waiting lists for expensive schools now. I always tell Dr. Drew, "What difference does it make? I got warehoused at North Hollywood High before getting put on academic probation at Valley Junior College, and I'm smart." He says school teaches kids how to think. I disagree. I think whether your kid is smart or dumb boils down to one thing and one thing only: Are they curious? If they ask questions, want to know how and why things work, they could do pre-K through 12 in Tijuana and turn out fine.

And when did this pre-K bullshit start anyway? I don't remember it from when I was a kid. Fucking pre-K is like someone finding a meal between breakfast and brunch. It's just another excuse to pay someone to raise your kid. And I have twins, so this goddamn pre-K is going to cost me 10K. And for what? So some chick can watch my kids run in a circle until nap time? I could get one of those plastic owls they put on the roof of seafood restaurants to do that.

I just had an idea. If you have a special-needs child going to a kindergarten for children with disabilities, it should be referred to as Special K. The parents will get a kick out of it, and let's face it, the kid could be in his thirties and he wouldn't know what the fuck you were laughing about.

On the other hand, if your kids are not curious, even with the finest education they'll still be the most boring people at the party. And as long as we're on the topic, what is smart anyway? Here's my simple definition, and I hope you're smart enough to appreciate it. The true test of brains to me is, Are you able to achieve your goals? In other words, can you get what you want? If all you've ever wanted was to be self-employed and you can't figure out how to do it, regardless of what your SATs say, I'm gonna label you dumb. And if you've always dreamt of backpacking through Europe and you hike to the grave without ever achieving that goal, then no matter what degree you've received, in my book, you're dumb. It's the only kind of smart I hope for my kids to have. Sometimes it's about money, but maybe it's about starting a relationship or climbing a mountain. Either way, the ability to have a goal and achieve it is the most important kind of smart there is. Now, if you'll excuse me, I have to find someone to finish writing this book.

We've created a society of validation monsters. All you need to do is look at bumper stickers. They used to just be on the backs of Volkswagen vans. And they fell into one of three categories—funny: DON'T LAUGH, IT'S PAID FOR, or BEAM ME UP, SCOTTY; sexual: HONK IF YOU'RE HORNY, or IF THIS VAN'S A-ROCKIN', DON'T COME A-KNOCKIN'; and pragmatic: DON'T TAILGATE, or GAS, GRASS OR ASS: NOBODY RIDES FOR FREE. But they were never grandiose. Nobody bragged about their kids' accomplishments in the classroom or on the playing field. And you never saw the license-plate frame that makes me want to hurl into my Audi's ashtray—PROUD GRANDPA OF AIDAN AND DAKOTA. We knew something back then that we seem to have forgotten today, which is that no one gives a shit about your grandkids or whether your fat son made the honor roll at his magnet school. Somebody decided ten years ago that more kids would make the honor roll if we praised them on our Volvo bumpers. I think it's quite the opposite. I think your kids would be much more motivated to make the honor roll if they knew your car was gonna get a big orange Styrofoam dunce cap on the roof if they weren't pulling at least a 3.0. We'll call it the Denver Dunce Cap.

Another example of how we're ruining our kids are Girl Scout cookies.

Sounds innocent enough: How can Girl Scout cookies be responsible for the demise of our civilization? It's not the cookies, it's the distribution network. When I was a kid, Girl Scout cookies were actually sold by Girl Scouts. Not that the Carollas ever bought any: A) They didn't take food stamps, and B) in the early seventies, my mom considered anyone in uniform the Man.

Quick aside: Let's take a moment and establish the power rankings of Girl Scout cookies. Tagalongs (peanut butter and chocolate), Samoas (caramel, chocolate, and what seems like pubes), Thin Mints, and everything else is a distant fourth. The one that needs to be removed from the lineup altogether is the Trefoils. These are the shortbread cookies—textureless, tasteless poker chips that are basically the Girl Scout version of the sacrament. How fucking low does your self-esteem have to be to skip past the Samoas and the Tagalongs to order a couple of cartons of this white-trash kibble? Are these the only ones you can eat without having to lift your Klan hood?

My point is, Girl Scouts don't sell Girl Scout cookies anymore. The moms and dads of the Girl Scouts do all the heavy lifting. When I was working at *Jimmy Kimmel Live!*, every year around February the beleaguered dads would corner you in the hall. "Hey, man, my daughter's troop is trying to get to Yosemite this year. Can I put you down for a couple of cases?" Can you imagine when you were a kid asking your dad to take a crate of cookies to work and sell it for you? He'd be like, "How about I take your fucking bike to the corner and sell that?"

Today's generation of Girl Scouts are not learning how to work, they're learning how to delegate. Dads: How about you show some goddamn self-respect and stop muling Pecan Sandies for the Girl Scout cartel? And girls: How about you show some dignity, get in that brown skirt, fill up that Radio Flyer, go to the entrance of the supermarket, and wait to be abducted?

WHERE HAVE ALL THE FELLAS GONE?

Far too many guys in their forties can't turn a wrench or swing a hammer nowadays. But they have tons of opinions about the new Silver Surfer movie. It's a sure sign of the pussification of America. What happened?

Forget about actually being a man's man—guys don't even bother to *lie* about being manly anymore. It used to be a fella would at least have enough dignity that when he was driving with the missus and the car wouldn't start, even though he didn't know what the fuck to look for, he'd say, "Pop the hood." He'd stand there and stare at the engine for a while, set his cigarette on top of the air cleaner, and yell, "Try it now." Of course the engine wouldn't start, but at least he looked like a man. Now the guy says, "Call Triple-A. I don't want to get my cuticles dirty."

It's the same thing with fighting. Guys used to have stories where they said, "This son of a bitch spilled a drink on my old lady at the bar, so I got in his face and said, 'If you're looking for trouble, you found it. You're in for a world of hurt.'" Now dudes tell stories that go, "I honked at a guy and he got out of his car so I called 911. But I got a busy signal, so I locked myself in and hit the OnStar button."

What happened to the bullshit factor where you at least pretended to be a guy?

Here's a good fight story. And it's all true.

I was about twenty-one and was with five buddies looking to get laid at a party. It was a nice house in the hills and someone's parents were out of town. The problem was I was the only one not getting laid, because I had hooked up with a nutty chick. So I wanted to leave. As I was walking down the stairs exiting the party, the chick told a group of tough guys who were just arriving that I had hit her. I had done no such thing but now I really wish I had. So they followed me down the stairs and were threatening me.

It was like some multicultural gang from a bad TV show—a big husky Mexican guy, a brother, and three white guys. I said I couldn't fight because I had arthroscopic knee surgery three days earlier; I still had stitches and just took the brace off. But the big Mexican guy responded, "I'm gonna break your other knee." I was drunk, so I said, "Okay, it's just me and you, right? You're the one with a beef. If your friends promise not to jump in, I'll fight you." He agreed, so we headed out to the street and I started beating him up. I was a good boxer. I was just hitting him and he wasn't hitting me back. Eventually I whacked him hard; he fell into his group of friends and didn't come back at me. Then I made the mistake of taunting him. "Hey buddy, you wanted it. You were Mr. Tough Guy on the stairs. You begged me to fight and now I'm out here kicking your ass, so come on, you pussy. I ain't done. Bring it on."

Mid-taunt, I felt a sting on my left shoulder and heard the sound of breaking glass. One of his buddies had thrown a beer bottle and it broke when it hit me. Six inches higher and I'm sure it would have ruptured my eardrum. But this thing just shattered and fell to the ground without so much as a scratch. But then out of nowhere his buddy, a guy I later found out was named Terry, took an aluminum baseball bat, came up behind me, and took a full swing at my knee. Maybe he was trying to keep his friend's promise to break my other knee. What the fuck is wrong with people? Who thinks, "I have no issue with this guy, I've never met him before, he just had knee surgery, but I'm going to come up behind him when he's not looking and take a full crack at him with an aluminum bat like they used to kill Joe Pesci in *Casino*"? He took a home-run swing, but thankfully it wasn't at the knee with the stitches in it. Instead he shot high and hit the fleshy part of my thigh. All it did was sting and make me curtsy. Then all five of them jumped on me and one of them hit me with a good uppercut that busted my lip open and spilled blood all over my nice white button-up shirt. I found the guy who hit me—it was the black guy, and interestingly enough he was the kung-fu guy of the group. We started going at it. It was one in the morning on a street in Studio City and we were reenacting a scene from *Enter the Dragon*. While we were trading kicks and punches, the cops arrived and it broke up.

In the end those guys thought I was a maniac because I had a beer bottle broken over me, been hit with a baseball bat, and after all five of them jumped on me and busted my lip open, I was screaming for more. The guy who wanted to fight in the first place was much worse off than I was. But I still, and rightfully so, wanted some revenge on the animal who had hit me with the bat. I knew he was a local guy, and I spent six months trying to find him.

Cut to New Year's Eve. I was at a party at my friend Umgad Abuzamzam's place making out with some chick in a bathroom. There was a violent pounding at the door. It was my buddy Ray. He was hammered and screaming at the top of his lungs, "It's Ray, get out here." I said, "Leave me alone." I was with a chick whose panties were around her ankles. I didn't have time for Ray. But he insisted, "Get out here, you've gotta see this." So me and the girl got our shit together and opened the door. Ray had Terry, the bat man himself, in a headlock. I can't imagine what was going through his head. Here it is six months later, Ray's got him by the neck, and he's staring at the guy who took on him and four friends, a beer bottle, and a bat, and was asking for more. Ray was offering Terry up to me like a cat when it catches a bird and drags it into the house. As a result of Terry begging for mercy, my lack of killer instinct, and my boner, I told Ray to let him go. So Ray flicked him away like a cigarette butt.

Then, five years later, I was standing on the street in front of my apartment building waiting for someone who was gonna check out the truck I was selling. I noticed a large moving van being unloaded by a new tenant. I remember thinking, This is a big fucking Mexican guy about to move into my building. I didn't recognize him. But he recognized me. He said, "I know you, man." So I asked, "Oh, did you play some Pop Warner football with me or something?" He said, "No, I know you." I replied, "Well, you don't look familiar to me. Did you grow up in North Hollywood?" He said, "No, we fought, man." Then it hit me who he was, the guy I had beat up. For a moment I was scared because I was standing in the street with a buff Mexican guy, and the last time we were in the street together, we were throwing punches. But I quickly realized I was the one who beat him up, and I knew all those guys thought I was a maniac anyway. So sure enough, he just walked into his apartment.

In 2006 we tracked down Terry and called him on my morning radio show. He's now a professional pilot. I hope you're reading this on a plane that he's flying and just shit your pants.

Now that's a fight story.

You ever see one of those movies from the fifties where every guy is wearing a hat and the same gray suit, and every woman has her hair styled the same way? That was back when we had something called a society. Now we have *individuals*. The notion seems evolved, but the execution is starting to piss me off. That being said, here's a list of guys I can't hang out with.

WEIRD FACIAL HAIR GUY I don't mind a guy with a beard. And I love a guy with a mustache. I'm talking about the a-hole who has the Sharpie-thin stripe going ear to ear and over the top of his upper lip. Never have more calories been spent achieving a worse look. Why would somebody cultivate a look that required an extra hour in the mirror each morning? Exactly. It's because this narcissistic fuck gets to stare at his Jersey Shore ass for an extra hour in the mirror. Is it a coincidence that the more elaborate the facial hair, the bigger the narcissistic dick that's rocking it? I don't think so. I shave twice a week, and that's way too much mirror time for me. These guys start every day with a meticulous sculpting of their mug, which I'm sure is followed by a homoerotic pose-down.

MY-WIFE'S-MY-BEST-FRIEND GUY I know I sound like a jaded dick, but your wife's not supposed to be your best friend. She's not even supposed to be in your Fave Five. When's the last time you begged your best friend for a blow job? I don't believe these guys. I think they're just saying it to score points with their wives and to make the rest of us look like assholes. Your best friend is the guy you go to to bitch about your wife getting fat. Plus you can't brag to your wife about the handy you got in the champagne room.

I DON'T OWN A TV GUY If you can't afford a TV or you pawned your TV because of a gambling debt, you get a pass. But this is the guy who doesn't own a TV for the sole purpose of announcing he doesn't own a TV. This is his way of declaring he's better than you. He acts like everyone who has a TV just sits around staring at *Night Court* reruns and Ashton Kutcher commercials. He would never admit there's provocative, informative, entertaining programming such as my favorite new reality show *I'm a Pretentious Asshole Who Tells Everyone I Don't Own a TV.*

GUYS WHO ANNOUNCE THEY "RESCUE" DOGS You didn't go into a burning warehouse or the roof of a flooded barn to get the dog. You went to the pound, because you were too cheap to go to the mall. You don't love dogs nearly as much as you love the idea of people thinking you're a hero. You ever notice people who buy their dogs rarely discuss how they got them, versus these assholes who work the phrase "She's a rescue" into every fucking conversation? What do you want? Spielberg to make a movie about you? I'd love to follow one of these douchebags around for a year with a clicker counter bouncers use at the door of the club, and find out how many times they utter the phrase "She's a rescue." Over-under would be fifteen thousand. When I was a kid, all the sofas in my house were freebies we got from other people who were throwing them out. My mom never once referred to them as "rescues."

THE GUY WHO WANTS TO KNOW WHERE YOU GOT YOUR COLD He's McGruff with a box of Kleenex and a bottle of Robitussin. As soon as you tell him that you have a cold, he tells you the date of his last cold and where he got it. Then he's gonna need to know where you got yours. "I don't know" is not an acceptable answer. He's a regular Sherlock Holmes who's gonna follow the trail of mucus until he breaks the case wide open. He asks, "Do you have kids? They probably picked up something at preschool and brought it home." "Have you traveled recently? The air in those planes just recirculates. They're like flying petri dishes." Thanks, Cold and Flu Case. What does he want me to do with this information? "As soon as this fever breaks, I'm giving those kids away! And the next time business takes me to Chicago, I'm going by mule!"

I'VE NEVER DRANK GUY Close asshole cousin to I Don't Own a TV Guy. Now don't get me wrong, if you don't drink now because the last time you got drunk you drove your Pontiac Aztek through a Gymboree or beat the shit out of Tina Turner, or screamed at a trooper, "What do you have that Taser set on—pussy?" then you have an excuse not to drink. I'm talking about the a-hole who's never been drunk a day in his life. He says he doesn't like to feel out of control. Call me old-fashioned, but I don't want to hang out with a guy who won't pass out long enough for me to draw a cock on his forehead.

GUY WHO SWIMS BEFORE WORK This guy is always bright-eyed and bushy-tailed. You didn't think your hangover could get any worse? Try standing next to the guy who's never felt more alive. No matter how early the job starts, he finds time to squeeze in six or seven hundred laps over at the Y. This asshole never misses an opportunity to let you know he's a superior person.

YOU: Wait a minute, didn't you go to the U2 concert last night?

HIM: That's right, I didn't go to bed till one thirty, but I still got up at four forty-five and hit the Y.

YOU: If I stay up till ten fifteen beating off to *Blame It on Rio* I'm calling in sick the next day, you prick.

GAY GUY WHO ACTS SO GAY HE'S THOUGHT OF AS A CHICK AND THUS GETS OUT OF ALL THE HEAVY LIFTING

I've been kicking around this theory for a while. There are two kinds of gay: *I love to chug cock* gay, and *I'm not going to help you move* gay. This guy's the latter. Speaking of ladders, don't ask to borrow one. He doesn't own a fucking tool. And he isn't going to help you or anyone else do shit. He's essentially presented himself to society as a frail woman. You wouldn't tell Céline Dion, "Grab that forty-pound sack of kibble out of the trunk and bring it up to my apartment." This breed of gay is well aware of this and relies heavily on it. Kind of like those assholes with the handicap plate going to the water park.

ROCKABILLY SKULL GUY He's the guy who needs to let you know exactly what decade he's trapped in. No matter what the calendar says, it's always 1955 to him. Whether he's at a club or the supermarket, he's dressed like the fourth member of the Stray Cats. And he's in love with skulls. From the tattoo on his arm to the shift knob on his Mercury to the chrome one on his key chain. This asshole loves skulls more than Hamlet. Hey, Fonzie, you're a forty-four-year-old house painter, not one of the Outsiders.

The person I really feel sorry for is this guy's girlfriend. This poor bitch has to dress like Betty from the Archie comics or they can't go out. I bet every Saturday night they have the same argument: "Can't I just wear my Juicy sweatpants and leave my hair down?" "Fuck that, put on that poodle skirt and those saddle shoes, we're going to the mall to get you a skull tattoo."

GUY WHO TELLS YOU WHAT CAFFEINE DOES TO HIM A close cousin of the Guy Who Tells You What Red Meat Does to Him. He's scared he's never going to sleep again. If you handed him a wedge of jicama he'd ask if there was caffeine in it. He'd tell you a horror story about the time he went to the diner for breakfast, ordered a decaf coffee, and couldn't sleep for three days. That waitress must have given him regular! You could give him a cup of stream water and he'd ask you three times if there was caffeine in it. We get it, you're a lightweight. But I must admit I'm secretly jealous. Wouldn't it be nice to be a thimbleful of Maxwell House away from being able to drive an 18-wheeler from Los Angeles to Vermont nonstop?

PANTIES IN A BUNCH GUY This is the guy who is looking for an excuse to be offended. Every action, no matter how harmless, is a personal attack. He's the guy who's walking his dog down a narrow street with no sidewalk when I come around the corner at nineteen miles an hour and gives me a look like I drove through his living room while he was reading *Where the Wild Things Are* to his special-needs grandchild. By the way, his wife is the bitch who uses the phrase "Excuse you," and his brother is the guy with the huge put-upon exhale when you ask him to switch seats on the Southwest flight. Hey dick, not everyone is out to get you. We wouldn't even know you existed if it wasn't for your overdramatized approach to life. But I suspect you already know that.

LAZY FLIP-CAP GUY At some point a few years ago, somebody invented the ketchup bottle with the flip cap so you could avoid the ketchup going skunky when one of your coworkers was too lazy to twist the metal cap back on the Heinz. But the lazy flip-cap guy's lethargy has overcome this new technology. Every job I've ever had with a communal kitchen has had a ketchup, and now a mayo squeeze bottle, where the cap was left open at a 90-degree angle. I find it satisfying to hear the snap of that plastic cap after I've doused my fries in ketchup. But this guy is so lazy or passive-aggressive that he refuses to complete the simplest task on the planet. What's this asshole's strategy? Obviously he's using the ketchup—why does he want it to get all dry and crusty at the top? Is he high? Or is it a fuck-you to everyone he works with? Imagine how devastated the inventor of the flip cap would be if he could travel through America's kitchens and see the millions of unsnapped caps. I'm sure when he invented this thing, he thought, "Eureka! That's it, there'll never be another open, crusty ketchup bottle. I've created a utopia for generations to come!" But there's one thing he didn't count on . . . just how lazy, self-absorbed, and narcissistic we actually are.

WE'VE BUILT A MINIMUM-WAGE GILDED CAGE

We made a mistake in this country that will rank right up there with slavery and Japanese internment camps. We deputized a bunch of minimum wagers and placed them in every guard shack, behind every counter, at every gate, and gave them carte blanche to fuck with us. We're essentially prisoners in a penitentiary that we paid for.

Let me give you two quick stories that would have never happened in this country fifty years ago. Last year I went to the X Games to watch a friend race in the rally competition. The race was gonna begin momentarily, and I was running late. I was met in the parking lot by a guy who had my credentials, and we started jogging toward the entrance. When we got to the entrance, there was an eight-dollar-an-hour guy in a yellow windbreaker standing between a two-foot gap in the barriers. We showed him our credentials and he said, "You can't get in this way." At first we were confused. These were all-access laminates. He said we had the right laminates, but that we had to enter at the end of the barriers on the other side of the parking lot. I looked to the right and saw that if we did that, it would lead us right back to the same spot just on the other side of the two-foot barrier he was standing in front of. There were no metal detectors to pass through and no paperwork to sign. He simply wanted us to go a hundred yards to the right and then back to end up in the same exact place we were already. Keep in mind, all he needed to do was move a half step to the left and we could have passed straight into the venue. And there was no line, so we weren't cutting in front of anyone. He just wanted to watch us dance. There's no way our grandfathers would have put up with guys making ten cents an hour fucking with them. They would have pulled a derringer from their boot and shot them in the face. And there wouldn't have been a court in the land that would have convicted them.

The second incident happened over the holidays at Disneyland's California Adventure. (Quick note if anyone who's in charge of the music selection is reading. The weird Muzak version of "California Girls" is fine, but perhaps you should think about pulling the Mamas and the Papas' classic "California Dreaming" from the set. I was eating a frozen banana with my daughter on my lap thinking, I wonder if Papa John Phillips was fucking his daughter when he wrote this song?) Anyway, back to the minimum wager who'd waged war on our happiness. We had been waiting in line to ride some zip-line device with a tire on the end of it for about twenty minutes. My son had pussed out early on, and now it was just me and my daughter. When it was her turn, the diesel dyke in the khaki slacks and matching ranger hat said, "She has to be at least forty-two inches tall to go on the ride."

Another quick sidebar: That fucking arm that measures kids' heights should be at the back of the goddamn line so you don't have to wait half an hour to find out you're not Splash Mountain material. You probably know where this one is heading.

So Rosie O'Donnell's husky doppelgänger says, "Step under Jiminy Cricket's arm." I knew this was merely a formality, since we'd just got off another ride and Natalia made the forty-two inches with plenty to spare. This time, however, the minimum-wage maximum bitch said she wasn't tall enough. I got down on one knee to get a better look, and I'm telling you a Pop-Tart dipped in Astroglide would not have made it between the top of my daughter's head and the bottom of Jiminy's arm. Her fucking hair was touching the arm. I said, "She's tall enough." The diesel dyke just said, "Next." I said, "Wait a minute. We've been waiting all this time and you're just gonna kick us out?" She said, "She doesn't meet the height requirement." I said, "By three thirty-seconds of an inch. And if she knew how to stand up straight, her scalp would be bleeding." It was at this point that Ranger C-Word dug in. What the fuck has our society come to when people armed with only a windbreaker and a name tag can fuck so royally with the people who pay their salaries? And what is that instinct to dig in over nothing? She's taking a moral stand against my daughter enjoying her afternoon?

Lawyers, unions, and wrongful-termination lawsuits have created our own little slice of Russia right here in the U.S.A. We've made it almost impossible to fire people and have thus enabled all the angry, frustrated douchebags whose names you never remember at the high school reunion to fuck with our pursuit of happiness.

When Jimmy was doing *Win Ben Stein's Money*, I would go by the lot to visit him and it was always the same routine: He would leave my name at the guard shack at the entrance. The following is an exchange I've had 350 times with every guard on every lot in this town. "Hi, I'm here to see Jimmy Kimmel." "Who's he?" "He's on *Win Ben Stein's Money*." "What's your name?" "Adam Carolla." "Let me check the list . . . you're not on the list." I don't know what the fantasy is at this point—that I'll just go up in a cloud of smoke, or that I'll admit that this was all part of some horribly conceived ruse and apologize. Or shall I just throw the car in reverse and drive back up the hill to my home? But it seems to be the expectation. I tell him to check the list again. He then asks what my name is a second time. At a certain point when he realizes I'm not going anywhere, he asks one more time, "Who are you here to see?" and then picks up a phone and says, "Yeah, I have . . . [points index finger at me]." I shout my name for the third time. He repeats a facsimile of what I shouted at him into the phone, and then begrudgingly opens the gate with a look that says, "You may have won this round, Mr. Capolla, but don't worry, Alan—I'll be back."

Here's what I would like to scream at all the people who put themselves into the gatekeeper position. First, remove that plate of shit someone put under your nose and act like you fucking want to be there. Second, I'm not asking for entry into your fourteen-year-old's vagina, I'm trying to drive onto a motherfucking lot. Third, it's not your goddamn lot. Your job is not to stop *all* people from getting onto the lot, it's to prevent *certain* people from getting onto the lot. Points four through twenty-seven: Drop your motherfucking attitude. Just because you control a white piece of one-by-six from a telephone booth with a wall-mount air conditioner doesn't make you General fucking MacArthur.

This country is being overrun by these assholes, and no one wants to say anything because they're getting minimum wage to park our BMWs. I'll tell you the same thing I tell my embarrassed wife: When I dig into these ass-wipes with their GEDs dipped in attitude, I'm doing them a goddamn favor. Somebody needs to settle their shitty hash, because they're not going anywhere with the attitude they currently possess. Obviously, it has not served them well. Here's some advice for you people: Shake yourself like an Etch A Sketch and start over. You've already spent your thirties in a terrarium holding a clipboard with a pencil tied to it and sucking up carbon monoxide. Would you like to be buried in it?

Here's another parking-lot-related anecdote. The reason I'm telling this story is to hopefully inspire you and to kill pages. I was going to an event in Hollywood at the Palace Theater. As I was pulling into the lot adjacent to the theater, the guy with the flag yelled, "Twenty dollars." Not "How are you? That will be twenty dollars." Just "Twenty dollars." I said, "I'm sitting on my wallet, let me park in the spot that's ten feet ahead of me. I'll get out of the car and give you the twenty dollars." He said, "You give me the twenty dollars now." Keep in mind, I was wearing a suit, sitting on the tail of the jacket, and at the time I was driving a 350Z, which means my ass was lower than my feet. I said to the guy one more time, "Just let me park the car and I'll give you the twenty when I climb out." What did he think my plan was? To jump out of the car, laugh like Ray Liotta, and yell, "Sucker! I'm running to Mexico. Good luck selling that thirty-five-thousand-dollar car." He said, "No. I need the twenty now." And I said, "Screw it, I'm going across the street." I threw the car into reverse to pull out and park at the competitor's lot, so he said, "Fine, park the car, then give me the twenty." And then I did what I'm asking all of you to do and what makes me a hero. I said, "Fuck you," and I pulled out and totaled a van filled with retarded kids. No, I just went across the street and parked. I never thought I'd be cast in the role of Asshole Robin Hood. I always assumed I'd be trying to stick it to the Man. But as it turns out, the problem is not so much with the Man but with the men he's giving eight dollars an hour to.

The minimum wagers who were put on this planet to ruin your short stay on the same planet come in many different shapes and sizes. Usually they have penises, and huge guts that hang over the top of their penises to protect them from the rain. But once in a rare while they come in the form of a young petite female, and this next story is just such a case.

I had a hankering for Middle Eastern food, so I headed for the city of Van Nuys to a restaurant I frequent called Zankou Chicken. Middle Eastern food sounds horrible on paper and looks horrible on a paper plate but tastes delicious. And once you've decided you're in the mood for it, Italian, Chinese, or burgers just won't do. So I sped toward Van Nuys with visions of shawarma dancing in my head, jumped out of my car, ran into Zankou, and proceeded to order what I always get, the fifty-fifty shawarma plate—half chicken, half beef. For those of you who've never heard of shawarma, let me A) explain to you what it is and B) thank you for being heroes in the fight against terrorism. Shawarma is slices of beef or chicken piled high on a vertical spit that rotates in front of a red-hot three-sided space heater. An electric knife is used to carve off morsels that usually end up in the provided pita and eventually in your belly. In the case of Zankou, their shawarma station had the two spits side-by-side just inches apart. It's important to note that the price for the shawarma plate, be it chicken or beef, was the same—$7.99. And with that in mind I happily ordered my fifty-fifty shawarma plate.

The seventeen-year-old Armenian she-dwarf who weighed all of ninety-eight pounds, and if you subtracted the eyeliner would have been well into the low seventies, said, "We don't do half and half, it's either all chicken or all beef." I said, "I know for a fact you do the fifty-fifty shawarma plate, because that's what I order every time I come here and I've been here at least ten times." The curt cunt just repeated what she said the first time. I said, "I think you're misunderstanding what I'm asking for. Not more meat, just the same amount but with chicken and beef. If they're both the same price, instead of two swipes with the electric knife on either the beef or the chicken, just give one on the beef and one on the chicken." She then uttered the phrase that's the battle call of all shitty businesses: "Everyone asks for that." God fucking forbid you give the public what they want. As a matter of fact, we could avoid this whole mess if you just boarded up the doors and got on the roof with a hunting rifle like a Korean liquor-store owner during a black riot. Or you could just give everyone what they're asking for since it doesn't cost you an extra goddamn penny.

She explained that she could get into trouble. I said, "Go get your manager, we need to talk about shawarma and your attitude." She said, "He's not here." I asked, "Then how is he gonna know you gave me the fifty-fifty shawarma plate?" But Tammy-Faye Baklava wouldn't budge. At this point a lesser man would have ordered the falafel plate, but this American said "Let's roll" to the Zankou in East Hollywood. She just grunted and gave me the see-you-in-hell look. I left with the satisfaction of knowing that in a few short years her Armenian husband would be beating the holy shit out of her. And that's not a slight against Armenian men; if she married Carl Sagan he'd be beating the fuck out of this bitch on a nightly basis.

I hopped into my Honda and set sail for the Zankou Chicken on Hollywood and Normandy, which is nowhere near the Zankou on Sepulveda and Burbank in Van Nuys, where I was. A scant fifty minutes later, and now starving, I walked into the Hollywood Zankou Chicken, said to a guy who looked like Khalid Sheikh Mohammed, "Give me a fifty-fifty shawarma plate," and without any hesitation he said, "Would you like a drink with that?" My first impulse was to drive back to Van Nuys to settle that bitch's hummus. But by that time my blood sugar and resolve were both dropping quickly. So I settled in for one of the most, and simultaneously least, satisfying lunches of my life.

I'll leave you with another tale of a minimum wager attempting to ruin my life, but this one has a storybook ending. I was at a billiards hall drinking beer and shooting pool on a Friday night after a *Man Show* taping. It was a *Man Show* tradition. After every tape night we would go to a big pool hall and drink pitchers of beer until the PAs got drunk enough to tell you what they really thought of you. I was in the middle of a conversation with a PA about how Jimmy was the funny one when somebody ran up the stairs and yelled, "They're towing your car."

I, along with a couple of people, ran down the stairs and across the street to find my car hooked up to a tow truck that was ready to drive away. I'll bore you with a few quick details because they're important to the telling of the story. One, the car was a brand-new silver BMW M3, and two, the tow truck was one of those modern-style ones that had the two prongs that slid under your back tires and lifted the rear end of the car off the ground.

I ran up to the gentleman and said, "This is my car, how can we take care of this?" And he said, "You can follow me to the impound lot." I said, "How about we just take care of this right now? I'll pay you and we can both go our separate ways." He said, "That's not going to work," and began to drive away. I jumped into my car and mashed my foot on the brake pedal as hard as I could. He dragged me for a couple of feet, then jumped out of the tow truck and yelled, "What are you doing?" I said, "You're not towing the car. Let's just take care of this now." He said, "I have to tow the car. If I don't come back to the impound lot with a car, my boss will ask questions." I said, "Do you ever go out on a call and by the time you show up, the car is gone?" He said it happens all the time. I said, "Let's just make this one of those times." He said no and headed for the cab of his truck. I then headed for the driver's seat of my car and we began round two of *Dancing with the Tards.*

We both jumped out of our vehicles, got into it again, and at a certain point I said, "Why are you being such an asshole?" This could have been settled easily and nobly the way our forefathers would have done it—with a trip to the ATM. But no, this dick was going to make me follow him to downtown L.A. at one A.M. and fill out a bunch of paperwork.

All of a sudden I heard a voice yell, "Pull your tie-down off." It was the voice of one of our directors, Tom. (Tom wasn't exactly what you would call straitlaced. He once, in the middle of the AIDS hysteria of the late eighties, dressed as a junkie hobo and went into a crowded New York subway car and shot fake blood from a prosthetic penis at a horrified crowd of commuters.) I looked over and saw that Tom had taken the nylon lashings off the passenger-side rear wheel. I, without hesitation, pulled the lashings off the driver's side, and then Tom screamed, "Go!" Keep in mind the rear wheels of the car were at the height of a kitchen countertop. Maybe it was adrenaline, maybe it was fear of being squirted by a fake penis, but I jumped into the car again.

The car didn't budge. The problem was it's rear-wheel drive, and the tires were on a rack that prevented them from rolling forward. Tom was now slapping the hood yelling, "Go!" This time I threw some revs on the engine and dropped the clutch. The car lurched forward and landed on the ground with a thud, hitting something on the way down. I didn't have time to get out and assess the damage, I just hauled ass into the night, and so did Tom. I went home, poured myself a glass of wine, and did what I always do, waited for federal marshals to show up at the house.

The following morning I went down to the garage fearing the worst, and to my shock and delight the only thing wrong with the M3 was the spare-tire well in the trunk got converted from an innie to an outie. I pulled out the spare tire, climbed into the trunk, and jumped up and down on the sheet metal until it went back to its original form.

There are probably more than one of you at this point who feel sorry for the tow-truck driver. To you I say Suck it; this dick brought it on himself. This would have never happened in the past or today in New Jersey. We could have settled this with a couple of twenties and a handshake. But in the immortal words of John Rambo, "They drew first blood, not me." Tow-truck drivers are the worst people on the planet, second only to meter maids. The lion's share of the work these guys do consists of going on moneymaking sweeps with local cops and hanging out in flooded intersections to charge people fifty bucks to tow their stalled Hondas out of the drink. And the impound yards they work for are a bunch of extortionists. I got a motorcycle towed at eleven thirty on a Thursday night and went to pick it up at seven Friday morning and they charged me for two days' storage. Feeling sorry for these assholes is like feeling sorry for Uday and Qusay Hussein. Fuck those guys. And besides, isn't it nice to hear a story where the rich white guy wins for a change?

AIRPORT
2010

The airport simultaneously represents all that is right with our society and all that is wrong with it. The idea that I can be standing in front of my self-flushing urinal, evacuating my bladder with the gent to my right expelling a Diet Coke he may have consumed on another continent, while the sweet scent of the Cinnabon wafts under both our noses is nothing short of miraculous. Not to mention the most well-lit four hundred square feet on the planet, the duty-free shop, with its thirty-gallon Grey Goose bottles, oil-drum-sized containers of Chanel No. 5, and bricks of Toblerone in the window. Take that, terrorists. The airport is also a metaphor for why this country works: people of all shapes and sizes, from all parts of the globe, putting aside their religious and cultural differences for the common goal of getting drunk on a plane. There, I've completed my paragraph about what's good about the airport. Now I can dedicate the next thirteen pages to why it sucks.

Airports are one big rule followed by a pile of regulations. If you're not showing your ID, removing an article of clothing, or being patted down, there's still a very good chance that somebody in a uniform will be telling you you can't stand here or park there or leave your bag anywhere. Unless you're a fat guy in black Reeboks with a vest and a camera. Then you have run of the airport. I was walking through LAX and there was a guy from TMZ with a camera on his shoulder walking backward, filming me, weaving his way through a maze of wheeled luggage and weary travelers. I thought, This guy is one baggage handler tying his shoe away from killing himself and taking out three Asians along the way.

A moment on the paparazzi. Why are these douchebags able to exist? How can they profit off celebrities without their consent? When we used to do a man-on-the-street bit on *The Man Show,* we were not allowed to air footage of anyone who didn't sign a release form. And when we did *Crank Yankers,* we couldn't air even the voices of people we called without them signing a release form. And when I was on the radio, we couldn't do a March Madness bit because the name "March Madness" was copyrighted: Thus "Mad Marchness" was born. If Harvey Levin was a watchmaker, do you think he could just take a picture of George Clooney, Photoshop his watch onto his wrist, and use it for advertising? Of course not. You'd have to pay Clooney millions of dollars for that. But you can run a website, a TV show, or a magazine all for profit using nothing but celebrities who don't give consent to use their images, and there's not a fucking law on the books that this would fall under? Any sane person who had even a cursory understanding of our society and its laws would have to admit this should be illegal. So then why does it remain legal? One answer: Nobody feels sorry for celebrities.

I know it seems too simple and not technical enough, but that's the bottom line. That's the only reason this is allowed to continue. If these were Hopi Indians instead of Halle Berry, not only would they think you're stealing their soul but the public outcry would be deafening. The map of the stars' homes is another example of a clear breach of privacy. If you ever visit Hollywood, for ten bucks you can buy a map of the stars' homes, for twenty you can buy a fifth of Jose Cuervo, and for thirty you can buy a hunting knife and finish the job.

Whose idea was it to let these paparazzi jack-offs, most of whom have extensive criminal backgrounds or are at least deadbeat dads, have a retarded-fat-guy panty raid in the same place where they strip-search old women and force guys like me to empty the contents of our toiletry bags into the garbage? Am I the only one who thinks a bunch of guys who have no business at the airport shouldn't be allowed in the fucking airport? Ironically, if one of these guys left the airport and decided to film the Brooklyn Bridge instead of Renée Zellweger, he'd be arrested. Couldn't we just make one more rule in a place where if you light up a cigarette in a bathroom you're dragged out in leg irons? The only people allowed at the airport are people who have business at the airport.

Dear a-hole naysayer who thinks telling these guys they can't be at the airport is tantamount to wiping my ass with one of the founding fathers' wigs: The airport is already a civil-liberties-free zone. I can't make a joke about shooting pool with Osama bin Laden without being arrested and I have to pass through a machine that's manned by a nine-dollar-an-hour guy who gets a front-row seat to my botched circumcision.

Of course all this security would be unnecessary if we'd just start doing what everyone secretly wants to do anyway—profiling. We've turned *profiling* into a dirty word. Sort of like what the English did with cigarettes. We never stop talking about profiling and why it shouldn't be tolerated in our society. The problem is, as humans we can no sooner stop profiling than we can stop our fingernails from growing or our cells from multiplying. It's woven into our DNA. When you walk down the street and you see a dog coming toward you, you immediately begin the process of profiling. Is it a Labrador or is it a rottweiler? My holier-than-thou friends to the left would argue that since I don't know either one of these individual dogs personally, I should refrain from judgment. But we all know that the statistical likelihood of a Labrador attacking is far less than a rottweiler. I'll bet you if the guy in the Birkenstocks with the FREE TIBET bumper sticker on his Honda Insight was taking his teacup poodle for a walk and saw the rottweiler, he'd cross to the other side of the street. Yet when it comes to security, we're supposed to throw away the most important tool we have in the fight against terrorism. It's not racial profiling. It's including race as part of the profile, just like age, gender, weight, et cetera.

My cruel fantasy is that one of these assholes who rail against pro-filing as a crime-fighting tool gets his kid abducted. Then when he sits down with the FBI profiler, the guy says, "According to our data, there's a ninety percent chance your daughter was abducted by a white male between the ages of thirty-eight and fifty-two who lives within a two-mile radius of your home and has some previous rela-tionship with little Cindy . . . oh, wait a minute, I've just noticed your name is on our list of assholes who've taken a bullshit showboating stance against profiling. Well, now, that's different. Instead of going up the street and questioning the forty-seven-year-old unemployable loner who drives the primered van, we're going to have to talk to ev-eryone in the city. The other statistic we've learned in our profiling is that there is usually a forty-eight-hour window before the search turns into a recovery. But we're going to waste a whole shitload of time talk-ing to people who obviously didn't commit this crime so that we don't hurt the feelings of a few."

And speaking of blanket policies that make no sense. I was at the Phoenix airport in 2008 coming back from shooting the *Top Gear* pilot and decided to go into the bar and order a round for the guys I was traveling with. The bar was empty except for one heavyset, gray-bearded, grizzled guy who looked like he just rode his donkey into town after a long day of panning for silver in them thar hills. He ordered a Jack Daniel's straight up, and that's when I overheard the young guy with the earring behind the bar asking Charlie Daniels if he had ID. At first the old sea captain just laughed—he probably hadn't been carded since he was trying to join the merchant marine in World War II. But the guy with the twinkle in his ear asked again. At this point it became apparent that he was serious. Dan Haggerty's dad fired back, "You've got to be shitting me, son." The bartender replied, "New policy. Everyone has to show their ID. No ID, no drinks." Then I watched Burl Ives reluctantly reach into his dungarees and pull out his ID. This may sound like nothing to you, but I saw it as a very sad testament of our times, and also an eerie harbinger of what the future holds. Obviously this is corporate lawyering at its worst.

I was carded myself leaving Burbank airport a few days earlier. The guy said, "Hey, *Man Show.* I used to love watching that. Now let's see your driver's license." Does he think I shot *The Man Show* when I was fourteen? No. He knows I'm twice the legal age. It's just some asshole who went to law school decided to take the ability to make decisions away from the poor fuck who makes the Bloody Marys. On the other hand, I could be wrong. Maybe the old man at the Phoenix airport was in reality a local teen with a diabolical plan that involved purchasing an airline ticket and seven hours in a makeup chair having prosthetics applied for the opportunity to spend eleven bucks on a well drink.

And the legal insanity doesn't stop once you get on the plane. As soon as your ass hits the seat, you hear this familiar refrain: "Tampering with, disabling, or destroying the lavatory smoke detector is against FAA regulations." I have this fantasy where sometime after "tampering" and before "disabling" I spring to my feet and yell, "Shut the fuck up! You just said 'tampering.' You're covered. We certainly don't need the 'disabling,' and we sure as fuck don't need the 'destroying' part of your retarded soliloquy. You've somehow managed to make the Sky-Mall catalog a rich and compelling alternative to your flight-cabin State of the Union. Nice work, toastmaster."

Was there an incident that necessitated this run-on sentence about the smoke detector? Was there a case fifteen years ago on a Pan Am flight where a guy went into the first-class head, lit up a butt, and took an ax handle to the smoke detector and his case had to be thrown out of federal court because his dream team argued "the stewardess only said 'tampering with' when, in fact, my client disabled and destroyed the smoke detector, and thus no jury in the land can convict him"? I know it seems trivial, but someone's got to point out every droplet in this ocean of time-wasting legal bullshit.

45

This next tale is another condemnation of attorneys and what they force the airlines to do. I was flying back from a college gig in Florida and sitting in first class attempting to get drunk when I realized we hadn't moved in an hour. I looked up and found out what the problem was. It was an overhead storage compartment. The latch was broken, and the spring-loaded door kept raising on its own. The flight attendant said we couldn't take off until all the overhead compartments were securely closed. At that point I said, "Why don't you just take the luggage out of it—that way nothing can fall on anyone's head and we can take off." She replied, "Oh, it's empty." I said, "Fine, then let's take off." Now I get the answer that's prefaced with "sir." "Sir, we can't take off until the overhead bin is securely closed." I again point out that it is empty, and that the law is only in place to prevent Samsonite from crushing midgets. She once again, but this time with a little more emphasis on the "sir," tells me we can't take off until the hatch is secured. At that point I suggest holding the lid closed with a piece of duct tape.

Fast-forward to an hour and a half later. The maintenance guy has boarded the plane, attacked the latch with a screwdriver to no avail, and finally settled on my original suggestion . . . duct tape. We've removed the ability to reason from the people who are supposed to be in charge.

Of course, post-9/11 the airlines get to use safety as an excuse for all this stupidity. A quick funny story related to 9/11. I know what you're thinking, Aren't all stories related to 9/11 funny? Of course, and this one is no exception. I was flying to New York with Jimmy to do the Hugh Hefner roast. This was in September 2001, mere days after the attacks, so everybody was understandably a little bit nervous. Jimmy declared at the airport that his head was on a swivel; he was ready to roll, and if he saw anyone darker than Tom Petty heading toward the cockpit he would spring out of his seat and tackle him. As the plane was taxiing, I put my magazine down and glanced over at Jimmy. His head was tilted back, his mouth was wide open, and he was sound asleep.

Another thing I can't wrap my mind around is the fact that you can fly with your dog, but if I have more than three ounces of Prell, I end up on a terrorist watch list. Every time I go to the airport there's some guy holding my toiletry bag upside down over a trash can, shaking it. Meanwhile Paris Hilton and her menagerie stroll right past me. What the fuck is that? You can't bring your dog into a Starbucks, are you really allowed to bring it on the plane? It's especially unbelievable with all this allergy nonsense. There's got to be more people who have dog-dander allergies than people with peanut allergies.

But of course no more peanuts on the plane. They've been replaced with fiesta mix, whatever the fuck that is. Apparently *fiesta* is the Spanish word for "crap that tastes like a ground-up bouillon cube." It's essentially the crushed and broken stuff someone swept off the floor of the Frito-Lay factory and put into tiny bags. This stuff doesn't exist on the ground. Have you ever met anyone who's eaten fiesta mix below thirty thousand feet? Of course, people make the financial excuse. But is there anyone who wouldn't pay an extra fifty cents on their ticket price for real snacks? Halfway through a six-hour flight I'd suck a guy off for a bag of Cool Ranch Doritos.

A decision that makes no sense logically or financially is the lack of a sleep channel on the plane. Airlines would love it if everyone just passed out as soon as they boarded. If you get on a plane later than nine in the evening, they immediately hand you a pillow and shut the lights. Obviously they want you to sleep. And they program the stations. They have two country stations, classic and contemporary rock, hip-hop, probably even a ranchera station. But no sleep station.

The closest channel they have is the classical one, but even that's ineffective. Just as you are nodding off to Pachelbel's Canon, a douchebag who sounds like James Lipton chimes in with a long-winded history of the song. "You've been listening to 'Air on the G String' from Orchestral Suite Number Three in D major by Johann Sebastian Bach. Originally written for strings and piano, it was later arranged by violinist August Wilhelmj, who transposed the key of the piece from D to C major and lowered the melody by a full octave. Therefore

Wilhelmj was able to play the piece solely on the G string of his violin. Thus, 'Air on the G String.' A fascinating piece of musical history. I'm glad I could share it with you. You are listening to Classics in the Air."

If you manage to get past the lecture about Bach and Prince Leopold without rushing the cockpit praying a sky marshal would put you out of your misery, you might attempt to drift off to a soothing Beethoven sonata only to be jarred awake by a John Philip Sousa march or some Tchaikovsky piece with cannons. Did the airlines research this? Did they hand out a survey to their frequent fliers and realize that while 19 percent of their patrons said they prefer to sleep on the flight, a rousing 81 percent said they wanted a master's-level education in chamber music? What the fuck is wrong with these people? There's been two hundred different airlines over the last fifty years, and not one goddamn one of them has a sleeping channel on their prerecorded radio station. Why not a channel with just light classical, crickets, and rain-forest sounds?

You'd think that a way to avoid a lot of these hassles is to cough up for a first-class ticket. Wrong. Flying first class actually makes the process longer. One of the so-called perks of paying a king's ransom for your ticket is that you get to board first. You pay *more,* yet you have sit there *longer.* Your flight is as long as your ass is in the seat. If you get on the plane last, your flight from New York to L.A. is six hours and five minutes. If you're the first guy on the plane, your flight is six hours and fifty-five minutes. And there's no movie showing, there's no booze flowing, there's no stewardesses blowing. It's not like you're getting a foot massage, a reach-around, and a martini the whole time. The flight attendants are helping the person who paid one tenth the price you paid get his luggage into the overhead bin. As long as you're on the ground, you ain't in first class. You're not getting your Bloody Mary until you're at thirty thousand feet. People think it's a champagne fountain up there, but what's really happening is you're getting the stink-eye from the economy-class passengers as they shuffle by and whack you in the shin with their luggage.

Here's what first class should be: Get me when everyone else is on the plane. Send the stewardess out to the bar to say, "Mr. Carolla, we're ready to leave." What if this was a bus instead of a plane? There's nobody who would pay ten times more for a bus ticket if he had to sit there while everyone else was loaded on. Imagine the bus driver says, "Because you paid three hundred dollars, you get to sit on the bus and watch everyone else drag their asses on board before we leave. And by the way, this bus holds two hundred and eighty-three people, so it's gonna be a while." You'd say, "Fuck you, I'm going to a bar, come get me when the people who paid thirty dollars are buckled in."

After you arrive at your destination, the torture continues. The first thing most people do when they get off the plane is head to the bathroom. Big mistake. From an olfactory perspective, you'd be better off heading to a Porta-John at the nearest construction site. The damage done in the airport bathroom is worse than any terrorist action that could happen on the plane. What happens in those bathrooms is the work of an international all-star team of shitters. It's a combination of bad airplane food meets nervous flyers meets "I've been holding this in for six hours" meets "Who cares? No one in my country of origin will ever know about this." It's how you treat a rental car: It's not mine, therefore I don't give a fuck. People file off the plane, see that bathroom, and think, "Not my home turf. Let the games begin."

Then it's time to go home. The airport shuttle, at best, probably saves you twenty bucks over a cab. But the cost to your time, soul, and sense of smell will never be recovered. I was in New York covering the Video Music Awards for KROQ when I got the call to come back and audition for *Loveline* on MTV. I was poor back then, so opted to take the shuttle to my apartment. My shuttle smelled like a burlap sack of BO had been thrown onto a hibachi. Just this whoosh of hot air and foreigner funk. Different parts of the world have different stink. It's a curry-based diet meeting synthetic-based rayon. They're all wearing disco shirts, their beards are down to their chests, and they haven't washed their hair in six months. That shuttle van smelled like I walked into an asshole. There shouldn't have even been double doors; there should have just been cheeks that opened up. Of course,

I'm the first guy in the van and we have to do that thing where you circumnavigate LAX twenty-eight times to fill it. So we're doing that circle and I'm hanging my head out the window like a dog on a country road. The other four or five couples eventually pile in. Since I was the first guy in, I felt like I was the lead man, like I was at a deli and pulled the first ticket. But no, because there's a guy whose apartment is between LAX and where I live. So we eventually drop off a couple of people and it gets down to me and one other guy. We head down the 405 and toward the 101 interchange. He lives out in Calabasas, which is fifteen miles north on the 101, and I live in Sherman Oaks, which is two miles south. We're coming to the fork and I realize if we veer to the left, I'm going to this guy's house in Calabasas with this smelly motherfucking driver. I literally grabbed the wheel and pulled us to the right.

The shuttle is the worst twenty dollars you'll ever save. It adds ninety minutes to whatever a Town Car or cab would have been. You have the unenviable choice between being dropped off last or being dropped off first and having a bunch of losers who can't afford cab fare and have no friends or loved ones with cars knowing exactly where you live.

Here's a story from the road that encapsulates all the misery associated with air travel. In the late nineties, when Dr. Drew and I would do the college circuit, often we would leave town for four or five days at a time. One evening before such a trip, during a commercial break from *Loveline*, I suggested to Drew that we carpool to the airport. No sense in us both paying for expensive long-term parking. I said, "Since you live in Pasadena and I live in Hollywood, how about you pick me up on the way to LAX?" He explained that wasn't going to work because he had to go to the hospital on the way to the airport and make the rounds. I said, "It's a seven A.M. flight—what time do you expect to make the rounds?" He said, "About five A.M." By the way, we were having this conversation at eleven forty-five in the evening. This is why Dr. Drew is currently hard at work on his ninth TV show and your fat ass is sitting around reading this dumb book. Anyway, he suggested me sleeping over at his house that night and then waiting in the car while he made the rounds. I sarcastically asked if he was going to crack the window.

It was at that point I took one of my many retarded stands. As we came out of commercial break, I made the proclamation that I was not going to drive myself to the airport and that if Drew would not pick me up, then a loyal listener would. The only requirements were that you were female and had a road-worthy SUV. A young lady immediately called in to the show and said she had to be at work at six thirty in the morning so she was up at that hour anyway, and it would be an honor to transport me and my luggage to LAX. I said great and put her on hold. I didn't want to give my address out on the air, but as I was speaking to her on the phone I realized I didn't want to give out my address off the air, either. So I told her to go up Beachwood Drive, past the market, and I would meet her down at the bottom of the thousand stairs that connected Beachwood Canyon to the street far above it—and that she needed to be there at five thirty sharp. Since it was almost midnight, I told her to get some sleep and I'd see her in a few hours.

I then got back on the air, and before saying good night to the millions of troubled teens I proudly boasted to Drew that I, in fact, would not be paying for parking at LAX. He laughed and said, "Good luck. I'll see you at the American Airlines terminal about six fifteen."

Five hours and eight minutes later, my alarm went off. I quickly drank my cup of coffee, pulled on a heavy overcoat since it was drizzling and cold, and grabbed my suitcase with the week's worth of underpants and socks crammed in it. I walked out of my house and up the street to the mouth of the staircase. I then dragged my heavy suitcase down the steep, dark, wet stairs on my way to rendezvous with the mysterious young lady with the SUV. Using my luggage like a barstool, I sat on the sidewalk under a streetlight with my collar pulled up, wishing it would either stop drizzling or she would arrive. I checked my watch. It read five thirty-seven. I started to become concerned. I thought maybe I should jog down Beachwood, around the bend, to see if she was waiting at the market. But then I thought, Should I drag my luggage with me or should I just leave it unattended? I decided to drag it behind me. She was nowhere to be found. Now I'm beginning to sweat profusely under my many layers of winter gear. I once again picked up my luggage and this time charged up the canyon to see if she was waiting at the next corner. Again nothing. By this time it was approaching six A.M. I worried that something tragic may have happened to this kind-hearted stranger but then quickly decided the cunt had stiffed me.

I ran up the stairs. Again, these are novelty stairs, the kind that trainers send their clients/victims up and down. I threw my luggage into the trunk, jumped into the car, and hauled ass toward the airport. It was now well after six, and the airport is at least a half hour away. I drove there like an old man drives through a farmer's market, ignoring all laws of man, nature, and God. I screeched around the corner and into the long-term parking lot about six forty-two, grabbed my luggage, and sprinted toward the security line. This was pre-9/11 so I still had a chance.

I'd made it through by about six fifty-three and started scurrying down the endless terrazzo-covered corridor toward the American Airlines gate. When I arrived I was surprised and relieved to see Dr. Drew standing at the check-in counter. I looked to the left and saw our plane was parked right behind him with the gate still hooked up. I was weak from fluid loss but still had enough energy to let forth a celebratory "Hell yeah!" And that's when I noticed Drew was arguing with the woman. "Sir, the door has been shut. We can't reopen it." I found out later their "on-time" schedule is based on when the door shuts, not when the landing gear goes up. And since it was the first flight of the morning, it affected the entire day's schedule. I started in on the woman. "It's two minutes to seven, the plane is parked, the jetway is still attached. Why are we standing in front of the plane arguing?" This bitch was clearly not going to let us onto our airplane.

Drew took this opportunity to make a couple of points. One was that his brand-new camel-hair overcoat was still on the plane because he got off to look for me. Two—the gig we were going to was at the University of Florida at a nine-thousand-seat basketball arena. This was easily the biggest show we'd ever done. As I began a third round of shouting/pleading with the unhelpful representative from American Airlines, Drew turned his ire toward me. "You couldn't have driven yourself to the goddamn airport? You had to get a listener to do it? That jacket cost my wife two grand and this is the first time I've worn it. It was a gift." (Quick side note on gifts: Why does everyone get caught up in the that-coffee-mug-was-a-gift argument? Doesn't that make it more expendable?) I fired back at Drew, "If we could have just carpooled like human beings, I wouldn't have had to rely on the listener with the heart of gold and the alarm clock of marzipan."

As the arguing wore on, I realized the plane and the jetway still had not budged. I pointed out to the bitch in the blue blazer that I could have been on the plane and drunk by now. She repeated for the fourteenth time, "Sir, the door has been closed." Then the final indignity. I saw a worker walk out of the jetway. The door had been open since we'd been there. At that point, I went into a fugue state. I don't remember much after that, just that whenever Drew tells the story he says all I kept repeating to her was "Get me the guy from the commercial. Get me the superhelpful guy that makes everything right. The guy who chases weary travelers through the terminal with the attaché case they mistakenly left behind. That guy. Go get that guy." This argument went on and on while the plane didn't move and the jetway didn't move. It's another one of those letter-of-the-law, spirit-of-the-law arguments. Thank you, dickhead lawyers. The door not opening was no different from the overhead compartment not closing.

Almost every form of transportation has improved over the last forty years. Cars are safer and more comfortable, trains are faster and less expensive, and even buses have improved—not counting the whole segregation thing. Airline travel's the only mode of transportation we've taken a step backward in. The passengers dress like defendants on *The People's Court,* the stewardesses have gotten uglier or gay, and a flight from New York to L.A. still takes six hours, exactly the same as it did in 1963 except that now you have to get to the airport two hours earlier for the prison-style pat-down and delousing. And instead of sitting across from guys with ascots, I'm sitting across from an ass named Scott.

THAT'S ENTERTAINMENT?

I've had the good fortune to work in a variety of jobs in Hollywood—radio, television, film, the Internet, gay pornography—you name it. And I've always been a fan. So I feel well qualified to tear the mass media a new asshole.

TV AND OTHER MISCELLANY

I love television. I wasn't raised on television, I was raised *by* television. I watched nine hours a day back when there was nothing on. Imagine how much I watch now. As a matter of fact, it kills me to write this book because I'm not watching TV right now. If only someone could make a TV show about me writing a book, that would be awesome.

Network television followed about the same arc American car companies took from the early seventies till now. Back in the seventies when there was no competition like cable, satellite, et cetera, you got such gems as *The Brady Bunch, Hawaii Five-O, Dukes of*

Hazzard—the list goes on and on. Now, I know a lot of you wax nostalgic about those shows, but it's not because they were good. They were pieces of steaming shit. The reason you like them is because these shows were all on when you still had hair and weren't in a loveless marriage. But make no mistake, *The Brady Bunch* sucked. What's this have to do with cars? Well, before cable hit our televisions and Toyota hit our shores, we had *Hart to Hart* and the AMC Matador. Two American piles of shit. Now we have *Lost* and the Z06 Corvette. See what you can do when you're pushed by competition?

THE BIGGEST LOSER

I've never seen *The Biggest Loser,* but I have seen the commercials because they play the shit out of them around seven P.M. when I am trying to eat. A cavalcade of morbidly obese dudes with D cups, stretch marks, and manhole-sized areolae are herded in front of me and my spaghetti and meatballs. When did it become okay to show man boobs on prime time? I could make a pretty fucking compelling argument as to why it was more offensive and emotionally scarring for my kids than seeing chick boobs. Couldn't they throw a wife beater on these fat motherfuckers? The guy already has to go to the zoo to be weighed. Do you think five ounces of cotton would make a goddamn difference? I don't care whether you have a penis or a vagina, either you need a sports bra or you don't. Of course the chicks wear a top—they're covering up the one positive side effect of obesity, which is big jugs. So let's quickly review the retarded society we've crafted. If I turn on *Survivor* and a hot female model is scrambling up a cargo net and a half inch of her ass crack can be seen over her bikini line, it needs to be pixelated by the network. But the lactating male long-haul trucker on *The Biggest Loser,* whose jugs are bigger than anything Russ Meyer's ever beat off to, is perfectly fine, according to Standards and Practices? Does anyone else want to kill themselves? I'll tell you who the biggest loser is: my junk!

M*A*S*H HAIR

I was watching a rerun of *M*A*S*H* the other day, a show I've seen two thousand times. As I was marveling at Alan Alda's huge, dry mop of seventies hair and B.J. Hunnicut's pube-fro and walrus mustache, it dawned on me: This show was supposed to be about the Korean War. The Korean War took place from 1950 to 1953. Not only did no one in the military have that hair, no one in society had that hair. Trapper John was rocking a full-blown Jew-fro in what was supposed to be 1950. Back then no guy left the house without a handful of pomade. And the only guys with mustaches in the fifties were either carnival barkers or Latin band leaders, and theirs were dripping with wax. At least on *Happy Days* they attempted to look like their hair was living in the same decade, until somewhere around season three when Ralph Malph said, "Fuck it, I'm getting a blow dryer," and that's when everyone's hair jumped the shark. I blame Elvis for this. He made 425 movies in nine months, which meant that whether he played an Old West gunslinger or an Egyptian pharaoh, his hair always looked like Dick Clark's circa 1955. By the way, *M*A*S*H* aired from 1972 to 1983. The show lasted nearly four times as long as the event it was portraying. The only other time in television history that happened was *Roots*.

THE VIEW

I know I'm a guy so I'm supposed to hate *The View,* but I don't hate *The View* because I have a dick. I hate *The View* because I have a brain. *The View* is going on what feels like its thirty-fifth season. It has numerous Emmy nominations, and even an Emmy win, and it's a disjointed, scattered piece of shit that's hosted by some of the least compelling, most untalented people that have graced a television set. If this show consisted of five guys sitting around talking over each other with the occasional hackneyed joke awkwardly shoehorned into the meaningless conversation, it would have been yanked off the air years ago. You see, at ten in the morning all the smart people are at work, and that leaves *The View*'s audience.

Barbara Walters is about as interesting and funny as that one old teacher you had in junior high. I know everyone treats her like some kind of national treasure, but she's clearly past her prime. And no one at that show would dare utter a word. It's about the same relationship Saddam Hussein shared with his coworkers. When she finally decides to hang up her dentures and call it a career, there will be a silent celebration akin to what the guards did after the Wicked Witch got the bucket of water tossed on her. On her last show, the lavaliere mics will be recording a lot of "We'll miss you, we'll stay in touch, we don't know how we'll carry on without you." But the internal monologues will skew a little more toward "Have fun on the Greyhound bus to hell, bitch."

Sherri Shepherd is dumb. She's read one book and it's the Bible. She's not "ha-ha" funny, she's more "We need a fat chick who's not funny" funny.

Elisabeth Hasselbeck gets a pass. She's already being punished on a daily basis. Could you imagine if your lot in life was to be wedged between Barbara Walters and Sherri Shepherd? She's the lunch meat between a stale piece of sourdough and the dumbest slab of pumpernickel to ever hit the day-old bin at the bakery.

Whoopi Goldberg. What happened to the unstoppable force of comedy that had us doubled over with spun gold such as *Burglar, Jumping Jack Flash,* and *Eddie*? An Emmy for *The View* and an Oscar for *Ghost*. She deserves those about as much as Elvis deserved his black belt in tae kwon do.

Joy Behar—she's the funny one. That's like saying Marwan al-Shehhi was the funniest of the 9/11 hijackers.

CARTOONS

Now I know what you're thinking: Why would an old fuck like me waste a bunch of time writing about cartoons? Two reasons. One, I was forced to stare at these things every Saturday morning throughout the seventies. This was a by-product of my inability to read and my dad's inability to throw a goddamn baseball. And two, now that I have young twins and still can't read, I'm forced to watch cartoons in my forties.

Where to begin? Let's start with the most prolific, Hanna-Barbera. They're responsible for such gems as Magilla Gorilla, the Hair Bear Bunch, Jabberjaw, Hong Kong Phooey, and Grape Ape. Now, I know all you haters are going to say, "What about *The Flintstones?* What about *The Jetsons?* What about *Jonny Quest?*" Those shows all sucked, too, they just didn't suck as hard as a big purple ape that kept repeating the phrase "grape ape" over and over again. These shows blew ass while Hanna-Barbera got rich and we got dumb. Hanna-Barbera didn't do programming for kids because they loved kids; if they loved kids, they would have created programming that was interesting, entertaining, informative, anything but that fucking purple ape. They did entertainment for kids because they weren't talented enough to create programming for adults. It's like those bands for kids. Do you think the guys in the Wiggles were sitting around their dorm room twenty years ago and thought, "Well, we could be the next U2 or Nirvana and bang all the groupies we wanted. Or we could make music for five-year-olds and get some of that sweet, sweet Guatemalan nanny poontang"?

It's a topic we rarely talk about in our society. We've decided that since the children are our future (I disagree, I say it's the hovercraft), that every single thing done for kids is above reproach. I contend these jack-offs are just preying on the stupidity of children. I've read two hundred *Peanuts* cartoons and never even cracked a fucking smile. Yet Charles Schulz made more dead last year than I made in the last decade. Even the legendary Dr. Seuss wasn't exactly Ernest Hemingway. He rhymed *box* and *fox*, everyone! Big goddamn deal! You don't think you could have written that when you were high?

Back to being robbed of my childhood. The guys who churned out almost as much shit as Hanna-Barbera were Sid and Marty Krofft.

There should be a class-action lawsuit against these two numbnuts. Hey, if you can sue Union Carbide for poisoning well water, why can't we sue these two assholes for poisoning our brains?

I was on the CBS lot last year and we were walking to the stage where I was shooting my sitcom. Somebody said, "There's Sid and Marty Krofft's office!" Then, with a certain amount of pride, one guy said, "Marty's there, would you like me to introduce you to him?" I said no. He said, "Why not? The guy's a legend." I said, "A legendary hack." The guy stopped walking. He was shocked. He said, "Do you know how many shows Sid and Marty Krofft got on the air?" I said, "I know, I watched them all when I was a kid. *Far Out Space Nuts, Land of the Lost, Sigmund and the Sea Monsters*—artistically vacant, derivative, hackneyed garbage. Basically a big bowl of Styrofoam packing peanuts that came in a brightly colored box with a shitty prize in it." He said, "How can you say that? The guy's a pioneer. He's eighty-five and still hard at work every day." I said, "Hard at work doing what? Warming over steaming piles of cat shit like *Land of the Lost* so that a new generation's IQ can be collectively lowered while this imbecile hammers another check?" Then he said, "Why are you so angry at Sid and Marty Krofft?" I said, "Because idiots like you are trying to turn these guys into deities. They're rich, isn't that enough?" They came around during a time when there was no competition and monopolized Saturday mornings with shows like *Sigmund and the Sea Monsters*. One of the worst shows, nay one of the worst creative endeavors ever undertaken. And now they want respect? I'll give you two scenarios. One is they actually thought they were artists and that the shit they were crapping out every Saturday morning was good, which makes them delusional hacks. Or two, as I suspect, they knew they were providing shit, they knew the checks would clear, and they didn't give a fuck, which would make them evil hacks.

Either way, you watch an episode of *Far Out Space Nuts* and tell me if the label "legend" applies.

SITCOMS

Let it be noted that when the history books are written and future generations want to know why we're still doing shitty live-audience four-camera sitcoms in 2011, they can blame *Two and a Half Men.* The genre was almost dead. I was like Jamie Lee Curtis in the first *Halloween,* catching my breath on the sofa and thinking, Thank Christ this horrifying ordeal is over. And then from behind the couch popped up Sheen, Cryer, and that kid with the thyroid condition and set the movement back ten years.

I did a sitcom pilot for CBS. It was run by five women who were sort of like friends of your mom when you were in high school. A little bit scary, not particularly funny, and you weren't exactly sure what they did for a living. But you figured you ought to be nice or you would get in trouble. Indulge me on a quick sexist rant for one minute.

Most of the comedy executives that I've dealt with at the network level have been women. Close your eyes and tell me, how many really funny women have you come across in your life? Thank you. I fantasized I'd be talking comedy with a bunch of fat Jews named Murray who knew exactly what I was talking about. The reality is you get your choice between postmenopausal women, gays, and Harvard grads. The network landscape is littered with people who have never made another human being laugh, not counting the time they tried to throw a softball. But don't worry, they're experts. Like an expert on great white sharks who's never left Wichita. I don't know why it's an accepted fact in this town that you can be an expert on funny without having a funny bone in your body—and I'm including their funny bones, which I'll downgrade to mildly amusing bones—but somehow they all get away with it. And if you knew how much money these guys/gals/gays made, you'd never stop vomiting.

CAR COMMERCIALS

I love cars. I hate car commercials. So why would a guy who loves cars hate slow-motion beauty shots of cars cruising down winding roads? Because of the disclaimer: "Closed course, professional driver. Do not attempt." Do the goddamn lawyers have to get involved with every fucking aspect of our society? They used to just be on the commercials where the guy pulled an e-brake and slid into a parking space in front of a busy café. Now the disclaimer is in every shot of any car driving. I've seen them on minivan commercials where the van was going fifty-five in a straight line on an empty highway to Vegas. Hey assholes, if I'm not allowed to attempt to drive the vehicle in a straight line on an empty highway, what the fuck am I buying it for? There was a Subaru commercial a few years ago that showed their competitors' cars driving around on the front wheels with the rear ones six feet off the ground, illustrating they are front-wheel drive versus Subaru's all-wheel drive. And then came the disclaimer: "Do not attempt." How the fuck could you attempt to drive a car with the rear wheels eight feet off the ground? It's sad that we've regressed as a society to the point where we have to put warning labels on shit that's physically impossible.

HERPES MEDICATION

You always know it's a herpes commercial when the chick is kickboxing, mountain biking, or riding a horse on a beach. I wish I could get genital herpes just so I can start living. Whenever I see a herpes commercial I always think, Poor actress. People in snuff films are making fun of you. But then I realize the worst gig in TV is not the chick playing the herpes queen, it's the stooge boyfriend who has to stand next to her and look understanding while she's talking about not letting breakouts control her life. If you do the math, it's fairly clear she didn't get the herpes from this guy—her last beau gave her the big H during one of their very frequent pound sessions. And after her first outbreak, he probably moved on to some European lingerie model who was clean as a whistle. Now this sap is left behind to pick up the pieces and use a condom for the rest of his natural life. I wonder how the audition process goes. Here, put on this flannel shirt and try not to look too judgmental. Just a thought: You know how Native Americans get pissy when Mexicans play Indians in movies? I wonder if people with herpes get angry when nonherpes actresses depict them. If I was in charge, I would only hire actresses with herpes. And the good news is there's no shortage of them.

DUMB GUYS IN COMMERCIALS

Look, let's face it, guys are smarter than women. Ladies, please debunch your panties and open your ears. Men build all the bridges, all the dams, go to the moon, et cetera. It's a fact. I don't want to argue about it. If you don't believe me, go down to the patent office, where, by the way, Einstein and his penis used to work, and see all the great innovations women didn't come up with. But commercials depict men as simpleminded buffoons. The wife's out of town and Dad's left alone to prepare breakfast for the twins. Smash cut to the guy dumping the waffle batter into the toaster. Or how about the famous Carl's Jr. campaign about how guys would starve without them, featuring a dunce in his mid-thirties attempting to make guacamole by putting a whole avocado in a blender? (You ladies are lucky I'm too lazy to look up what percentage of Michelin-rated chefs are men.) Or the same guy wants to lounge on the sofa all day watching arena football, but his lady convinces him to go with her to Home Depot to remodel the basement. We would complain about this unfair depiction, but we are too busy running Home Depot and the plant that makes the television the guy on the couch in the commercial is watching. And building, designing, and operating the camera and satellites that make it possible for you to see the commercial that makes us look like retarded chimpanzees.

Speaking of inaccurate depictions, I've seen seventy-five ADT home-security commercials and I've never seen a face darker than Conan

O'Brien's involved in the home-invasion scenarios. Imagine if an alien came down to the U.S. and just watched TV for a year and then took a tour of our prison system. He would be like, "These white criminals are the shrewdest of them all. They commit one hundred percent of the crime and almost never get caught."

PUBLIC SERVICE ANNOUNCEMENTS

We've all seen PSAs. When I was a kid it was Smokey the Bear talking about campfires and Woodsy Owl telling us not to litter. My kids can look forward to Fergie warning us about online predators and Zac Efron explaining the dangers of huffing copier toner. Radio and TV stations don't run these PSAs out of the goodness of their own hearts or because they're civic minded. The FCC mandates that they run a certain number of them a year or they'll pull their license. We all make fun of the *Reefer Madness*–type PSAs of yore, but how kind do you think history will be to ones of today like David Schwimmer telling you to talk to your kids? (Little-known piece of TV trivia: Schwimmer's character was the only one of the Friends who actually had a kid—you just wouldn't know it because he never spoke to him.) Dick Van Patten wasn't available? Or even the guy who played Joey? You had to get the one Friend who was a deadbeat dad? He spent more time with the monkey. And by the way . . . talk to your kids? This is all you could come up with? How fucking lazy can you be? "I used to just grunt at my kids and use semaphore, but ever since the guy who ignores his kid on TV and has no kids in real life told me to talk to mine, Harvard, here we come!"

The most popular PSA on television these days is the "Over the Limit, Under Arrest" one for drunk driving. Now, I know what you're thinking. How can this asshole have a beef with a drunk-driving PSA? Well, this is why I'm the *writer* and you're the *readee*. Simple: gender bias. This commercial shows cops pulling over six or seven drivers. All males. Women don't get DUIs? I'm sure the makers of these PSAs would argue that more males get DUIs than females. Fine, but from here on out, every AIDS PSA has to start with "Attention fags."

PSAs aren't limited to your TV set. Hopefully your town has not degenerated to this point, but half the municipal vehicles, garbage trucks, cop cars, and so on in Los Angeles have a bumper sticker that reads STOP SENIOR ABUSE. (Between these bumper stickers and the barbed wire around the freeway signs, L.A. has to win the award for the most depressing city to drive in. A stroll through the Holocaust Museum would be more uplifting.) Does this bumper sticker actually stop anyone from abusing a senior? "I was on the way to Shady Acres to beat the shit out of Nana, got caught behind a street sweeper, and really did some soul-searching. Took a long look in the rearview mirror and didn't like what I saw staring back at me." Obviously this bumper sticker doesn't prevent senior abuse. I bet if anything, it reminds people to abuse seniors. "Jesus, that's right, it's been almost a month since Grandpa's felt the cold sting of his own slipper across his weathered face."

But it gets worse. Next to that bumper sticker on the same street sweeper is one that reads DON'T ABANDON YOUR BABY. Is this what it's come to? I don't know why this is written in English. (I know that sounds like I'm a racist, but who's the one assuming I meant it should be written in Spanish?) This is not asking you to raise your baby, it's basically saying drop it off at the firehouse instead of the Dumpster. In the final tally, I'm sure these bumper stickers do way more harm to the collective psyche of the community than they do good.

Thousands of hours and millions of dollars are squandered each year on ineffective, no-shit-Sherlock PSAs. Meanwhile, barrels and barrels of oil are wasted and most of those rollover deaths in a Ford Explorer a few years back could have been prevented if the tires had been properly inflated. But nary a word about that. Maybe they'll get to it when they're done with secondhand smoke and self-esteem. Obviously our government, the FCC, and the Ad Council (the anemic, semiretarded, hypocritical, money-wasting morons who come up with the PSAs) have little to no interest in having a positive impact on society. I gotta go. I gotta get Schwimmer's agent on the line. I want to see if he's available to cut a PSA on wasting our most precious resource—my fucking time.

MOVIES

I love movies. I love good movies, I love bad movies. I just don't like mediocre movies that are supposed to be great. Let me give you a couple of titles of movies that were mediocre but were huge successes.

LITTLE MISS SUNSHINE Nominated for best picture, best original screenplay, best supporting actor, and best supporting actress. It won for best original screenplay, and Alan Arkin won for best supporting actor. As far as best original screenplay, this is like giving song of the year to "Mary Had a Little Lamb." And Alan Arkin was in the first half of the movie; his corpse was in the last forty-five minutes. He played a junkie, sexually addicted grandpa who taught his fat granddaughter to dance like a whore. He didn't have a lot to do in the movie, and it's a role that your grandfather could have pulled off. (My grandfather has been dead for ten years, so he'd require a little more time in makeup.) Alan Arkin was fine, but giving him the Oscar for this role was like awarding the Nobel Peace Prize to a guy who broke up a bum fight with a garden hose.

LOST IN TRANSLATION Another film that qualifies for the Emperor's New Gay Clothes Award. A boring, look-how-cool-I-am movie made tolerable by Scarlett Johansson in her underpants that won for best original screenplay. I'll bet when Alan Arkin and Sofia Coppola see each other at Oscar parties they exchange those knowing glances that couples who are fucking around on their spouses with each other do. "Can you believe what we got away with?"

TYLER PERRY MOVIES I don't blame Tyler Perry—it's not his fault he's a horrible writer. It's not that hard to write horribly. It's Oprah's fault for making a star out of a guy who's built an empire around a gun-toting, 250-pound grandmother whose conflict-resolution strategy involves threatening to put her foot up your ass.

Dear black community: You don't have to support this guy's subpar products just because he's the same color as you. It's not like I sit around and say to my white friends, "Rob Schneider's got a new piece of shit coming out this weekend—let's head to the multiplex. By golly, he's white and we need to support our own." (If you think I'm being too hard on Tyler Perry or Rob Schneider, I challenge you to watch *Diary of a Mad Black Woman* or *Deuce Bigalow 2*.)

Here's a handful of my favorite movies. I left out the *Gone with the Wind*s and the *Godfather*s because I figured you've seen those.

PAPILLON Steve McQueen at his best. And if Arkin had an ounce of dignity he'd drop off his ill-gotten Oscar to the guy who is missing one, Dustin Hoffman, for his work in this movie.

LOVE AND DEATH Woody Allen's funniest joke-for-joke movie.

BREAKING AWAY Funny, understated, and a great performance from Paul Dooley.

DEFENDING YOUR LIFE Funny, poignant, smart, inspirational. Sad that most of you have seen *Happy Gilmore* and *Tommy Boy* 250 times but have never seen this one. Best comedy of the last twenty-five years. *Lost in America* is another Albert Brooks masterpiece that never gets shown on TV. Why *Billy Madison* has to play on a fucking loop and *Lost in America* pops up once an Olympic season is not only confusing but cosmically wrong.

FARGO No better Coen brothers movie. William H. Macy was excellent. Arkin, after you've dropped off the Oscar at Hoffman's place, grab one of the loose Oscars he's using to hold down the tarp on his barbecue and bring it by Macy's place for his role in *Fargo*.

SAVING PRIVATE RYAN Best opening twenty minutes of any movie in the last thirty years. Important, moving, almost made us forget we hate Vin Diesel.

ELECTION Quirky, funny, dark. All the things *Little Miss Sunshine* was trying to be.

CARS (AND ALL THE PIXAR STUFF) Entertainment for people four to ninety-three. I know you thought I was gonna say ninety-four, but the cutoff is not a day over ninety-three. Sorry, rules are rules.

OVERNIGHT This is a great documentary. But I could have picked twenty others. The point is, you're almost never gonna go wrong with a documentary. P.S. Don't call it a "doc." Now that Papillon's made it off of Devil's Island, there's a vacancy for all you people who say "doc" and "*Curb*."

NO COUNTRY FOR OLD MEN No better Coen brothers movie.

MUSIC

I love music. I don't know anyone who says they don't. The problem for me is I love good music, but based on what's playing on the radio, the music everyone else likes sucks. So I'm forced to listen to that shitty music on the radio. Music is one of those topics that's very personal and that people claim is subjective. But if you like "I Need to Know" by Marc Anthony or you don't feel like you've heard the Oak Ridge Boys' "Elvira" enough this week, you're a brainless fuck who doesn't know shit about music. The problem with those people is they're dumb, and dumb people respond to repetition. Thus, they end up thinking songs that blow ass are good because they were beaten into their heads by corrupt program directors.

Here's how stupid people are. "Having My Baby" by Paul Anka was number one in 1974. In '06, CNN announced it was the worst song of all time. One of the best songs of all time, "Rosalita" by Bruce Springsteen, came out a year before but did not chart. On a positive note, it's comforting to know that people had no taste and were nimrods almost forty years ago. Everyone always talks about today's youth, how ill-informed they are and how bad the music of today has gotten. At least our parents were fucking idiots too.

How did we get into this mess? Rod Stewart comes up with an abortion of a song like "Passion" or "Hot Legs." The label he's on drops off a sack of cocaine and some money to a DJ and/or program director. They agree to play "Passion" three times an hour, you assholes hear it on the way to work two thousand times, and the next thing you know, you're hooked on a subpar, piece-of-shit song. There's no way, based on its own merits, that "Shout" by Tears for Fears would be a number-one song. Somebody had to get paid off.

You measure a good song the same way you measure architecture, fashion, or any other artistic endeavor. Time. You know when you see a picture of yourself from the eighties with a horrible hairdo and some stone-washed jeans and you think, "How embarrassing—what the fuck was I thinking? Why didn't somebody stop me?" It's the same thing Mick Jagger and David Bowie should be thinking every time they hear their cover of "Dancing in the Streets." The point is, at the time it seemed like a good idea, just like kitchens with burnt-orange Formica and avocado appliances, den walls covered with fake brick paneling, and segregation—all horrible decisions that we now universally recognize as wrong. But somehow when it comes to music, we can't just admit we made a mistake with "Emotional Rescue." There's always some dick who defends the past. "Hey, man, I lost my virginity to 'Careless Whisper.'" I'm sure there was somebody who got laid for the first time on 9/11 but they don't get a boner when they see the footage of the planes going into the tower.

Let's start with a list of songs I never need to hear again:

"ADDICTED TO LOVE" BY ROBERT PALMER Robert Palmer is a guy who flies under the shit radar. He had three or four horrible songs made tolerable by the coke whores pretending to play guitar behind him. "Addicted to Love" is a shitty, repetitive song that, sadly, I could belt out on karaoke night even if the monitor was broken. That's the tragedy, that's where the lawsuit should come in. I know all the fucking lyrics to "Addicted to Love" and "Bad Case of Loving You" and "Simply Irresistible" even though I've never bought a Robert Palmer album. When the first lick in "Addicted to Love" comes on the car radio, I pounce on it so fast I've almost gotten into accidents. If the knob broke off and I couldn't change the channel, I would drive into the first eighteen-wheeler traveling the opposite direction. This is the essence of this chapter—all the shit that's foisted on us, how we can't escape it because it's ubiquitous in our retarded culture, and all of the imbeciles who not only defend these hacks but turn them into millionaires while my ears are being raped.

"COCAINE" BY ERIC CLAPTON Superslow and super-repetitive. The song should be called "Quaalude" or "Ether Rag." It's also ironic that just a few short years after Ed Sullivan told Mick Jagger to change the lyrics from "Let's spend the night together" to "Let's spend some time together" and told Jim Morrison not to say "Girl, we couldn't get much higher," Eric Clapton is allowed to do a fifteen-minute homage to booger sugar.

"I SHOT THE SHERIFF" BY BOB MARLEY "But I did not shoot the deputy." "Oh, our mistake. Sorry for the inconvenience." Bob Marley's a legend and so is Eric Clapton and there's something progressive, evolved, and cool about a British guy covering a reggae song. It still does not prevent the song from blowing hippo ass, not rhyming, and not making any fucking sense whatsoever. He shot the sheriff but he didn't shoot the deputy? Bob Marley would make an awesome attorney. "Your Honor, while it's true my client murdered the sheriff, he did not, however, shoot his lower-ranking partner. We'll take our apology in the form of a check. Thank you."

"I LOVE ROCK AND ROLL" BY JOAN JETT AND THE BLACKHEARTS This song is a one-two punch of shitty and fucked-out. It's the melodic equivalent of getting crabs from a fat chick. Lose-lose. It's a simplistic, repetitive, uncreative chorus that never ends. If that isn't bad enough, I've heard it 235,000 fucking times.

"BORN IN THE U.S.A." BY BRUCE SPRINGSTEEN (SORRY, LYNETTE) Bruce has got a lot of good songs—this ain't one of them. Somewhere around the 166th time he screams he was born in the U.S.A., I start wishing I was never born at all.

"ABRACADABRA" BY THE STEVE MILLER BAND "Abra, abra, cadabra/I want to reach out and grab ya." Lyrically, this song is an abortion. Steve Miller gets some kind of free pass musically, and I'm not sure why. His songs suck, whether it's the joker-toker song, or "Take the Money and Run." His lyrics sound as if they were written by an eight-year old who was stricken with fetal alcohol syndrome. Have you ever uttered this phrase: "I could go for a good Steve Miller song about now"? I've had notes left on my car windshield with more complex rhymes. Is there something I don't know about Steve Miller? Did his wife drown his five kids in a bathtub? Does he have full-blown AIDS? Is there some reason why we can't all say out loud how much his music sucks and what an insult his songs are to everyone's collective intelligence? Right about now you're saying, "Ace, don't be so hard. 'Jet Airliner' is a pretty good song." He didn't write that one.

"STUCK WITH YOU" BY HUEY LEWIS (SORRY, JIMMY)
Jimmy Kimmel's favorite artist and one of the nicest guys in the world. So I'll keep this short and give Huey the benefit of the doubt. I'm sure he was extremely high when he wrote this retarded nursery rhyme and never thought in his wildest dreams it would get picked up for airplay. This, by the way, is how you know you're popular—when even your shittiest songs are getting a ton of airplay.

"THE GIRL IS MINE" BY PAUL MCCARTNEY AND MICHAEL JACKSON
This song is lame enough while they're singing, but when they start talking to each other and using each other's first names, it goes into the gay stratosphere.

"BRASS MONKEY" BY THE BEASTIE BOYS
It's hard for me to bag on this song because if I couldn't sing and had zero musical talent yet insisted on being in a band, I guess this is the kind of shit I would crank out too.

"BEAUTIFUL GIRLS" BY SEAN KINGSTON
A great example of a modern shitty song. A lot of new songs sound as if they're synthesized and it's intentional. In the past, when they found some hot chick who couldn't really sing, they'd clean it up in the studio—but the whole plan was not to let you catch on. Now there's a whole new brand of music that sounds as if it's being sung by a Roomba, which goes against the very essence of music. No soul, no human beings, no connection. When I was a kid, all the futuristic movies would show humans sitting down for dinner and on their plate would be a pill that said "Turkey" on it and another pill that said "Stuffing" next to it. That is what this feels like. Plus it's just a straight rip-off of Ben E. King's "Stand by Me."

"AMERICAN WOMAN" The Guess Who recorded the eight-minute version of it in '69 and Lenny Kravitz did the four-minute version that feels like eight minutes in '99. If you want to have fun, you can play a little musical Who's on First: "Who had the shittiest song of 1970?" "The Guess Who?" "That's what I'm asking. . . ." To be fair to Lenny, I don't think he likes the song; he picks his music based on a complicated algorithm that boils down to what song he looks coolest playing in front of a full-length mirror.

"MANEATER" BY HALL & OATES I know you guys love "Sara Smile" and "Rich Girl" and expect me to give Hall & Oates some sort of pass based on the work they did before "Maneater." Well, guess what? O.J. has a Heisman and he rushed for two thousand yards. This is not only one of the worst songs ever created, it's one of the worst artistic endeavors ever undertaken, and I'm including "Piss Christ" and those enema painter guys. It uses a shitty metaphor to illustrate a fucked-out theme, and just when things couldn't get worse, there's a horrible generic eighties sax solo. Call me old-fashioned, but I like my sax solos to have some relationship to the song they're in. That sax solo sounds as if Hall & Oates reached into a pillowcase that said "Eighties Sax Solos" (picture Rob Lowe in *St. Elmo's Fire*). The whole song was done on a Casio and represents everything that's wrong with music. Imagine if you resurrected Hayden, Tchaikovsky, Janis Joplin, and Wes Montgomery, sat them down in a room, and played them that piece of cat shit rolled in AIDS jimmies known as "Maneater." Then you told them, "This song made it all the way to number one." They would never stop vomiting. Other than that, it's an okay tune.

I know what you're saying. Hey, man, those are good songs, I like some of those songs. Please let me address this. None of these songs are good. They suck by all units of measurement. Cosmically and artistically, they all represent horrible work by the artist. The fact that you like them is a combination of the man pounding them into your brain and your brain being malleable enough not to fend off the shit barrage that program directors constantly bombard it with. My brain has a hard candy outer shell that is able to ward off the John Cougar Mellencamps and absorb the John Hiatts. That's why I get to write a fucking book.

The eighties were simultaneously the best decade and the worst decade for music. Everyone always does that "Oh, you were in high school in the early eighties, and that's why you like all that music." I don't like the cars from the early eighties, I like the cars from the sixties. I hate the architecture from the early eighties, I like architecture from the twenties. Are you starting to get the picture? So shut the fuck up. I like the music from the early eighties because the Pretenders' first albums and Joe Jackson's first albums and Elvis Costello's first albums were great, not because I was fifteen. But you wouldn't know there was this much great music in the eighties if you ever tuned in to the eighties station on satellite radio or watched any VH1 flashback eighties shows or listened to any eighties weekend on your local radio station. Then it's a lot of "Union of the Snake" by Duran Duran, Wham's "Young Guns," "Tainted Love" by Soft Cell, . . . it's all the soundtrack to a really shitty Adam Sandler movie. It's like we're punishing ourselves. It's called the Eighties Station, not the Super-Shitty Fucked-Out Horrible Songs from the Eighties Station. We could be hearing "Clubland" by Elvis Costello or "Stupefaction" by Graham Parker, but instead we get "The Safety Dance" by Men Without Hats. This is the equivalent to getting a sack of trail mix, picking out all the smoked almonds and peanut M&Ms, and just eating the raw sunflower seeds. Why are we fucking doing this to ourselves? There's tons of great music out there. Why are we forced to listen to the biggest mistakes of the decade? If we're going to go this route, shouldn't we take a number-two pencil and shove it into one ear until it pops out the other?

Indulge me for a moment while I directly address the gentleman who programs the Sirius XM eighties channel that's in my wife's car.

Dear Fuckstick:

You obviously don't know shit about music or you're a maniacal madperson who is trying to sonically punish those who pay a premium for satellite radio. If I hear "People Are People" by Depeche Mode one more fucking time on your piece-of-shit eighties station, I'm gonna buy a black-market Soviet ballistic missile and shoot down your fucking satellite.

THEY WERE SO GAY AND WE WERE SO NAÏVE

The Village People broke when I was in junior high. And even though they all had bushy mustaches and were singing about cruising YMCAs and shipping out with the navy, none of us had a clue they were gay. One of the guys was just dressed as a leather homo. He didn't even have an occupation other than sucking cock. And we were still like, "Those guys must pull down a ton of chicks. It'd be awesome being one of the Village People. You must get pussy every night." It's not as though we didn't know what gay was, we just couldn't do the Village-dude math. And none of our dads or older brothers did it for us. Somehow in the era of disco, everyone was gay and no one was gay. Between the coke and the mirror ball, we were all temporarily blinded.

Another swish we should have seen coming was Rob Halford from Judas Priest. He dressed like an extra from *The Beastmaster,* no wife, no kids, man-gina goatee, and a studded codpiece. "Ram It Down," "Point of Entry," and "Hell Bent for Leather" are just a handful of their super-obviously gay titles that we didn't get.

When Queen came out with that album that had all the nude chicks on the bicycles, I was like, "Freddy probably personally nailed every one of those bitches." Freddy was giving us obvious clues, we just weren't picking them up. It's like we were standing under a gay basket, he threw us a no-look pass, but we missed the layup. His balls just clanked off our rim. The band was named Queen, he adopted a massive overbite and a biker-cop mustache, and yet we still didn't get it. So he finally threw in the towel and said, "Fuck it, give me AIDS."

REGGAE MUSIC

Reggae music sucks but no one except me will say it. Bob Marley's "Jamming" is one of the shittiest songs ever made. And no one ever utters a word about it because somehow you're either uptight, racist, or square if you don't like reggae music. Here's my problem with reggae music : You only need one reggae album in your collection to officially own every reggae song ever recorded because they are all the same.

Having a collection of reggae music is like having a collection of garbage disposals in your kitchen. If you've got one, you're covered. Here's how you know reggae music sucks. Whenever you argue with someone about reggae music they go, "Are you telling me that with your feet in the sand and the Caribbean as far as the eye can see, sipping rum out of a hollowed-out pineapple, that reggae music doesn't sound great?" Of course it does. A recording of my mom getting raped would sound good under those circumstances. What if I made that argument? "Are you telling me you don't enjoy Ben Folds when you're getting your cock sucked?" Nobody else works where you are and what you're doing into the music argument, just reggae defenders.

LED ZEPPELIN

Not only one of the greatest rock bands of all time, but one of the most secure. We're living in a time of shameless self-promotion, where Ed Hardy T-shirts have "Ed Hardy" printed on them 250 times, Fergie's first single was called "Fergalicious," and every player in the NFL refers to himself in the third person. (I have a theory on the whole athlete-third-person phenomenon. They don't do it because they're pompous, they do it for when their wives confront them with a pile of text messages from their mistresses. That way they can say,

"Debrickashaw Jackson doesn't cheat. Debrickashaw loves his family. That doesn't sound like the Debrickashaw Jackson I know. But if you want, I can talk to him next time I see him.") So it's refreshing that Led Zeppelin intentionally made their song titles confusing. Here's a list of Led Zeppelin hits. I guarantee you know every one of them, but not by title, because they're not mentioned in the lyrics of any of these songs.

Black Dog

D'yer Mak'er

Immigrant Song

Moby Dick

Over the Hills and Far Away

Four Sticks

Trampled Under Foot

The Wanton Song

The Battle of Evermore

This is why "Stairway to Heaven" is Led Zeppelin's most requested song. Because no one wants to call the radio station and say, "Could you play that one that goes 'Da-da-da, I live for my dreams and a pocketful of gold.'" The song titles are complex, but when it comes to the album titles, they lay them out like IKEA instructions: *Zeppelin I, Zeppelin II, Zeppelin III, Zeppelin IV.* The fifth album, *Houses of the Holy,* is where they regain their insanity. Just to fuck with you, it does not contain one of their few hits that has the title in the lyrics, "Houses of the Holy." That's on *Physical Graffiti.* The antithesis of this is another great rock band from the seventies. The name of the band: Bad Company. The name of the first album: *Bad Company.* The name of the first single . . . wait for it . . . "Bad Company." Paul Rodgers also named his first daughter Bad Company.

Here's a tip for all you folks who enjoy Kenny Chesney or Céline Dion but are scared you'll get your ass kicked by hipsters at the cool-guy party. If anyone asks you what's in your iPod, you just tell them

Motorhead and Radiohead—or if you like, you can put the word *early* in front of any artist's name, and it works. "I'm into early Clapton." "I'm into early Billy Joel." "I'm into early John Tesh . . . before he went corporate and lost his edge."

In conclusion: Artistically, we humans are capable of such great work as *The Wizard of Oz, Songs in the Key of Life,* and *All in the Family.* Yet we choose to drown ourselves in a sea of *Paul Blart: Mall Cop,* "Every Rose Has Its Thorn," and *Cougartown.*

MOTHERFUCKING NATURE

I'm fascinated by nature because it's got a lot of range. On the one hand, it seems boring. It's got a lot of browns and oranges and colors from furniture in the seventies. And then once in a while you'll see some multicolored fish from an exotic locale and think, Holy shit, how did nature come up with that one? Sometimes nature's so straight, Republican, and uptight, and other times it's like the gayest guy ever. The peacock? Come on. That's a gay-pride parade on two legs. The word *peacock* even sounds gay.

It's not just animals. Think about the range pumpkins have. There's the minipumpkin you put out for the table centerpiece on Thanksgiving that's the size of an apple, and then there are the ones that collapse the suspension of the farmer's truck they're sitting in. The ones you see at county fairs. There are big humans and small humans. But the smallest go sixty pounds and the biggest go six hundred. With pumpkins it's seven ounces versus seventeen hundred pounds. And they look exactly the same.

And we have a lot of range in our reactions to nature, and it doesn't necessarily follow logic. Take our feelings about bats. All bats do is eat grasshoppers and mosquitoes and sleep in a belfry, yet we're completely freaked out by them. Even Hollywood can't decide how to feel about the bat. Think about Count Dracula and Batman. No other animal has had that kind of cinematic range. There's no manatee that either saves a city or comes in at midnight through the French doors and rapes an ingenue.

Or bugs. We've decided there are good bugs and bad bugs. For some reason we hate cockroaches, but what did a cockroach ever do to anyone? Bugs really tell you a lot about human nature. If you live in the United States, unless you're one of the four people ever to be killed by a black widow spider, bugs should be neither here nor there. Yet we spend a lot of time thinking about them, talking about them, and figuring out ways to get rid of them. They're almost a metaphor for how our psyche works. They're small, mean us no harm, and pose no discernible threat, yet if we know there's one in the bedroom with us we can't go to sleep. Also, we don't really define bugs along the lines of whether they're dangerous or not; we define them aesthetically. What's the difference between a moth and a butterfly except one is gray and one looks like the gay flag?

SPIDERS I love the idiots who say you should be happy to have spiders in your house because they take care of the bad bugs. That's like saying, "I like to keep a Crip around the house. It keeps the Bloods out." Also when's the last time you walked into the kitchen in the middle of the night and saw a spider locked in mortal combat with a silverfish? I used to put them outside, but then they would just go out, fuck, get pregnant, and come back in. There's a reason they're inside. They're not lost. They came inside for the same reason you came inside. It's warm and there's food.

There's nothing that makes you look stupider than walking into a spiderweb. When you step out of the house and get one in the face, your neighbors think you're having a seizure because they don't see what you hit. They just see a crazed maniac throwing punches in the air. And it comes out of the spider's ass. If it came out of a seagull, you'd have to take a shower.

DUNG BEETLES This is a bad draw in the animal kingdom. This is your whole life—you roll around a pile of shit until a hawk eats you, which is a sweet relief. The dung beetle would be one of those insects other insects couldn't complain in front of. Like when you tell a guy how miserable you were at Boy Scout camp and he tells you he did three tours in Nam. A pill bug couldn't be like, "Oh, man. I have to live under a rock," or a moth couldn't go, "Goddamn. Every time someone turns on a porch light, I have to go flying at it," because a dung beetle would be like, "Cry me a river. I have to roll around a ball of elephant shit that's three times my height." Could you imagine how low the self-esteem of a dung beetle must be? If I get a zit I won't even leave the house. This is worse than Sisyphus: At least he was pushing granite, and not rhino flop.

ALLIGATORS Every time I turn on the TV there's some jack-off in khaki shorts diving off a boat onto an alligator or wrestling one at an amusement park in Florida. This has to be really confusing for the alligators. Five million years of people being scared shitless of you, but in the last five years every asshole with a fan boat and a roll of duct tape is jumping on your back. I'd love to be a fly on the wall at the next alligator convention: "What the fuck? I used to just slide up on the shore, yawn, and scare the bejesus out of any native within a hundred miles. Now every yahoo with a video camera and a Red Bull wants to throw down. What the hell? Does anyone know what the fuck's going on? Why aren't these goddamn people scared of us anymore? One of your guys in Florida is gonna have to eat a toddler. Get these assholes back in line." I bet when Steve Irwin died, they were pissed that a stingray got him. "It should have been one of us, man."

FISH I love the hypocrisy of the people who for "moral reasons" won't eat beef or poultry, but when you press them on it admit they eat fish. To me a swordfish is much more majestic than a chicken or a cow. And the way you catch and kill them is usually less humane than what a cow gets. A cow will get a bolt to the head, quick and easy. A swordfish gets a hook through its mouth, is dragged out of the water, and essentially drowns on the deck of the boat while guys with beards hit it with those weird small boat bats. If it's lucky, it gets its head cut off first. Either way, it was alive and now it's dead, and someone served it up to you with a side of mashed potatoes. So what's the difference? Get a fucking steak, you pussy.

Recently I was thinking about fishing and I realized why I don't like it. It's because you use little fish for bait. Fish are essentially cannibals. They eat smaller versions of themselves. This would be like me saying, "I'm hungry. Somebody get me a midget."

DOLPHINS It's too bad dolphins can't get laid by humans. There isn't a hot chick alive who doesn't love dolphins. Dolphins are the only thing that lives in the sea that women would actually have sex with. If there are any single guys reading this and you're trying to get laid when you're on the first date and the chick asks you, "What do you do for a living?" say, "I work with special-needs dolphins." They are the only creatures that live in the ocean that make us brag, "They're smarter than us, you know. If you're ever out and there are sharks around, they'll ward them off. They're family oriented and highly intelligent." They're very curious and we love that. It's funny because when dolphins or otters or something that's cute are curious, it's adorable. When it's rats, roaches, or fat chicks, we want to put them down.

WHALES Every year or so, a whale gets lost and ends up in a river or a bay and the news covers it 24-7. Why is it that whales used to be lantern oil, but now if one goes astray the whole world shuts down? And when a whale tries to beach itself we all go apeshit? Big whoop. It's decided for some reason it does not want to continue to live. Can't we respect that? Imagine if one day you decided you were just too tired to go on living but a bunch of guys in bandannas and Birkenstocks dragged you out of your house and forced you to get a job and start dating? Why can't we just let whales kill themselves? Why do we have to have whale interventions? "You have too much to live for. There is so much krill left to eat. Think about your pod."

BEAVERS I think it's cool that beavers live in lodges. Gophers live in holes, beavers live in lodges. It sounds as if they're in there smoking pipes, watching sports, and bitching about their beaver wives.

DOGS I have a sad relationship with dogs. I wanted one my entire life. All I wanted was a German shepherd. But my cheap parents didn't even want to feed me, never mind a dog. And maybe they were too liberal: German shepherds are the most racist dogs. Watch one episode of *Cops* with the K-9 unit and you'll know what I'm talking about. My parents were divorced and my dad was living in an apartment. I bugged him and bugged him and bugged him. He said one day when we moved to a house, he would get me a German shepherd. My father never made promises he didn't keep. Not because he was a man of honor, but because he never made a promise. We moved into a house in North Hollywood that cost my father fifteen thousand dollars. Now to be fair, those were 1975 dollars, but still, the average house was going for between sixty-five and eighty-five thousand. So you can only imagine what that piece of shit looked like. I woke up every morning and ran downstairs. Actually it was only one story. But I'd go into the living room with the indoor-outdoor carpet praying to see a German shepherd puppy with a bow on it. The dog never showed up. Eventually my dad remarried and moved into a house with one and a half bathrooms and I let go of the dream of ever getting a German shepherd puppy.

Twenty years later when I was living in my first house in the shadow of the Hollywood sign, working on *Loveline* and *The Man Show* and making a good living, I thought, "What ever happened to that German shepherd puppy I wanted so many years ago?" I decided to go out and rescue one by giving six hundred dollars to a bull dyke in Arleta who ran a puppy mill. I named her Lotzi after my beloved Hungarian stepgrandfather who died a few months earlier.

Lotzi

And a love affair began. She was beautiful and rambunctious and had one ear that wouldn't stay up. When she turned six months old, I dropped her off at the vet to be spayed, was due to pick her up that afternoon, and got a call from the vet saying that she was dead. Some sort of liver problem. I never got to the bottom of it. I was now in my early thirties. I'd had one dog in my life for a total of two months. It's a sad tale, but I tell it in case there are any kids reading this book. The message is: never follow a dream.

After Lotzi died I swore I'd never love again. Unfortunately for my wife, I expanded that proclamation outside of the canine realm. Almost ten years later, after moving into another house, a package showed up at the door. It was a car cover I'd ordered online. But just behind it was a blond Lab named Molly. She was shipped out from Chicago: A combination of neglect from my wife's nieces and nephews and their mom getting new furniture meant a one-way ticket to Hollywood for Molly girl. We immediately bonded and a love affair soon began. Sweet, energetic, and loves to play. My wife, whose biological clock

Molly

was ticking so loudly that it was more of a tell-tale heart than a clock, poured all her maternal energy into Molly as well.

One summer about five years ago after a particularly rousing episode of *Oprah,* she walked into the den and announced, "We've got to get Molly rattlesnake training." I said, "For what?" She said, "We're in rattlesnake country and it's summertime." I pointed out, "We're also in earthquake country and this is earthquake weather. Should we also be training her to work one of those wind-up flashlight-radios?" She replied, "There are rattlesnakes all over these hills. If one bite's good enough to take down a horse, that's plenty good to take down Molly girl." I said I would be goddamned if I was going to pay some guy in desert boots with his ponytail pulled through the back of his cap to come over here and shake a rubber snake in front of my dog. She came back one more time with a "What about Molly girl?" and I gave her the speech she's probably memorized like the Pledge of Allegiance by now: "Just because we live in Hollywood doesn't mean we're going Hollywood. All that nonsense is for paranoid Whitey who's got too much money and too much time on his hands. We don't need to buy into Oprah's scare-of-the-month club." I put my foot down, into a pile of Molly's shit, and that was it.

85

Two days later we were sitting in the den watching *Entertainment Tonight* when Molly came into the room and plopped down in front of the TV set. She seemed lethargic. Even though it was dark and the room was only illuminated by the television set, my wife noticed some swelling on the left side of Molly's snout. (You probably know where this is going.) Then she noticed two bloody red dots about an inch apart on her nose. It didn't take that guy who was eaten by grizzly bears to know those were puncture wounds. She'd been struck by a rattlesnake. Lynette immediately sprang into action by screaming at me. Then she jumped up to grab Molly girl, obscuring my view of a shirtless Matthew McConaughey sea kayaking. She yelled, "I told you! This is your fault!" and threw Molly into the car and sped off into the night. Four thousand dollars and zero blow jobs later, Molly was saved. Once again she cheated death. She's known around the neighborhood as the Osama bin Laden of blond Labs. The vet explained that if it had happened during the morning or afternoon when we weren't home, Molly would have just curled up in a ball and died. This didn't help my case. And between the antivenom serum and the multiple trips to the vet for follow-up, the guy with the magnetic sign on the Vanagon that said SNAKE WHISPERER would have been a real money saver.

I love Molly, but I do have a complaint. She sleeps everywhere except in the two-hundred-dollar bed we bought for her. I would love this ability—I'm envious. It usually takes a good fifteen beers before I could fall asleep on a bathroom floor. She'll sleep on the cold tile floor right next to her super-expensive suede bed lined with angora and stuffed with camel hair, I assume to mock me. I'll say, "Why don't you sleep in your bed, Molly?" And she'll look up like, "Nah, I'm good here on your sweatpants." I end up getting angry: "Get in the fucking bed, we paid for it and it's too small for the kids. Listen, you goddamn dog, you're going to be comfortable if I have to use my boot to mash you into that bed." If Molly had balls she'd just rest them on the edge of the bed to fuck with me. Why not sleep on the comfortable thing that's built for you? I've never gone to a hotel, seen the bed, and thought, "Hey, look at that. Goose-down comforter, California King mattress, soft pillows. Wow . . . Okay, I'm gonna go sack out next to the toilet."

I like a big dog. But then there are the people that are into Great Danes. Is a golden retriever not big enough for you? Who needs a dog the size of a donkey? I'm not going to hook it up to a plow. I need companionship, not something to pull my car out of a ditch. I don't want a dog that's so big that if it decides to have sex with me, there's nothing I can do about it. And if a week of the dog's fecal matter weighs more than you, you shouldn't be allowed to own it.

CATS While we're on a fecal tangent, let's not forget about cats. People, especially guys, don't like cats. But let's give credit where credit is due: Cats bury their own crap. A cat, with quiet dignity, lets himself out of the home, goes in the yard, drops a deuce, and then covers his tracks. If I were a publicist for cats, that's all I'd be screaming about. Humans are so horribly insecure. If the pet doesn't run up to us when we get home and literally start kissing our ass, like a dog, even if it just wants to get food from us, we can't handle it. We're like, "I don't like her. Why isn't she worshipping me?" Pets aren't here to make you feel better about yourself and your shitty life. That's what drugs are for. But cats bury their dook. Does anything say "I love you" better than that? Let's give them their props.

SQUIRRELS I've seen two hundred million squirrels in my life but I've never seen one take a shit. I walk my dog and she shits every nine feet. (I'll share my thoughts on bird shit shortly.) But I don't even know what squirrel shit looks like. There are as many squirrels running around the trees on my property as birds. Shouldn't I come out to my car in the morning and say, "Fuck, I just had it detailed and now it's covered in squirrel shit"?

BIRDS Okay, one last shit-related thought. I hate birds because they hate us. It's clear they hate us because there is more crap on cars

than there is on the ground. To me this is evidence that they're aiming. They're acting with malicious intent. There's constantly bird shit
all over my car. And if you own a restaurant by the ocean, you might
as well just paint your roof white. They should just call those restau-
rants Bird Shit by the Sea. I love when the plastic owl they put on the
roof to scare off seagulls is covered in bird shit. The seagull is saying,
"Hey tough guy. I'm on to your ruse. Hold on, I ate Mexican last night."

Let's be honest—if you could fly, you'd shit on things too. You'd be
like, "Hey, there's the mayor's motorcade," or, "My ex-girlfriend is
walking in the park with her new man. It's about time for an aerial
deuce dropping." Imagine the damage you could do. If birds were as
big as medium-sized dogs, we'd all be dead.

Let's talk about Pegasus for a moment. I know mythical flying
horses don't really exist, but it is an animal, after all. Have you ever
seen a pile of horse shit? Imagine that coming down on you from
two thousand feet. I have this fantasy of getting a Pegasus and flying
it over the cars and homes of my enemies. I'd spend a week feeding
it lunch-truck breakfast burritos and Dodger Dogs. Then I'd steer it
toward my neighbor's house, the one who called the cops about the
noise from my place at nine on New Year's Eve, and drop a bunker
buster. When he came over the next day to complain, "Hey man, your
Pegasus shit a hole in my roof," I'd be like, "Wasn't my Pegasus."

PANDAS Pandas hate us. All we want them to do is mate, and they
won't. They are the only species on the planet that refuses to screw.
Every other species loves fucking so much it has become a problem.
We have to spay and neuter dogs, thin the deer population, and beef
up the border, all because we can't stop the screwing. (I didn't say
which border, so that makes you the racist for thinking Mexico.) All
but the pandas. We actually have to show them panda porn to try to
get them to mate. This is more than just erratic mating habits; they're
openly mocking us. I witnessed it firsthand.

I went with some zoologists to a panda-bear habitat and had the rare privilege to observe two pandas mating. The male panda mounted the female panda from behind, and after about ten minutes he looked up, made a grimacing face, pulled out, and came on her back. Later in the day I witnessed the same panda being blown while he wiped his ass with the American flag.

We should breed them with dogs. Dogs never stop fucking. We need to invent a pan-dog.

I also don't like that we can only lease them from China. They won't give them to us, they'll only let us borrow them. Why are they so stingy with their bears? Not only do they eventually want them back, they come with a list of sanctioned names, and Todd's not on the list. We have to give them names like Ling-Ling and Ching-Ching. Fuck China. If we gave them a buffalo and they named it Pan-Pan, we wouldn't give a shit. We get their panda and we have to name it Mitsook or some other stupid Chinese name. Let's give China a bald eagle and force them to name it Gary.

LLAMAS My only problem with llamas is I don't know if we can ride them or not.

BULLS I envy bulls. Not because of their power or strength, but their psyche. Let's face it, we're all miserable because we got dumped by our prom date, or our Little League coach benched us, or our folks didn't pay enough attention to us when we were growing up. We just can't get over our shitty past. Bulls don't cling to their past. They are locked up in that stall and there's a guy on top of them tugging a rope that's wrapped around their balls. They're thinking to themselves, "When that guy opens the gate, I am going to buck this asshole off of me, and once that hundred-and-forty-pound shit kicker hits the ground, he's gonna feel two thousand pounds of bull horn going right through his sternum." Then the bell sounds and the gate opens, and for eight seconds all the bull can think about is, "I am going to kill this motherfucker for humiliating me. Once I get this

89

guy on the ground, he's dead." And then he bucks him off, sees him lying on the ground helpless in front of him, and thinks, "Now I am going to kill you for what you've put me through." He lowers his head and prepares to finish him off, but at the last second a guy wearing Wrangler shants, rainbow suspenders, and clown makeup jumps in front of him and the bull thinks, "Huh. Maybe I should kill this guy instead." In a split second all is forgiven, and the bull's entire focus is on killing a guy whose only crime was stealing Robin Williams's suspenders. While we're all punishing ourselves for our past, the self-actualized bull looks toward the future.

A quick tangent on rodeo clowns. Is there a more dangerous job that doesn't translate into an ounce of poontang? Chicks love firemen and there's danger involved, but not every day. With rodeo clowning, every day your job is to dress up like you're in a Telemundo skit and jump in front of a pissed-off one-ton murder machine. But at the end of the night you go home, alone, to a trailer and remove the makeup with your own tears.

BATHROOM DOOS AND DON'TS

This chapter is my attempt to get us all on the same sheet of toilet paper. Society runs because we have certain agreed-upon rules and standards. Red means stop, we read left to right, and with the exception of a few stoned celebrities, we don't enter the freeway on off-ramps. But when it comes to this great nation's bathrooms, it's anarchy. A lawless free-for-all of urine and fecal matter. I'm gonna try to put an end to this by laying down some simple guidelines.

RULE #1: THE BATHROOM DOOR SHOULD ONLY BE SHUT WHEN THE BATHROOM IS IN USE.

I can't tell you how many hours I've wasted standing in hallways at parties waiting for someone to leave a bathroom that was empty. The problem is when the door is shut, we assume someone's pants are around their ankles, so we wait. And after a few minutes we do that sheepish palm-toward-your-face, single-back-knuckle knock. That's followed up by the more aggressive, multiknuckle, hope-you're-not-mid-dump knock. When you finally enter the head and realize it's empty, you feel violated. You stood in the hall, this close to shitting yourself, while every attractive person at the party walked past you for nothing. Why the fuck would you shut the goddamn door on the way out in the first place? It's not like there's a fucking raccoon in the bathtub. You're not letting in a draft. Even if you shit the place up, why are you sealing it like Tupperware? Leave a few inches of daylight between the door and the goddamn jamb just to get some cross ventilation.

Quick anecdote: I was at a party where some wildebeest had destroyed the bathroom with his ass moments before I was to use it. I walked in the john with a lungful of party air, shut the door, and headed toward the commode. When I exhaled the party air, which smelled of sangria, and inhaled the bathroom air, which smelled of ass, I realized the shrub in the backyard would have been a much better alternative than the shit pit from *Slumdog Millionaire*. I immediately turned around, flung open the door, and there was a hot chick waiting to use the bathroom next. I gave her a halfhearted "It wasn't me," but the music was loud and we were both on the move in different directions. I'm sure when she was watching *Dancing with the Stars* a few seasons back she was like, "Oh, man, can that guy shit up a hallway bathroom." The point is, this wouldn't have happened if we could all just agree that closed door means occupied, open door means come on in, and cracked door means enter—but more like a cop entering a warehouse at the docks.

RULE #2: NO LOUD CELL-PHONE CONVERSATIONS IN PUBLIC BATHROOMS.

I was burned two times in the same week because of people ignoring this rule. First time was at a steak joint with Jimmy Kimmel. I was standing at the urinal with my back to the door when I heard a loud "How's it going?" I, never wanting to be antisocial or one of those aloof celebrities, immediately answered back, "Going great." Of course a second later, a guy who looked like Suge Knight's scary older brother pulled up to the urinal next to mine and continued his cell-phone conversation. If he had been familiar with this rule, I wouldn't have made an ass of myself interrupting the hit he was putting on his business partner. Three days later I was backstage at *Dancing with the Stars* when I walked into a small bathroom, with a single urinal and a single toilet, and began evacuating my bladder. Roughly about a pint and a half into the piss I heard a voice come from the stall, "How you doing?" Assuming it was one of the many people who work on the show recognizing my Capezios, I promptly answered "Good" and followed it up with a "Getting paid to take a shit. Not too shabby." A second later a loud voice rang out from the stall, "I'm on the phone." I know it's a free country, but you can't use your cell phone for the two hours you're in a theater or the six hours you're on a flight—how about you stay off it for the three minutes I'm taking a piss?

RULE #3: SOUNDS OBVIOUS, BUT FELLAS, LIFT THE FUCKING SEAT BEFORE YOU PISS.

When you're in a public men's room and you don't lift the seat, you're essentially peeing on some stranger's ass. It almost makes you gay. The only reason the seat's there in the first place is for those unlucky souls who have to take a dump in unfamiliar surroundings, and you've now compounded their problems by making them have to mop up your piss before they can off-load. Part of the blame falls on the manufacturer of the toilet seat: A) All the toilet seats used for commercial applications are wishbone shaped. They're not shaped like a doughnut like the one you're sitting on right now. They have a two-inch gap in the front that gives guys false confidence. "I don't have to lift this seat. I can thread the needle. I'm a regular Lee Harvey Oswald. Why, I wouldn't be surprised if my cock had rifling." And it's true, 96 percent of the stream finds its target. But that doesn't mean there's still not some collateral whiz damage from the final rogue burst or the drizzle created by the Fosbury Flop you do with your cock before you holster it. Now I'd be more, pardon the pun, pissed at you people, but it's not entirely your fault. This gets us to part B of my beef with the toilet-seat manufacturers: There needs to be a handle to lift the toilet seat. Preferably one that could be operated by foot, like the kick pedal on a drum kit. Do you jerk-offs really expect people at a gas station to blindly reach down between the bowl and the bottom of the toilet seat to lift it? People as a rule will do the right thing, but not at the risk of getting a stranger's piss on their fingers. Everyone I know recycles, but that percentage would go down quite a bit if the lid of the blue barrel was covered in trucker piss.

RULE #4: AND SPEAKING OF THE SEAT, LADIES, QUIT BITCHING ABOUT US LEAVING THE SEAT UP.

A) We take eight pisses to your one; B) It takes more energy to lift the seat than it does to put it down. Hell, you just have to get it started. Once you get past 90 degrees, gravity kicks in and does the rest of the work for you; and C) Guys don't like exiting the bathroom with the seat down because it makes the next person who enters think you just took a shit. In the fecal game, it's what we call a tell. I know what your argument is, ladies. When you use the toilet at night and it's dark you've sat down, felt the cold bowl, and almost fallen into the toilet. I have two things to say about this. One, if you almost fell into the toilet, congratulations on not having a fat ass. Nobody from the cast of *Precious* would be in danger of falling into the toilet. And two, how about you suss it out before you plop down. I've gone into plenty of bathrooms at night that had the lid down, but I didn't shit all over the top of it. No wonder you guys are only making seventy cents to our dollar.

RULE #5: KEEP YOUR FEET ON THE GROUND.

A lot of guys I know, when in a public restroom, admit to flushing toilets and urinals and opening doors with their bottom of their foot. This is great for you, Jackie Chan of the Can, but horrible for me, who uses his hands to do things like flush urinals and open doors. I know what your plan is, but in an effort to realize your retarded goal of not touching anything, you've managed to destroy my simple goal of not touching things that have piss on them. You see, the piss was not on the door or the urinal handle until your fucking Reebok put it there, you asshole. And it's not like you're a fucking surgeon, douchebag. You're not transplanting a goddamn liver. The next thing you touch is gonna be your computer's keyboard, which I guarantee is filthier than the push plate on the bathroom door. And are you finished, or perhaps you'd like to rub your balls on my car's door handle or wipe your ass on my son's Buzz Lightyear pajamas?

RULE #6: THE COURTESY FLUSH.

This is something that should be taught in schools. First you learn the courtesy flush, and if we have time left over, we can work on the Pledge of Allegiance. Not enough people employ this simple, nostril-saving technique. You simply flush the toilet as the first load of rubber meets the road. Now I'm not gonna lie to you and say it gets rid of the entire funk problem, but when timed properly it could get rid of up to 40 percent of it (your asshole may vary).

RULE #7: TIMING IS EVERYTHING.

When I was doing morning radio, I can't tell you the number of times I walked into the bathroom at six thirty in the morning only to realize some coworker had pulled the pin on an ass grenade moments earlier. And I would think to myself, Jesus Christ, you showed up to work ten minutes ago and you already shit up the bathroom? People do this routinely in the workplace. Could you imagine doing this anywhere else? It's not like you pull up at church and take a dump before the morning sermon or go to the movie theater— "Honey, get me a Diet Coke and some Junior Mints. I'm gonna go shit up a stall." No, you time it. You do your off-loading at home. Look, I understand if you're pulling a double shift and you ate dinner off the roach coach, but these are people who've worked at the same place, on the same schedule, for years and they refuse to dial their asses in. If I owned a business I'd give all new employees a two-week grace period for their asses to acclimate, and then after that if they shat up my bathroom, they'd be getting a pink slip—except this one would have a brown stripe running down the middle of it. And right next to the sign in the warehouse that said DAYS SINCE LAST ACCIDENT, I'd have a DAYS SINCE SOMEONE SHIT UP THE COMMUNITY HEAD sign.

RULE #8: NOT ALL URINALS HAVE THE MAGIC EYE.

We've fucked ourselves up as a society by retrofitting half the nation's urinals with the automatic-flush infrared eye and leaving the other half manual. It's why at least half the time when I hit a public urinal, there's a nice frothy effervescent pot of gold waiting for me.

Whoever took that piss was used to the urinal that flushed itself. It's like if the ATM you normally use spits your card out before the money, you'll never lose your card. But if you're on the road and you use a machine that spits your card out thirty seconds after the cash, you'll be in your car by the time the card comes out. This only excuses half of you. The other half of you know exactly what you're doing but are too lazy or inconsiderate to flush. And for you gents I'd like to say the following: What the fuck is wrong with you Purell pussies? I know you look at yourself as royalty and your policy is His Highness can't soil the royal cuticles with a handle. Great, so all us knaves can stare at your piss and have to flush the toilet twice? I know in your world other human beings don't exist, but I wish a group of these imaginary people would beat the shit out of you.

RULE #9: URINAL PARTITIONS.

This is less a rule of thumb and more a building code. I was at American Airlines's multimillion-dollar, brand-new, state-of-the-art terminal at JFK. Went in to use the bathroom with the polished nickel-plated fixtures and extensive granite and marble only to realize they'd skimped on the most important piece of equipment in a public bathroom: the divider between the urinals. The thin sheet of vinyl-coated plywood that protects my cock from judgmental prying eyes and protects my slacks from the scourge known as secondhand whiz. For basically what it costs to build a birdhouse, I don't have to look at another guy's wang or worry about the "dick-ochet" when a guy built like John Candy sidles up next to me to unload the seven Heinekens he had at the bar.

RULE #10: NO DESECRATING THE BATHROOM.

No pissing on the toilet-paper roll, no boogers on top of the urinal, no carving your gang tag into the toilet seat, no kicking in the stall door. (Ladies, I know you're all appalled right now, but this is common-place.) You know when you're driving and you're eight miles from your house and you have to shit so bad your teeth hurt and you screech into a gas station and ask the guy if you can use the bath-room and he says it's for employees only? Do you think that's the policy they started out with, or the one they put into place after all the dickheads treated their bathroom like an enemy village their platoon had overrun? Thanks to you assholes, my asshole's gonna have to wait until we get home.

BONUS JOKE

On one of the construction job sites I worked on, there was a Porta Potti. On the outside, written in Magic Marker, it said MEXICAN SPACE SHUTTLE. On the inside, above the toilet-seat liners with the same Magic Marker, it said FREE COWBOY HATS.

WOMEN, HEAR ME ROAR

I get labeled a misogynist all the time. But I'm simply pointing out that men and women are different. Or at least they used to be.

WOMEN ARE BECOMING MEN

We've done away with gender roles. As a culture we decided the smaller the chasm between male and female, the more evolved our society would be. But there's a reason you have cooters and we have peckaroos. We're different, and that's a good thing. Why is it that the same people who beat the celebrate-differences drum when it comes to cultures refuse to acknowledge the biggest cultural difference on the planet? Men and women. I guarantee you Japanese men, German men, and black men have a fuck lot more in common than your average dude and chick. Let's face it. Women are better with the kids when they get a boo-boo, but when it comes time to disarm the roadside bomb, that's where the fellas come in.

I have a theory that I think will put things into perspective. Look at society as a giant X. Women on one bottom leg, men on the other bottom leg. The date: 1950. Women cooked, cleaned, took care of the kids, and mended torn dungarees. Men provided, fixed the car, patched the roof, and warded off intruders with a baseball bat. Then the sixties arrived. Each gender moved a little higher up the leg of the X. Women stopped shaving their armpits and men grew their hair out. Women started going to work and men started taking their car to the mechanic. Now we get into the eighties. Figure we're about halfway up the X leg before the cross. Men start applying mousse and eyeliner, women are more worried about having rock-hard abs than they are about their kids. Now the nineties. School districts are being sued for girls' rights to play on the boys' football team, and being a woman trapped inside of a man's body is as real a medical diagnosis as Hodgkin's lymphoma. In the 2000s, we officially hit the intersection of the X. Men are "metrosexuals" getting mani-pedis while their wives drive a jeep to their job as an NFL sideline reporter. If you go to a store today you can find unisex fragrances. This idea would have never worked in the fifties. Women's perfume came in a glass slipper and smelled like baby powder and lilacs; men's cologne came in a ship or a football and smelled like a pine cone.

I grew up in the seventies with a steady diet of "the reason girls play with dolls and boys play with trains is because of the Man's homophobic agenda." Bullshit. My son loves trains. All boys love trains. They can't help it, it's in their blood. It's amazing that the train wasn't invented earlier, considering that young boys have been around for millions of years. It's heroin for them—they go berserk for it. If you put a boy alone in a room with some Thomas the Tank Engine toys and some Barbies and don't say a word, I guarantee that he'll go right for the trains.

What the fuck were my mom and her angry hippie friends thinking? And why haven't they apologized?

CHICKS ARE DUMB/EVIL

We're constantly talking about the Man and how the worst people on the planet are Republican sixty-year-old white guys. The Dick Cheney type. I'm now sure the worst people on the planet are twentysomething white chicks. Like the chicks from *The Hills* or Hugh Hefner's ladies from *The Girls Next Door*. At least the evil white guy in his fifties punches a time clock every day. These chicks aren't even doing anything. They contribute nothing to society except, if we're lucky, a bootleg sex tape. If anything, they're making us dumber. I'm not saying every girl needs to aspire to be Hillary Clinton, but let's aim a bit higher than Khloe Kardashian.

Chicks, especially hot ones, have learned that by looking good they can get guys to do the work for them and thus never learn anything. They're dumb and they don't need to get smarter. I had the blondes who currently play the Doublemint twins in the commercials on my podcast last year. At some point in the conversation, the movie *Young Frankenstein* came up. I asked the Doublemint twins if they liked Mel Brooks and, I shit you not, they asked if Mel Brooks was a dude or a chick. At that point I wanted to commit a double murder. "Yeah, that's Mel B's full name. Scary Spice also directed *Blazing Saddles* and *Spaceballs*."

This happens constantly with young women. They don't know shit, and when you try to correct them you become Weirdo Grandpa: "I wasn't even born when *Spaceballs* came out." And I wasn't born when *Citizen Kane* came out either, but I've still heard of Orson fucking Welles. (Not that *Citizen Kane* is half the film that *Spaceballs* is.)

Here's why guys are smarter than women. We're curious. We want to know shit. Men stared at the moon for twenty thousand years and thought, "What is that? How do we get there?" It came out every night, hung over us, and mocked us. "You think you can make it here? You're not man enough. How are you gonna land on me? What about the gravitational pull and the Earth's rotation? You ain't making it.

You don't have what it takes." So guys were like, "Fuck you, we're going to the moon." And we're competitive. It's not like we were racing the Russian *women* to the moon. There's no chick that stares at the moon and thinks, I need to hit a golf ball off that thing. I'm not saying the curiosity gene is always practical, but I am saying it's what motivates us. It gets guys killed, but it also gets the sound barrier broken.

It's not just intelligence, it's communication. Women do not have different tones. Everything is an emergency. Men have different vocal qualities for "Hey sweetie, I'm calling because you forgot your purse" and "There's a guy with a machete in the house." I've gotten the call where my wife is like, "Oh my God! Oh my God!" "What?!" "We're out of Sunny D." I thought one of my kids had been dragged off by a mountain lion. This is why chicks would make horrible air-traffic controllers. With them there's no difference between "A bag has been lost in Newark" and "Your wing is on fire." Or you'll hear them talking to their other hysterical friends: "Oh my God, Sheila. I'm so sorry, I'm so sorry. That's horrible." "What happened? Did Greg die?" "No, she forgot to TiVo *Ellen*."

WOMEN IN THE WORKPLACE

This emotionality is why women make seventy cents for every dollar we earn. (Are they pissed because they're making less or because they're getting paid in change?) One of the many reasons women are better at home with the kids than at the workplace is because they have something called feelings. We all know women who have cried at work. I've never seen a dude cry at work. Except that *Man Show* wrap party when a six-foot sub rolled off the board as they were carrying it in. It was like the Trail of Tears, but with white guys. On the other hand, when the kid brings home a piece of craft paper with some elbow macaroni glued to it in the shape of a pony, no dad has ever ripped it out of their hand and said, "This needs to go to the framing shop tonight." You see, we're better at work, and they're better at Scotch-taping horses made of elbow macaroni to refrigerator doors. It's just good science.

And no man has ever sued over a "hostile work environment." This soul-sucking nonissue takes up our time and money because anybody, especially if they have been victimized in the past, can claim sexual harassment. And of course that is the siren song of the lawyer. Anybody can sue for sexual harassment because it is completely subjective, which means the company's asshole lawyers have to make everyone jump through a bunch of bullshit hoops to protect the company from the "victim's" asshole lawyers.

Let me give you an example. Every workplace has a "cool guy" and a "creepy guy." Let's call the cool guy Adam. He's one of those guys where you just dig his vibe. The men in the office would like to talk cars, sports, or chicks with him over a beer. The women in the office will laugh at all his jokes and will give him every detail of their last date. "Don't worry, ladies, I'm not going to make a move. And if I did, you'd love it." Every office also has a "creepy guy." Let's call him [your name here]. Uncomfortable in his own skin, awkward. Picture the neighbor in the eighties movie who shows up to the blind chick's apartment and offers to set up her VCR while her Seeing Eye dog goes nuts and she says, "That's funny. Rondo never barks at anyone." Now here's the scenario. The attractive receptionist comes in a few minutes late on a Monday morning wearing tight new jeans. Cool Guy comments, "Somebody's been working out." She replies, "Oh, it's just the jeans." Cool Guy looks her up and down and says, "You do have good genes." She laughs and says, "We're doing a shot at the Christmas party." Now, same scenario with Creepy Guy. Receptionist walks in, Creepy Guy says, "Hey Kelly, nice jeans." And she marches straight off to Human Resources to file a report. This can't be taught in any sexual-harassment seminar because the women themselves don't even know it.

When it comes to these seminars, why isn't there more outrage? How many hours of our lives are squandered with this shit? Why are we being treated like criminals? You wouldn't need to attend a drug and alcohol counseling class if you had no history of DUI. I've been employed since I worked at McDonald's when I was fifteen and a half. Thirty years in the workforce and I have zero sexual-harassment claims against me. So with thirty years with no strikes, I still need to throw away two hours of my life to satisfy corporate lawyers? And I'm an atheist, so my life is more valuable than yours. You guys are going to have a rich, fulfilling afterlife, whereas I'm going to spend eternity in a pine box with a bunch of worms trying to stuff themselves into my ass like frat boys into a telephone booth. And here's what life comes down to—not how many years you live, but how many of those years are filled with bullshit that doesn't amount to anything to satisfy the requirements of some dickhead you'll never get the pleasure of punching in the face. If I told you you were going to live to a hundred, you'd say, "Awesome." If I told you you were going to live to a hundred but fifty of those years are going to be spent taking off your shoes at airports, sitting at sobriety checkpoints along the 405, and attending sexual-harassment seminars, you'd say, "Just kill me now." Isn't this what we're doing to ourselves? I think we should no longer keep track of our human life in years, but rather in hours. Your average person has six hundred thousand hours on this planet, and you want me to waste three of mine listening to some fat postmenopausal cunt talking about something that's never happened to her?

I have no prior history with sexual harassment, thus no need for this lecture. Should I also head down to the hospital for some prenatal care and lactation counseling? Everyone should stand up and refuse to go to these things. And if they fire you, hit them with a wrongful-termination lawsuit. Pit your lawyers against their lawyers in some dickhead version of Thunderdome. Because that's who to blame for this, the lawyers. As if these seminars have prevented one single lawsuit. In fact, I'd love to see the statistics on sexual harassment lawsuits filed. I guarantee there were ten times as many after these corporate-sponsored time rapings began. All the information they cram up your ass falls into one of two categories: A) No duh, or B) Not going to do that. I'm not and never was going to make the intern blow me for a promotion, but I am going to forward the e-mail link to the celebrity sex tape. Fuck you. What are you going to do about it?

You know a group that doesn't have to worry about being sexually harassed nowadays? Nurses. Remember in the seventies, in every episode of *Three's Company* the neighbor Larry would hook up with a hot stewardess or a hot nurse? But look around. In the reality of 2010, stewardesses can barely back their fat asses down the aisle for the beverage service, and nurses are in worse shape than the people they're treating. Nurses are a good eighty to a hundred pounds heavier than the average person. They're sweating white country gravy while lecturing you about your cholesterol. These women are so fat that their skin color changes and you can't tell what race they are. Their ethnicity changes to fat. It's either those chicks or the big-muscled veiny gay guy. What happened to the hot nurses in the candy striper outfit? The scrubs these nurses are wearing now are why they're fat. They have room to expand. These scrubs are essentially a painter's tarp with a back pocket and a drawstring. You know how they say a fish will get as big as the bowl? These scrubs are the Pacific Ocean. It's the black-bouncer-in-the-velour-sweatsuit effect. Put that guy in a pair of tight Daisy Dukes, I guarantee he puts down the hoagie. If you put him in a sweatsuit, he'll just fill it out. I can solve America's obesity problem right now. From here on out, every Friday is Wear Your Swimsuit to Work Day.

And don't let the profession affect how hot you think a girl is. There are women who look good for their profession. That doesn't mean they're hot. Danica Patrick is hot . . . for an Indy driver. She's a 7. If she were hosting at Nobu, you wouldn't give her a second look. The "sexy" female athlete is an interesting phenomenon. I was watching some *Entertainment Tonight*–type show that was profiling "Hotties of the Winter Olympics." They put the speed skaters and cross-country skiers in Victoria's Secret underwear and snow mukluks. Then as they panned up their bodies, I was thinking, Hey, nice legs, good abs, she's hot. But when they got up to their faces, I saw that they were just a little bit off. It's sad, but they scrolled up the hot, toned bodies and the faces had a dusting of Picasso. The eyes were too close together, or the nose was a little crooked. Then it all made sense. I figured out why she's an Olympic-caliber athlete: If it were Heidi Klum's face at the top of that body, there's no fucking way she'd ever get up for one five A.M. workout. Hot chicks don't have that gene. So to all the wannabe Olympic moms and dads out there, if you want your little girl to be a champion, you're one well-placed snow shovel to the face away from the gold.

There has been a pleasant uptick in hot teachers having sex with their students. Where were these women when I was at Walter Reed Middle School? How come kids now get Debra LaFave and I got Mrs. Wolk, who literally had a hygiene problem? I love the idiots who complain about the double standard and say we should punish these female teachers the same as we would male teachers. If the male gym coach has sex with the fifteen-year-old girl, she will be mentally and emotionally scarred for life. The only damage to a fifteen-year-old boy who nails the music teacher after class is carpal tunnel from getting high-fived by his buddies. Just like my grandfather used to say, "If you can beat off to it afterward, it's not a crime." This is another misguided attempt to treat the genders as if there are no differences. Little Billy who bangs the female teacher is gonna be all right. Little Suzie will end up working the pole at Olympic Gardens and won't be going by the name Suzie.

STRIPPER NAMES

Stripper names are out of control. Remember back in the day when you'd go to a strip club and the stripper was named Candy? You knew her real name was like Shelly or Brenda, but Candy sounded sexier. Now when you go to a strip club, you ask the stripper her name and she'll say Charisma, Allure, or Emotion. They used to use sexy names, but now they're just making shit up. "I'm gonna go to the champagne room with Cubic Zirconia." And you feel like an asshole because you have to use it. "Would you care for another Coke Zero and Captain Morgan, Fancia?"

And when they ask for your name, you always give them your real name, Jason. We should be the ones giving the fake names. I feel like we've got more to lose. You're at an Outback Steakhouse with the missus celebrating your twelfth anniversary, and here comes a drunken Charisma: "Jason, I didn't recognize you with your fly up. Don't you remember me? From Bob's Classy Lady? You bought me thirteen hundred dollars' worth of Champale!"

What would be the harm in them giving us their real name? Oh, your name is Nancy? Let the stalking begin! And would you really need to stalk someone who works in their underpants at a place that never closes? I'm just saying, why bother stalking Julia Roberts if you could show up at her work, pop in a Warrant CD, give her twenty bucks, and she'd get naked and hop on your lap?

Fellas, from now on we start using fake names. Next time you go to Jumbo's Clown Room and the stripper says, "I'm Essence, what's your name, honey?" you say, "I'm Colonel Duke LaCross. How's it feel, bitch?"

THINGS CHICKS ARE INTO

Chicks are into fashion. My wife watches those *Project Runway*–type shows where the model is strutting down the catwalk and Rachel Zoe is going, "Oh my God, Oh my God" about the dress. Lynette will give me the stink-eye because I say to the TV, "I could do that. I could put that dress together. I wouldn't want to put that dress together, but if you gave me a sewing machine and some taffeta, I could knock that shit out. Easily." It's true. Making a car or being an architect is much more difficult than fashion, but everybody goes nuts for these fairies.

Speaking of dresses, let's break down the myth of the thirty-five-hundred-dollar wedding dress. Every woman pulls this shit on her soon-to-be husband. Inevitably he'll complain about the cost of a dress that she is only going to wear once, and she'll reply that it will be an heirloom and that her daughter will wear it on her wedding day. Really? Then why aren't you wearing your mom's dress? You know she pulled the same shit on your dad in 1975, right? And with fashions going out of style from year to year and season to season, what are the chances that the burnt-orange, crushed velvet shower curtain your mom wore in the mid-seventies is going to be all the rage thirty or forty years later?

And what's with women and the dress they can wear only once? My wife will be like, "I wore that to Howard Stern's wedding—I can't be seen in it again." First off, *I* don't remember the dress you wore to Howard Stern's wedding, and everyone else there was shit-faced. You're the only one who knows you wore that dress. Second, this is insanity. You just paid nine hundred dollars for three yards of cloth and sequins that you think the queen from *Project Runway* made, but that was really stitched together by some husky Nicaraguan mother of five for a quarter an hour. The true cost of this dress is $38.50, but you're dipping into the kids' college fund to buy it because the nearly identical dress that was good two months ago is now expired. This is the argument I would make to all the feminists who get pissed when someone points out that men are better at math than women. Crunch those numbers. Nine hundred dollars for a dress you're going to wear once, or the seventy-five bucks we pay to *rent* a tux?

And women won't fill us in on what a size-14 dress is versus a size-2 dress. It's their own little secret language, so we're constantly confused. Why can't they just use inches like we do? For us it's easy: If a guy has a thirty-two-inch waist, he's slim; if he's got a fifty-five-inch waist, he's a lard ass. If a chick is a size 8, I have no idea if she's Kate Moss or Kate Smith. They're doing that to keep us off guard. It's sort of like what Europe does with the metric system. I heard an interesting study once. Plus-size models are usually size 12 through 14, and the average woman is size 14. So the average woman walking around the United States is at the upper end of what we would call a plus-size model, except she's got an ugly face.

Of course, they wouldn't want to be models anyway. These girls always say that they didn't want to get into modeling—someone signed them up for the International Model Search competition, or they went along with a friend who was auditioning for a Maybelline campaign and the casting agent pointed at them instead. They'll say anything but admit they looked into the mirror on their fifteenth birthday and saw a piping-hot chick staring back and thought, I could really cash in on this great genetic hand that was dealt to me. The reason you know their story is bullshit is because if they wanted to stay in school and become veterinarians, they would have done it. There's no federal mandate that says: All hot chicks *must* model. And of course the ugly male version of this is the stand-up comic. He can't admit he thinks he's the funniest motherfucker on the planet, so when you ask him how he got into comedy, he says he went out to a comedy club and some friends "pushed him up onstage." What kind of club is this where you can take a guy who's never held a microphone in his life, push him up onstage, and have him do a set? The few times I've seen a guy take the stage who wasn't supposed to be on it he was immediately dragged off it by a large Samoan man. And can't you just say no? What if your buddies signed you up to do some gay porn? Would you just shrug your shoulders and say, "Well, I guess I'd better start lubing up."

The reluctant comedian and the reluctant model would be perfect for each other because her *Playboy* profile says she loves a guy with a sense of humor. My ass. I've seen the guys you're with. You hooked up with Lorenzo Lamas, bitch. You love a guy with a shaved chest and a spray tan who talks about himself in the third person.

ADAM CAROLLA

Every time I interview one of these six-foot blondes and say, "You must have driven the boys crazy in high school," they always give me the sob story about being "awkward" and not being asked to the prom. I'll buy that with your Sarah Silverman types or that chick who played Juno. But if you're Cameron Diaz or Jessica Biel, you're either lying or went to school with a bunch of fags.

And apparently modeling is a miserable life. I remember hearing a few years back Tyra Banks talking about going to France when she was sixteen and how lonely it was and blah blah blah. Fuck you. You know where I went when I was a teenager? The Lawry's Seasoned Salt factory in Eagle Rock. I left with a shirtful of tears and a packet of taco seasoning. I never left the county, much less the country.

Let me take a minute to officially nominate Tyra for Blowhard of the Century. I train with a guy named Terry Claybon. He is a boxing trainer to the stars. At his gym, he has signed pictures of some of his clients thanking him. Matt Damon thanked Terry. Nicolas Cage thanked Terry. Joe Rogan thanked Terry. But not Tyra. While everyone else had a picture of themselves with their arm around Terry saying thank you, she brought in her own picture of just her looking all greased up in a bikini with the following message:

"Thanks for making me strong, confident, and powerful. Can't nobody fuck with me now." And she signed it "Butterfly," after Muhammad Ali.

This is the height of blowhard narcissism. First, I'm sure the "Butterfly" nickname was self-applied. This is something hacks do: They attach themselves to people with actual talent in hopes of some reflected glory. But more egregiously, her thank-you did an e-brake-slide 180 and turned it right back on her. I wonder if she does this everywhere? What about the dry cleaner's? "You guys are the best. Thanks for making me look so smoking hot in the blouses you cleaned."

When Tyra isn't thanking herself while thanking someone else, she's doing a hidden-camera sting in a fat suit. This just in: Being fat and ugly makes your life harder. I know, shocking. Why is it always the hottest actresses and models telling us how beauty comes from within?

I used to go insane over one of NBC's "The More You Know" PSAs, in which *Sports Illustrated* swimsuit model Molly Sims says, "What makes you special is not what you wear or who you hang out with. Being proud of yourself is what really counts." Thank you, hot skinny blond successful actress. I'm sure the chunky teenager behind the counter at the Quiznos in Tustin heard you loud and clear. Do you have no sense of hypocrisy? You're only asked to make the goddamn PSA because you're hot. We'd have no idea who you were if we didn't want to fuck you. If I've learned anything from supermodels, it's that as long as you "feel" sexy, men will be magically attracted to you. It doesn't matter if you are pockmarked and weigh 550 pounds, and sixty-five of those pounds are neck goiter. It's all about how you "feel."

We've all bought into this retarded adage about beauty coming from within. Has anyone ever stopped and thought what an asinine statement that is? I like cars. But if somebody ever asked me what makes a '69 Ferrari Daytona so beautiful and I said the engine block, I'd be a lying asshole.

Women also perpetuate this retarded myth where "I wear lingerie for *me*—it makes *me* feel beautiful." Then why don't you wear it around the house when you're alone? It's such bullshit: Everything you do is for someone else. If I heard women were attracted to a fecal-matter swastika on my forehead, I'd be sticking my index finger up my ass shortly after I found out that information.

So since you're clearly doing it for us, let me give you a list of things we're *not* into.

GIANT HOOP EARRINGS Who is this for? This is tribal ornamentation. We're not Kalahari Bushmen. And it is going to work out terribly for you when you get in a fight and the bitch at the club uses them as a handle to smash your face into the bar.

If you're going to do earrings, just go with the simple stud in the lobe. And that's it. We're not into the weird piercings, either. We don't like the dumbbell going through the nipple, the spike in the tongue, or the clitoral-hood piercing. Or that little stud in the nose that looks like a giant blackhead or a clove pushed into a Christmas ham.

TATTOOS Tattoos are wasted effort. Every time I look in *Playboy* I want to shout at Hugh Hefner that we want the girl next door, not the whore. The college student looking for an extra hundred bucks for books, not the skank who gets teamed on the pinball machine. Every girl in that magazine now has fake tits, is thinner than the coke rails she's doing in the bathroom at the club, and has a tramp stamp. Also, tattoos have totally ruined period porn. And by period porn, I mean that it's set in a different time period, not some disgusting fetish. You're supposed to be Cleopatra. I sincerely doubt she had a Tasmanian devil on her left ass cheek.

FINGERNAILS We almost never notice your fingernails. And that's a good thing. It means you've either done nothing or gone with some simple, subtle polish. When we do notice your nails, it's because you look like Edward Scissorhands got a job at Earl Scheib. No guy is attracted to the three-inch press-on nails with a unicorn emblazoned on them. I would love to build a giant digital counter billboard, like the one they use to keep track of the deficit, showing the amount of time women have spent on their nails. I'd build a billboard next to it that says GUYS GIVING A SHIT ABOUT CHICKS' NAILS. The first one would have millions of hours registered, and the only thing on the second billboard would be pigeons.

BIG JEWELRY How do you define big jewelry? Like the Supreme Court defines pornography: I'll know it when I hear it. If I can hear you getting out of the car from inside the restaurant, you're wearing too much of it. This isn't the Old West—we don't need to hear your spurs jingle-jangle-jingle. Though it is nice that we can hear you coming down the hallway when we're on the computer looking at

YouPorn. The jewelry acts like a cowbell that gives us a fifteen-second heads-up to close the laptop. I'm not interested in fucking Mrs. T.

ARMS Chicks never stop talking about Madonna's arms or Michelle Obama's arms. I've never met a guy who's given a shit about a chick's arms. Don't get me wrong, guys aren't into fat arms, but fat arms are usually attached to fat women who have fat asses. Now back to Madonna. No guy wants to be with a chick who has arms like a junkie on a crew team.

HAIR Big hair has been out since Reagan used his DeLorean to beat the Russian hockey team in the Olympics (my recollection of the eighties is a little fuzzy). But for some reason a lot of chicks still do their hair like they're gonna party like it's 1989. We don't want the crispy hair; we want to be able to run our fingers through it without breaking them.

There's also the weird multicolored hair with the skunk stripes. Just like the fingernails, we don't want anything that draws attention to itself. A little highlighting is one thing, but we don't want your hair to look like a bag of Skittles.

And short haircuts. This is a thing chicks like on other chicks. Girls always tell other girls how cute they look with a short haircut. But they're really thinking, That's one bitch I ain't gonna have to compete with. I've never heard one of my male friends say, "That girl would be hot if only her hair looked like Moe Howard's."

MAKEUP By all means put on a little foundation, but the closer to natural the better. Nobody wants to be seen entering the club with the sad hobo clown from a velvet painting. Again, just like the nails, the hair coloring, and the muscles, moderation is the key. We don't want the caked-on mascara that makes you look like a crazy Armenian bank teller. We're not into the fake painted-on eyebrows or the two-tone lipstick where you line the outside of your mouth with a Sharpie.

Just give me a woman in her natural form. I don't need the rodeo-clown makeup, the giant hoop earrings, the tats, the piercings, or any of that other shit. It's not the Mexican lottery show. I don't need that much going on.

RELATIONSHIPS

Let me close out this chapter by making the best case I can for how men and women are, and always will be, inherently different. One need look no further than the bedroom. Men take their sexual mentality and apply it toward women. A guy thinks, "I love it hard and fast. I'd like to be yanked off by a paint-can shaker with tits. So she must love it that way too." Wrong. When it comes to sex, men and women are as different as dogs and cats. Think about how you are with a dog. You're rough and tumble with it. You grab it by the ears, chase it around, play tug-of-war, roll it over on its back and slap its belly. You go after the dog. A cat has to come to you. It has to be in the mood. It will rub itself against your shin when it fucking feels like it. And think about when you pet a cat. They will apply pressure where they want and will move their body so you're rubbing whichever part they want. And it has to be slow and rhythmic. This is why cats will jump onto the fridge when a toddler bounds into the room. They don't know how to be gentle.

Ladies, I know it sounds like I was a little hard on you in this chapter. But anytime you start feeling sorry for yourselves, remember this—you're worse drivers than we are but you pay less for car insurance, and you're worse people than we are but you live five years longer.

A MESSAGE TO THE FAT CATS IN WASHINGTON

I'm convinced I could win any election by just repeating the phrase "I'm going to send a message to those fat cats in Washington."

People constantly label me a conservative. It's part of that all-or-nothing mentality. The majority of my opinions are liberal. I'm an atheist. I'm in favor of legalizing pot, prostitution, and gay marriage. But because I hold a couple of conservative opinions about national security, the death penalty, and how the government wastes my tax money, I'm considered somewhere to the right of Reagan. I just get behind whatever I think is the smarter idea; I don't arbitrarily pick a political team. Depending on where they grow up and what their parents' beliefs are, people get assigned to either the blue team or the red team and have to hate everything the other guys stand for. But it's not the Red Sox and the Yankees. I don't need to be forced into picking a side. I root for whichever team has the plan that's going to fix shit and against whichever one will continue to hold us back. So let me take a moment to bash both the left and the right, starting with the left.

OBAMA, HOPE, AND CHANGE

When Obama got elected, everybody was talking about hope and change. At the time I said, "You won't even notice the fucking difference after Barack is voted in. Your life will not be different." Don't get me wrong. Barack's a good, smart guy. I think he's doing a decent job; I have no problem with him. But don't give me that shit about hope and change and daylight at the end of the tunnel. You're still at the same shitty job you had, your life sucks just as bad as it did, and your old lady is still as fat as she was when W was in office. I've been around long enough to know nothing ever changes. If you were locked in a closet from before the election until now and I let you out, walked you up and down Main Street, showed you your 401(k), told you what was going on in international news, and then asked you, "Who won, Obama, McCain, or did Bush get a third term?" you'd never know.

How much change do we really need, anyway? I can think of several places that need change more than we do. China needs to change, Darfur needs to change. We're cool. Liberals are obsessed with the notion that we could be better. Yes, we could be 10 percent better, but Africa could be 95 percent better. We could do less polluting and be a little bit better, but those guys could lighten up with the raping and the AIDS and be a shitload better. We're like someone who got 2200 on the SATs. Yes, we could do better. But hello? Colombia, Yemen, Bosnia. Those guys are in the single digits. They got an eight. Combined. When they get into triple digits, then we can talk about how America needs to change.

And philosophically, it's wrong. The only person who can change anything in your life is you. You want change? Stop crapping out kids, get some vocational training, then get a job and fight to keep it. It's so naïve and pathetic every four years when an election comes up and I have to watch all the formerly intelligent people around me start going bananas for one candidate. As if that candidate gives a flying fuck about their lives, as if any policy that candidate enacts is going to affect their lives in any discernible way. A good economy and not being depressed are the only things anyone should ever care about.

THE PATRIOT ACT

When the Patriot Act came back in the news in 2005, every single one of my faggoty, lefty Hollywood friends squealed like a stuck pig. "I don't want the government eavesdropping on my e-mail exchanges or listening in on my cell-phone conversations." Everyone had their cargo shorts in a bunch over it. I was the only one I knew who was like, "Hey, Agent Double-O Douchebag, if the government intercepts any of your e-mails, all they're going to find out is that you're not funny. And how about spending a little less time worrying about the government and a little more time focusing on your narcissistic disorder, the one that leads you to believe the government actually gives a shit about you."

That's what it is. It's narcissism. The government wants to listen to *my* calls. They want to invade *my* privacy. This is the religion of the secular. You never hear this Patriot Act shit from the religious right. Religious people don't fear Big Brother; they already have a personal relationship with the biggest brother of all. Here's the deal. The human brain can't handle the idea that there is nothing. There's no God and there are no rules. We can't deal with our own responsibility for our actions and choices. So we invent an eye in the sky that is watching us. For some people it's Jehovah, Allah, or Santa Claus. To the San Francisco atheists, it's a government satellite.

Not that the conservatives don't have their own form of narcissism. The counterpart to the privacy pussies on the left are the paranoid gun nuts on the right who think that Obama is going to take away their AK-47s. He's coming into *my* house for *my* gun. Listen up, dipshits of all political stripes . . . No one from the ATF is coming for your gun, and no one from the NSA is reading the e-mail you wrote your life partner about *Top Model*.

And this is the challenge I always make to the contrarians: It's the same one I offer to the secondhand-smoke idiots. Cite me one instance, one time when you or a family member or even a coworker got their computer confiscated, and I'll apologize. You can't. So shut the fuck up and focus on your Master Cleanse.

Unlike you, I don't believe the government is evil. I know there's this fear that once the government is allowed to monitor your cell-phone conversations the next thing you know it becomes *Soylent Green* or *Logan's Run*. When I was born, I was assigned a number. When my two twins were born, they each got a nine-digit number assigned to them. And guess what, when you were born, the government gave you a number, too. It's a Social Security number. They assigned it to you so they could keep track of you and take money from you your whole fucking working life. So we should all be over this. Don't pay taxes for a couple years and see if you don't receive anything in the mail from the government. Believe me, they know who you are and where to find you. And if you don't pay them the money you owe them each year, they'll take it out of your check without your permission.

To all my Hollywood liberal friends who are worried about their civil liberties being invaded, I've got news for you: You're already living in a police state, you just don't know it. Don't believe me? Try converting your garage into an office without asking the city for permission first. And if you go through an intersection a millisecond too late, a camera will take a picture of you and send it to your home address. You can't even smoke a cigarette on the beach. If you grow a pot plant in your backyard, you'll be arrested. Your stoner flunky kid can't apply for a job at the post office without a background check and a urine sample. Yet you fucks are worried about the Man reading a couple of your e-mails? It's one of the few activities the government participates in that doesn't involve extracting money from us and may possibly prevent a commercial airliner from hitting a football stadium. And you narcissistic douchebags want them to stop? If you really want to focus on the government and your civil liberties, how about the fact that every cent I make from January 1 until the middle of May each year goes to the government? How about you self-righteous fucks start working on that?

BIG PHARMA

Another thing my liberal friends like to complain about is "Big Pharmaceutical." I like big—big grapes, big linemen, big houses. I don't understand why when you put *big* in front of anything except *tits* it becomes bad. I want the drug companies to be loaded. For some reason, as a society we understand there are certain things that you pay for—cars, homes, vacations, and things like that. And then there are other things that we just think are God-given rights, like health care. So if you make luxury yachts, you're not a bad guy, you're just trying to make a buck. If you're Donald Trump and you want to open a championship golf course in Scotland, you're an entrepreneur. But if you're a drug company and you're trying to get rich, you're the devil. I want them trying to get rich. I want them motivated by greed. Everyone thinks the drug companies should just pour a bunch of money into research and development without a payday. I love the fact that almost all the innovative drugs come out of this country because in other countries the government has gotten involved to such a point where there's no entrepreneurship. AIDS isn't a death sentence anymore because drug-company guys are greedy. I know there's a balance that needs to be struck so they don't rape the rain forest or whatever, but overall, when the dust settles, I want the greediest guys in the world trying to cure cancer. I want the greediest guys in the world trying to make a car that goes two hundred miles on a gallon. I want the greediest guys in the world trying to get me to New York in one hour instead of five. I want the greediest guys in the world trying to do all this shit so it will actually get done.

Let's talk about AIDS pharmaceuticals. I find it ironic that the people who were most vocal in bashing the pharmaceutical companies are the ones whose lives were saved by those same companies. All the tears Liz Taylor shed, all the wisdom of the Orient, and all the quilts strewn across the National Mall in front of the Capitol didn't cure one AIDS patient. It was big, greedy pharmaceutical companies. Once again, the evil white devil intervened and saved lives. All your coffee enemas and holistic healers couldn't replace a couple hits of AZT. I only wish the big pharmaceutical companies would take the same approach to handing out the AIDS triple cocktail as I suggested with the profilers. "Hey, Mr. HIV positive. Sure, we'd love to rid you of your death sentence using our wonder drugs. Let me just check my clipboard. Oh, I'm sorry. You called us greedy capitalist pigs. Have fun butt-fucking your herbalist, and I'll see you at your funeral."

WELFARE

Welfare doesn't work. It's monetary methadone. Let me explain. You either need to kick heroin or OD. But methadone is just a perpetual circling of the airport in a plane with shitty seats and a Kate Hudson movie. I believe most people who need welfare are depressed. The welfare lowers their self-esteem and compounds their depression, making it even more difficult to find a job. I've seen enough promos for *The Biggest Loser* to know that even the laziest and most pathetic individual is capable of soaring to great heights given some structure and motivation. Welfare is the equivalent of the government sending them a jumbo bag of Bugles in the mail twice a month.

The Carollas have a rich history of not being rich. My mom was depressed and on welfare. One time when I was a kid I asked her about getting a job and her response was, "And lose my welfare?" People need to get out of the house and find some work and the sense of purpose and dignity that comes with it. Ironically, this wasn't a problem during the Great Depression. People went down to the docks or the factory every morning and tried to find some work to provide for their family. Again, purpose and dignity. If you took that same person and told them, "We're gonna drop off a check, just enough to get by on," they'd stop moving. They'd completely lose their sense of pride and spiral deeper into hopeless apathy.

I don't care if you're sweeping out parking lots or scraping bird shit off of awnings, you're doing something. It doesn't matter if you come home at the end of the day with ten dollars in your pocket, you're doing something. When you remove that part of life, you end up with people lying around who then turn on themselves and eventually, and ironically, the government. Constantly bailing people out does nothing but create resentment for the people giving them the money. Has anyone on the dole ever seemed thankful? Never. It's more like, "How am I supposed to get by on seven hundred and forty dollars a month? I have six kids." You're not supposed to get by, you're supposed to fucking work. But you're trapped in the quicksand of the welfare system.

SCHOOL LUNCH PROGRAMS

People say, "Oh, Adam. You're so heartless because you're not for giving free lunches at school." Yes, I want the parents to cook their kids a fucking meal. I don't want them to have a free corn dog at school. I want the parents to boil some beans and make their kid a goddamn lunch. It's the superliberal a-holes who grew up with silver sporks in their mouths who think, Oh, they're incapable of doing it. Yes they can.

Nowadays food is practically free. Nobody is so poor that they can't go down to the Food for Less, get a huge sack of rice, throw in a couple of chicken bouillon cubes, and whip it up. And believe me, that shit will be healthier than whatever mystery meat and Korean War–surplus canned green beans the school is cooking up. You'll hear the Tim Robbinses of the world defending this garbage by saying, "These kids need a hot meal every day." That's bullshit. Kids don't need a hot meal, they need a nutritious meal. Your kid would be better off having an apple and a hard-boiled egg than fried fish sticks, canned corn, and a box of purple sugar water. And the dickheads who are complaining about not getting a hot meal are the same ones who are complaining that the meals are not nutritious. I feel qualified to speak on this subject because I was a recipient of the meal-ticket program. It was a delightful trifecta of deep-fried empty calories combined with a soul-crushing "I guess my parents don't love me enough to pack me a fucking lunch" followed by a dignity-robbing "What's wrong with your loser family?" So mission accomplished, L.A. Unified.

And if you can't accomplish the simple act of feeding your kids, they need to go into foster care. If you can't provide an orange and a Triscuit with a piece of cheese on it, shouldn't your kids be taken away? It's literally pennies a day. Isn't that the most important yardstick to measure parents by? Providing food is the most basic of parenting requirements. In nature, if a mama bird can't feed her chicks, she is unfit and it's time for Darwin to take out the trash. Education and health care come well below feeding your kids. And if you can't muster the drive to provide sustenance for your children, God knows what other kinds of neglect and abuse are happening in that house.

One evening I was having a conversation with Olga, my Guatemalan nanny, about her past. She told me that she was at one time a struggling single mother and that all her friends told her to get on welfare and put her daughter on the free-lunch program. She told me that she didn't think it was right to take money without working for it, and more important, she wanted the dignity of feeding her own daughter. She didn't think that should be someone else's responsibility, and if it meant waking up a little bit earlier or putting a little more effort in the night before, it was worth it to say she was taking care of her child. I said how much I respected her and then told her to finish feeding my kids, I'd be in the den watching *SportsCenter*. My point is, nobody who's receiving free lunches is any worse off financially than Olga was at that time in her life. Yet we didn't rob her of her dignity by feeding her kid for her.

How did people get along before the school lunch program? We didn't have poor people at the turn of the century? How did those people feed themselves before the fucking food tickets? The goddamn parents cooked goddamn food.

TAXES

I've had an impacted assful of people on the left who bitch and moan about how the rich don't pay their "fair share" of taxes. You may not know who Maxine Waters is. She's a representative out here in California. Imagine Aunt Esther from *Sanford and Son* but stupid. I saw her on Bill Maher's show a few years ago saying it's time the rich paid their fair share and I thought, "Hey, bitch. I paid almost a million bucks last year and I use nothing. What do you mean 'fair share'?" I pay seventy-five times as much as a shop teacher. Should we make it 175? We already have the top one percent paying 40 percent of the taxes. I paid more last year than my entire family paid in their entire lives since their parents got here from fucking Italy.

Imagine there are two groups: a group with five people and a group with ninety-five people. The five people are paying for everything, but all hundred people get one vote each. So the five people who are paying for everything get five votes and the ninety-five who aren't paying for anything get ninety-five votes. If I asked, "Who thinks the five percent should be paying more?" of course the group of ninety-five will raise their hands and say, "Hell yeah, they should pay more." And because everyone gets one vote, the group of five would have to pay more. Fuck that. That sounds like a democracy, but it's not.

I'd like a system where you got one vote for every ten grand you put in. If you're a cop, schoolteacher, garbage man, or fireman, you essentially get one vote. If you pay a hundred thousand dollars a year, you get ten votes. Bill Gates would get two million votes. And why shouldn't he get more votes? He's paying for that many more roads, that many more M1 Abrams tanks, that many more schools. Bill Gates gets the same vote that my mom gets? She'll just use her vote to make him pay more taxes.

And if you don't pay taxes, you shouldn't get to vote at all. Criminals aren't allowed to vote. Why? Because they are no longer considered members of our society. If you don't pay taxes, you are not contributing to society. You can use the roads, the parks, or go to those places where they hide the books. (What are those called again? Libraries?) But you don't get to vote in shareholder meetings at companies where you don't own stock.

Every one of those people who says I don't pay my "fair share" thinks that every rich person got that way because of Daddy's money. My dad didn't own a tobacco plantation. I fucking earned my way to this tax bracket. I have more because I worked for it. And contrary to popular belief, the lion's share of people in my bracket and beyond are self-starters who busted their ass to get where they are, not one of the Hilton sisters. It's a convenient, uninformed view of our society that makes it easy for people to put their hand out.

So let's call it what it is. Envy. What they're really saying is "Why do you have so much stuff? Why do you need ten cars?" People used to look up to rich guys and aspire to be like them. Now they resent them because they feel shamed. Those guys used to wear ascots and monocles to flaunt their success; now they dress down to conceal it.

This is entirely what terrorism is about. They can't stand our lifestyle, they can't stand our prosperity, and they can't believe that their god is letting us prosper over here while they live on a dirt floor and use goat-flavored toothpaste. So what they do is pray to Allah. But Allah's not there, so what happens? Our skyscrapers get taller, our limousines get longer, our chicks' tits get bigger, and these guys get more pissed and fly planes into our buildings. It's all based on envy turned into resentment turned into low self-esteem turned into rage.

I probably wouldn't even mind paying more if I thought for a second the government was using my tax money effectively. I once talked to Heidi Fleiss about how much manpower it took to take her out and nearly lost my mind. How many hours can the cops waste on things we don't care about? If J.Lo hires security, they do whatever the fuck J.Lo tells them to do because she pays them. We're J.Lo. We pay the cops, so they should do what the fuck we tell them to do. We don't want them busting prostitution rings and cannabis shops. And I'll have to send my kids to private school because Maxine Waters and her buddies in the teachers' union fucked up our public schools so bad that they're unusable. If there was any direct link between the money I give you and my life, I'd gladly turn it over. But if you dial 911 you get a busy signal, and the only thing in this town that doesn't have graffiti on it is the potholes. I'd like them to focus on doing a better job with the hundreds of thousands of dollars I'm currently giving them instead of focusing on doing a better job extracting more money from me.

Why can't we just go with a flat tax? I think the government likes that no one understands how the system works. That way, we just dump our money in a hole, never expecting to see it again. The government is a giant corporation with no competition that is constantly trying to keep you off balance so it can siphon more money from you.

ADAM CAROLLA

126

THE ACLU AND "TORTURE"

The ACLU recently lobbied for some of the records about torture techniques to come out. And one technique that everyone on the left was appalled by is that some agents went into another room, fired a gun, and then told the guy who they thought bombed the U.S.S. *Cole*, "We just shot your partner." They didn't really shoot him; they just went into another room and fired the gun. Are we turning into such cock-chugging homos in this society that we're really upset about this? If this was a Bruce Willis flick and he did this, you'd be cool with it, wouldn't you? He'd still be the hero because he had to figure out where the guy planted the dirty bomb in Chicago. I always said that about waterboarding. When everyone was freaking out about it, I said, "Well, it doesn't harm them." And they'd reply, "But they think they're going to drown." You've seen those action movies where the guy hangs the kidnapper by his ankles off the twelfth-story balcony and he says, "Okay, okay. I'll tell you where your daughter is," and then he pulls the kidnapper back onto the balcony. Isn't it like that? Have we turned into such a nation of pussies? Why do we have to act upset? I feel as if I'm being waterboarded by your tears. Why can't we say, "That sounds like a good idea to me"? They're not just fucking around; they're trying to get information that will save lives. Why do we act as if we're just trying to get a recipe for gazpacho out of these guys? We're trying to prevent terrorist acts. What is your argument? The guy went into the other room and fired a gun and said, "We shot your partner." To me that's reason to say, "Nice job, CIA. You're not killing anybody and you're getting information." I wish other countries interrogated that way. Wouldn't it have been nice for our downed pilots who end up in some rathole in Tikrit to have their Republican Guard interrogators go shoot a gun and then come back in?

Things have quieted down lately now that we have a guy in office who shoots hoop instead of golf. But a few years ago when the golfer

127

was in office, it was nonstop bellyaching about "enhanced interrogation techniques" and lots of assholes with bedazzled iPhones who couldn't find the dipstick in their Prius explaining to the experts how torture doesn't work. I'm no expert either, but here's how I know torture does work. It's been around for twenty thousand years. Shit that doesn't work usually goes the way of the dodo after a few years. Think eight-tracks and waterbeds. Plus, in keeping with a rich tradition of bellyaching but offering no solutions, of course you dicks have no substitution for extracting information from people. Perhaps one of you ass-wipes could take some time out of your busy day and come up with a method that worked. Oh, that's right, I forgot, you don't do shit but complain.

These same experts are also telling us how "we're creating more terrorists." Of course, it's just good sound math: Whether it's terrorists or cockroaches, the more you kill, the more are created. Any exterminator would tell you that. This combined with the Patriot Act is why there have been so many terrorist attacks on our soil since 9/11. According to your retarded logic, the Marshall football team should have won the championship the season after the plane crash. Here's my point: It seems counterintuitive to me that killing terrorists is creating more terrorists. I know your argument is that it's being used as a recruiting tool. There's only one small problem with your argument: You don't know what the fuck you're talking about. Where are you getting your intel, and how is it getting funneled back to the Mac store you're working at in Pasadena?

Of course after the Huffington Post crowd raises a stink, all this stuff comes out in the news. So now terrorists know we're not shooting their collaborators in the next room. These people have this truth-for-everybody idea but are the same ones lying about your chances of getting AIDS and how many people die from secondhand smoke. They can justify lying about that stuff because in their minds, it's going to save lives. They can just say that AIDS is an equal-opportunity killer, a heterosexual is just as likely to get it as a homosexual, and that fifty-three thousand people die a year from secondhand smoke. When are we going to realize these assholes are undoing this country? Where's the class-action lawsuit against these guys? When Benny Laden and his Terrible Towels light off a dirty bomb in San Francisco and a bunch of your friends die, can we sue the ACLU because the NSA guys were scared to crack open Hamid's hard drive? Hey ACLU, how about we let the CIA do their jobs so you can focus on more important matters, like struggling with your sexuality and deciding whether to confront your stepdad?

I'd like to direct this next portion to the terrorists reading the book. I think if you're going to attack us again, you're going to go for L.A. because you already hit New York. If you hit New York again, people are going to think you're limited to the Northeast. But if you get both coasts, you're going to scare the shit out of everyone in between. So I'm assuming you're targeting L.A. On the other hand, some of your greatest supporters live here in L.A. Many of the actors whom I share this fine city with seem to be some of your biggest sympathizers. So I don't know if you want to piss off Barbra Streisand or Susan Sarandon. More important, if you blow up Los Angeles all you're going to do is kill a bunch of Mexicans. If you want to get the blue-eyed devil, you won't find him here. I'm just saying, focus on a red state. For instance, do we need a North Dakota and a South Dakota? Or the Carolinas. We've got two of those.

Go somewhere John Cougar sings about, where they shoot Chevy commercials. I don't know what town they filmed *Footloose* in, but that's the area you should be looking at. Then Oprah will come on TV the next day and say, "If it can happen there, it can happen anywhere," we'll all be officially terrified, and you can get back to the important work of throwing rocks at women who read.

Second only to "torture doesn't work" in the retarded-statement category is "fences don't work." So all those East Berliners who drove around in two-stroke cars and ate stale bread for forty years should have just strolled into West Berlin and gotten themselves a breakfast burrito? Boy, they must be embarrassed, having spent all those years trapped behind a fence that didn't work. And what about all those crazy Jews in their concentration camps? You want to talk about suckers. I have a serious question for all you dipshits that say, "Fences don't keep anyone out." What if we just removed the fence around your fat kids' private school so that any homeless guy or pedophile could wander onto campus willy-nilly? Would you have an issue with that? I'd love to torture one of these no-fence fucknuts until they admitted fences do work—and do it in front of one of those torture-doesn't-work idiots to kill two birdbrains with one stone.

As far as immigration goes, I can't speak for the rest of the country, but I do feel as though I'm well qualified to speak about California versus Mexico. First things first. There's nothing magical about the topsoil in San Diego or cursed about the topsoil in Tijuana. The border is just an arbitrary stripe that runs along a patch of desert that eventually drowns in the Pacific Ocean. The reason San Diego is better than Tijuana is that we made it that way. And to be fair, although it's going to sound unfair, Tijuana is a piece of shit because they made it that way. No matter how hard you lean to the left, or how much you agree with Al Franken, I think you'd have to admit that if your kid was picking out a college, or a dentist, or a place to have an emergency appendectomy, you would pick the U.S. over Mexico every time.

So far I don't think I've said anything that couldn't be construed as a universal truth, no matter what side of the aisle you are on. Now comes the part where you get to call me a bigot even though you know I'm right. I know that if you take a large enough group of anything—beavers, Mexicans, fire ants—and place them on the other side of an arbitrary line on the ground, it will be business as usual for them. And since we already agreed business as usual was not a great plan for our kids and their orthodontics, then something needs to be done. Mexicans aren't bad people and they're not good people. They're just a culture. And at some point when there's enough of them, our culture will be usurped by their culture. And somehow me not wanting that to happen makes me a grand wizard in the Klan. The problem is their skin color is darker than ours, and we've formed a culture where being called a racist is worse than being called a pedophile. People are afraid to speak up. So let's remove the skin color for a minute and replace "Mexican" with "Polish." The second-largest city in this nation, Los Angeles, has a Polish mayor. We have arguments over whether our teachers should instruct in both English and Polish. If you call information, the first five words you'll hear are in English, and the next seven are in Polish telling you to say "Polish" if you want assistance in Polish. When you go to the ATM, you have to pick English over Polish. Chances are if you call a wrong number, the guy on the other end will have a thick Polish accent. The top three radio stations will all be Polish speaking—and I could go on for another ten pages.

Now all I'm saying is we don't need another Polish restaurant. I'm not saying the Poles are bad people. I'm saying I don't want my kids to be raised in Poland. I believe in their heart of hearts the super-lefty, open-borders people agree with me. The problem is the only time they take their boyfriend's cock out of their mouth is to call me a bigot.

Now on to bash the right . . .

ANTIGAY POLITICIANS

A politician can say, "I'm against gay marriage. I'm traditional that way," and I think, All right. But when the guy starts really digging in and introduces legislation to ban them from holding hands in public, he's gay. He cares too much about something that doesn't affect him. I don't trust a guy who's extremely interested in shit he shouldn't care about. When my kid is old enough to go away camping, I want to get the group of dads in a room and say, "Who wants to take the kids up to Mount Pinos for the weekend?" And if one guy's hand flies up, he's out. I'll say, "Sorry, Bert, you're out. Your hand flew up too fast. I don't trust you."

As a straight man, your attitude about the gays should be "Great, more pussy for me." You should have the same feeling about gays as you do about a team you don't follow. So be it. You're rooting for your team. If they want to trade a quarterback and get a new mascot, who cares? That's their business. You should be aware that they exist, and when your team plays them you should hope your team kicks the shit out of them, but you didn't grow up in that town or go to that college, so who gives a fuck? Once you start protesting too much about what that team is doing, something tells me you might have some of that team's colors running through your blood.

THE HPV VACCINE

In 2007, Texas governor Rick Perry mandated that girls in his state get the HPV vaccine. But because of that he took heat from a bunch of right-wing Christians. My wife lost one of her best friends to cervical cancer. She was thirty-four. Is that what you want? You want that for your daughter? I know you're religious and uptight about sex, but it's not like if she gets vaccinated, the next day a bunch of truckers are going to tag-team her on a pool table. It just means she's vaccinated. If you get vaccinated for leprosy, you don't get dropped off at a leper colony the next day. These are just idiots trying to slow down progress. They're all nuts about God, but then accuse doctors of playing God. Well, which is it? Do you love the fucking guy or not? If you do love him, how about we play him? It's a tribute. Look at it as Halloween: I'm dressing up as God. Or a Beatles cover band. Not the real thing, but still a good time—Jesusmania.

ANTI-EUTHANASIA VOTERS

The playing-God argument comes up every couple of years when a state puts a euthanasia law on the ballot, too. Someone whose body is riddled with cancer or is in the final stages of ALS has zero quality of life. Imagine going to bed every night and not knowing if you're going to choke to death on your own saliva.

How about we let these people go out on their own terms? Taking them off the feeding tube is not playing God: Hooking them up to it in the first place is playing God. What about organ transplants? Or Dick Cheney's heart surgery? Isn't that playing God? A lot of these same folks are for the death penalty and just got done bombing an abortion clinic. Pretty sure that's playing God. Of course, these dummies will offer the slippery-slope argument—"Sure, one day you're removing the breathing tube from a brain-dead ninety-year-old. Then the next thing you know, your perfectly healthy son goes in for his peewee football physical and the doctor snuffs his life out with a pillow and there's not a damn thing you can do about it!" Dr. Kevorkian made it possible for people who are suffering with terminal illness to pass with dignity. The state of Michigan spent millions of taxpayer dollars prosecuting and eventually incarcerating him when just outside the courthouse on the streets of Detroit were boarded-up storefronts and a bunch of homeless people who should have been in mental hospitals or in rehab—but there weren't enough beds because all the taxpayers' money was spent on a bunk for Kevorkian.

THE WAR ON DRUGS

Politicians in both parties are guilty of perpetuating this, but the liberals are definitely on the correct side. I go nuts when I read about how much the DEA spends on pot versus what they spend on crystal meth. There are certain drugs that when you get beaked out of your brain on them, you look around for the worst imaginable thing you could do. Meth makes you do evil things. Weed makes you eat pie filling straight out of the can. I'll put it this way. Who would you rather have living next door to you, a bunch of Phish heads or a bunch of meth heads? The first group might keep you up one night with a twenty-five-minute guitar solo, but the tweakers are gonna steal your stereo, pawn it for meth money, then microwave and rape your cat.

A quick note on meth. We can't have twenty-eight different "meth capitals." Every time I turn on the news, I hear about the "meth capital of America." We need to have them fight it out. The biggest meth head from Lancaster, California, and the biggest meth head from Jackson County, Missouri, sort it out in the octagon. Get Michael Buffer to announce it. "In this corner in the heavyweight division, six foot seven, weighing in at one hundred and nineteen pounds . . ."

When the history books are written, the prohibition of marijuana is gonna look like the prohibition of alcohol in the twenties and thirties. Our grandkids will think we were idiots. There was an ad that came out shortly after 9/11 saying that if you smoke marijuana, you're funding terrorism. No, the fact that the government made it illegal funds terrorism. They created a black market. I can't believe it's 2010 and we're still arguing about this. It should have been legalized in the early seventies. We could have generated millions of dollars in tax revenues and saved billions of hours arguing about something that's not intrinsically dangerous. Here's my philosophy on pot in a nutshell: The people who smoke pot will continue to smoke pot, legal or not. The idea that the second they decriminalize marijuana my dad's going to go out and buy a bong and a Hacky Sack is insane. As a parent I would prefer my kids didn't grow up to smoke pot, but I would also prefer they not eat chili burgers, ride motorcycles, smoke cigarettes, drink hard lemonade, or play with samurai swords. Since none of those things are illegal, it'll be up to me to educate them on the consequences of those behaviors. But let's face it, eventually the kid's going to rip a bong load and go for that chili burger. It's not going to kill him—we've all done it and we're all still here.

The government thinks pot is a drug and that all drugs are evil. They're not. It's what you do with them. Like cars. You could pick up your kids at day care or plow through an outdoor swap meet and kill a bunch of people.

And by the way, if drugs are so awful, how is it that no one works harder than crackheads? There are drug-free people who can't manage to get their shit together, but crackheads always manage to score. They are the tip of the ingenuity spear. Think about when you see the homeless guy pushing the shopping cart with two dirigible-sized bags of recyclable bottles and cans. He spent two days Dumpster diving and three hours at the recycling machine in the grocery-store parking lot feeding those filthy cans into the crusher so he could get the equivalent of a packet of Sweet'N Low to put up his nose or in his veins. And he had to steal the shopping cart. It's testament to the tenacity and initiative of the American drug addict.

Back to attacking the government. Let's not forget the intent-to-distribute shit. If the cops pull a guy over with more than a couple of joints' worth of weed in his car, they hit him with an intent-to-distribute charge. Maybe he just loves weed. That's like the cops pulling me over when I have a boner and charging me with intent-to-rape.

Where's the NRA when it comes to this stuff? They're constantly squawking about your rights and the Constitution and big government. Charlton Heston used to shout about taking guns from his cold dead hands. Yet these hypocrites have no problem with me getting my house confiscated and auctioned if I grow a pot plant in my backyard. No issue with that, huh? What's more dangerous, a bong or a bazooka? Idiots.

My overall problem with the right is they're foot draggers. They don't understand that in the near future gays will be allowed to marry, marijuana will be legalized, and stem cells will be used to repair organs. It's called progress; it's what societies do. And history isn't kind to those who don't recognize that. In my mind, these topics are no different than the two sets of drinking fountains installed for whites and Negroes. We'll burn millions of hours arguing over it, there'll be a few rallies, a few people are going to get hit with fire hoses, and twenty-five years from now magically every politician will have been for gay marriage back in the day.

Then there are certain political issues that both parties participate in. They cover the dipshit spectrum all the way from liberal pussy to conservative dickhead.

Which brings me to the lottery. This is state-sponsored gambling. It's hypocrisy of the highest order. I can't play blackjack without driving to Vegas or an Indian reservation, but every time I'm at the liquor store I get stuck behind some dropout playing his "lucky numbers." First off, you're buying a pint of Malibu rum and lotto tickets. You don't have lucky numbers. Second, I know you don't have anywhere to go, but I do, so speed it up. I don't understand why it takes so long to play a lotto ticket. I know you've got an eighth-grade education and numbers are confusing, but pick up the pace. There should be special liquor stores with signs that say WELCOME IDIOTS where you can get your lotto tickets, Slim Jims, and malt liquor, and then ones for the rest of us smart people so we can get our booze and move on with our fucking lives.

The lotto is the pinnacle of Loser Mountain. This is a horrible message for elected officials to send to their constituents and a worse message for you to send to yourself. Participating in this government-run scam is you announcing, "I'm a loser. I can't get my shit together, get a job and an education, and pull myself out of poverty. I have one shot at life and that's to hammer my welfare check, put on my slippers and bathrobe, shuffle down to the liquor store, pick up some lotto tickets, and maybe God will smile on me." You've officially waved the white flag at life and declared, "I give."

Around Christmastime you'll hear radio ads for lottery gift certificates. This is assfoolery on a level that can't be measured by any test or instrument. Not only are you a loser for buying lottery tickets, now you're trying to indoctrinate your friends and relatives into your brain-dead cult. You're giving someone a slip of paper so they can haul their ass to the 7-Eleven to get another slip of paper. Why don't you just burn the five dollars in front of them and save the trip?

Recently I saw a TV ad for the local lottery. In it the Garcia family wins the lottery and rents out Dodger Stadium for a family-reunion barbecue. Think about how horrible this message is and who it is geared toward. The state of California is saying, "Let's tell the people who can barely make ends meet and have a fifty percent dropout rate that their only shot is to throw what little money they have into the lottery and pray to the Virgin of Guadalupe that it all works out." Even worse, they suggest that on the minuscule chance they do win that they should immediately blow the money on an extravagant party for mooching relatives. How about investing the money in T-bills or Microsoft stock? Nope, let's rent out Dodger Stadium, get a shitload of carne asada, and go to town on the world's largest piñata. The tagline for the commercial is "Imagine What a Dollar Can Do." I'll tell you what a dollar can do. It can go into the bank or a fucking mason jar toward a college fund or bail. This reminds me of a great joke I heard when I did *The New Gong Show*. "What has five balls and rapes Mexicans? The lottery."

And 50 percent of the money that goes into the pot never comes out. Plus if you do win, you get your choice between barely half of the money you won in a lump or a twenty-year payout. Can you imagine applying that math to a Super Bowl office pool? The employees would burn the fucking building down.

Of course the defenders will talk about how the schools benefit from the lottery proceeds. Oh, you mean the schools that I can't send my kids to because they won't get educated and will get shot? Those schools? Our public schools have metal detectors at every entrance, barbed wire on the fences, and textbooks that look forward to the end of the Korean Conflict and welcoming Hawaii as a state. Public schools are essentially coed prisons with worse food. So don't give me that bullshit about lottery money going to the schools. To you assholes who defend the lottery: one question. Were the schools in California better before or after the lottery? And am I the only one who finds it ironic that the proceeds from this state-sponsored Ponzi scheme go toward an institution that's supposed to exalt the virtues of hard work, dedication, and preparation? If a school counselor suggested to one of his students (sorry, I'm just picturing a dude) that the student should cross their fingers and play the lottery, he would be shit-canned.

THE SCHOOLS

Everyone wants to know what's wrong with public schools these days. The dropout rate is through the roof, the test scores are in the toilet. What happened to the teachers? Nothing. I'm sure the unions haven't helped and the teachers are doing a horrible job, but let's take a moment to focus on the families. First of all, what's a teacher supposed to do when a kid drops out? Jump onto a horse with a cargo net and go after the kid like it's *Planet of the Apes*? It's up to the parents to make sure their kids attend school each day. We love to blame the system for everything. The bottom line is the system isn't the thing that's changed: The families have changed.

Let me give you a quick, personal example. I went to North Hollywood High in the early eighties. It was a large public school with almost every culture represented. The teachers weren't great, the school was more than fifty years old and not exactly state of the art, and the football field was mostly dirt. My group of friends consisted of Mexicans from the north Valley, blacks bused in from Compton, white trash from the mid-Valley, and Jews from the hills. We all attended the same classes and had the same teachers. But at the end of our senior years, while my Jewish friends went off to Cal, Stanford, and UCLA, we went off to Wendy's, Carl's Jr., and Arby's. Why? Their families were intact, their parents cared, they made sure their kids did their homework, and they made education a priority.

So to be fair to the teachers, it's not their fault. I'm sure teaching in a public school now is exactly the same as being a guard at juvie. The job of a teacher in today's public school system is to prevent the students from raping each other in the coat closet. It is children of all races who come from shitty homes with absentee parents. These kids have no chance no matter how much money you pour into the schools. But there are other kids who are being brought down by the public schools. They're not being taught any necessary life skills.

In junior high I was forced to take horticulture, cooking, plastics, and sewing classes. When I was at North Hollywood High, we had majors. I was a ceramics major. And as you all know by now, before I got into show business I had a successful career in the fast-paced and lucrative world of pinch pots. Ceramics major: what a joke. Have you ever met a famous potter? Has anyone ever put an addition onto their house from the money they made from terra-cotta pots? No. It was such time-wasting warehousing. My buddy Ray was in the Future Farmers of America, a skill that serves him well to this day from his shitbox apartment on Kling Street in North Hollywood.

They should size kids up when they're in ninth grade, and if they're like me, Ray, or any of the guys I grew up with, take them out of the sociology class. That's not going to do them any good when, like me, they're carpet cleaning. Just pull them out one day and say, "You're not heading to Harvard, you're heading to Hamburger Hamlet to push around a carpet wand." Not everyone is college material, so let's teach them a trade. Train them how to be electricians and plumbers and make sure they're prepared for life and the workforce. I'm not talking about shop class. I mean full immersion in a trade.

And what about some training for how to do a job interview and fill out applications? Kids shouldn't be able to get out of school without knowing where to put their name and Social Security number on an application or that when you walk into an interview you shouldn't be wearing a My Chemical Romance T-shirt and say, "'Sup? Do I got the job or what?"

Why not have all kids take a full-semester course on basic financial planning? As I said earlier, you're going to be raped by the government on April 15 of every year. Shouldn't public schools have mandatory classes about taxes and how to fill out your forms? Or how to write a check and balance your bank account? The economy in this country has gone down the shitter because no one can understand credit-card interest and mortgage payments, and thus get fleeced by the dickholes on Wall Street. This affects all of us.

Or CPR and first aid. Teach them basic lifesaving skills. I don't mean a day devoted to it in health class, I mean an entire semester. Make it mandatory. We could turn the next generation into para-paramedics. Not necessarily someone who can administer an IV of morphine, but someone who could save your kid if he was drowning in a pool or put a tourniquet on you when you get shot by one of the other dropouts from the public school.

CHILD ABUSE

My biggest beef in politics on both the right and the left is that politicians won't step up and talk about the real issues—and journalists let them dodge the important questions. The government will spend millions letting us know about the analog TV switch, but not make a single mention of child abuse. Abused kids grow up and abuse the system, their wives, their children, and my children. It's my dog-and-owner theory. If a dog attacks someone, the owner needs to pay and the dog needs to be put down. If you beat the crap out of your kid, you turn him into a monster who uses violence to solve every issue. That kid needs to be incarcerated or put down, depending on what he or she does to society. Sadly, that kid was once a victim and is now a victimizer. We need to deal with that kid, but we need to deal with the parents, too. Whichever Doctor Frankenstein was creating that monster in their lab (which I'm sure is more of an apartment than a lab), I want that person dealt with, too. Not only are the kids gonna have problems later, but whoever is sitting next to them in a school bus is gonna have problems, and whoever is at the ATM when they show up drunk is gonna have problems. It doesn't even need to be physical abuse. Every culture has its own form of bad parenting. Ours has a lot of parents telling their kids, "Life's a bitch, everyone's out there trying to screw you, so you've got to screw them first." Thanks, Dad. Thanks for creating one more asshole who's trying to screw me when I'm *not* trying to screw him because I didn't have you as a dad telling me that everyone was attempting to screw me.

POPULATION/BIRTH CONTROL

When is a politician on either side of the aisle going to have the balls to pipe up and say, "Poor people: Stop shitting out kids"? If we solve this problem, we solve all the other problems. Who is it that's filling our prisons? Who is it that's filling our soup kitchens? Who is it that is uneducated and on the dole? Who is it that is getting pregnant as teenagers? Who has no insurance and is getting strung out and filling up the emergency rooms? Unwanted kids. When parents start focusing on raising a family and having two kids instead of nine is when all of the world's problems go away. That's when the prison guards get to go home; you get to leave your front door unlocked at night and your laptop on the dash of your convertible.

Then these unwanted kids go on to have their own brood of unwanted kids, and so on and so on and so on. But it never gets addressed. Half the guys in the NFL talk about how they never knew their dad and that they were one of twelve kids. And we just applaud his mom instead of saying this is fucked-up and that having that many kids is its own form of child abuse. When the politicians hit the campaign trail, there's a lot of talk about the hardworking families on Main Street and the single moms who have to hold down three jobs. Right. They have to hold down three jobs because they have thirteen kids. Thus they can't pay their mortgage. Thus the whole economy goes down the shitter.

We refuse to address the root of the problem. Politicians are always yapping about creating new programs and increasing aid to struggling families. But they never, *never* talk about putting on a condom or using the morning-after pill. Ironically, the only group they ever told to put on a condom was the gays. It's not just the Republican politicians from the Bible Belt who are scared of the religious ramifications; the Democrats won't address it because of the racial and socioeconomic overtones. So we continue to increase our population and bust our budgets. This problem compounds itself with each new generation of unwanted kids. This nation is sinking fast. The S.S. *Fallopian Tubing* is taking on sperm faster than we can bail.

In a nutshell, the problem with politicians is simple. They were all former oilmen, lawyers, actors, or, worst of all, politicians. Where are the psychologists, where are the sociologists? I want someone who understands human nature. Not how to manipulate people into voting for them, but how to motivate people into staying in school, raising a family, and paying their taxes. If these hypocritical fucks would see a shrink on Saturday instead of going for the photo op on the church steps on Sunday, we'd all be in a much better position.

Thank you. I'm Adam Carolla, and I need your vote.

GOD, RELIGIOUS TOLERANCE, AND OTHER SHIT THAT DOESN'T EXIST

I am an atheist. There are two types of atheists. There's the Adam Carolla–type atheists, who are logical, reasonable people who don't believe in anything unless there's proof provided. Then there's the my-dad-was-a-born-again-Christian-and-used-to-sodomize-me athe-ist, the one with the chip on his fucking shoulder. These are the ones that want "In God We Trust" taken off the dollar bill. And they want the cross that's on the Los Angeles crest, because it was settled by missionaries, taken off the mayor's coffee mug. They draw attention to themselves by being a pain in the ass. Ironically, these people have turned atheism into a religion. I'm an atheist because I believe God doesn't exist, not because I have a score to settle with him.

I understand why we invented God and why we cling to him with both hands—because we're the only species on the planet that's aware it's going to die. Pardon the pun, but I pray I'm right about this. Imag-ine how horrible it would be if cows and chickens knew where they were heading, not to mention bomb-sniffing dogs. "Let me get this straight. When you're nine I'll be sixty-three and when you're twelve I'll be dead? And you want me to go down to the airport to see if that duffle bag is filled with C4? Suck my balls. Never mind, I've got it."

This is why we have religion. That's the genesis of Genesis. We can't face our own mortality, so we concoct stories about God's plan and a place in the clouds where everything is perfect and you get reunited with your loved ones. What if the person doesn't want to be reunited with you? Maybe your dead husband's been banging Jayne Mansfield up in heaven and the last thing he wants is you showing up and ruining the party. The great cock block in the clouds. Or what if the deceased guy was married multiple times? When he gets up to heaven, which wife gets priority? When Larry King finally kicks the bucket, it's going to be a Chinese fire drill. And if you lose a leg to a land mine in Darfur, is it waiting for you when you arrive? What if you got a breast reduction? Are the rest of your tits waiting for you?

At every funeral, the relatives of the deceased are told, "He's in a better place." Awesome. So the rest of us are stuck down here in Shitsville? And if he's in a better place, why are you bawling your eyes out? Shouldn't you be blowing a New Year's Eve noisemaker and throwing confetti? You're crying because you know you'll never see that person again and that one day your number will be called, too.

How about when the seven-year-old rides his bike into the street and gets killed by a gardening truck? Rather than deal with the horrible truth that sometimes awful things just happen, the family will say, "God needed him up in heaven." Why? What does God need with a seven-year-old? Is he manufacturing Nikes? Does he need a right fielder for heaven's Little League team and saw that Billy had a cannon for a right arm? And even if he did "need" little Billy, couldn't he have taken him quietly in his sleep? He had to get dragged under an '81 Toyota pickup with a shark cage full of gardening equipment in the bed?

Another way we make ourselves feel better about people passing on is by saying, "He died doing what he loved." I'm sure that's a comfort to the guy who got hit by an eighteen-wheeler on his motorcycle: "He died riding his Harley, doing what he loved." I'm pretty sure if he knew that he was going to ride his hog right off this mortal coil, he wouldn't have loved it so much. And they'll say it no matter what. Yeah, I'm sure the guy who had a heart attack in his cubicle loved crunching numbers for the plywood wholesaler. That was what he was born to do. The only time they don't say it is when the guy actually did die doing what he loved, autoerotic asphyxiation. I sadly had to attend a funeral for a young man who died that way. I wouldn't say it was uncomfortable, but I'd rather have watched my mom attempt to set the gang-bang record from a dentist's chair.

My problem with 95 percent of religions is one they never speak of: They hate religions other than their own. They all claim to be innocent Steeler fans, but let's face it, they hate the Patriots, and once in a while a couple of rogue superfans think it would be a good idea to try to take down the Patriots' team plane. And the next thing you know, we've got a fight in the stands.

It's all just made-up nonsense so we feel better. A lot of people like to attack Scientology and say that it's not a "real" religion, that it's a cult. To me, all religions are cults. And here's my take on Scientology. Tom Cruise and John Travolta always look happy. If your religion gets you in a place where you can bang Katie Holmes or pilot a DC-10 to the America's Cup, then sign me up. I don't care if you believe in space aliens; my only interest is that someone doesn't blow me up at a disco.

Most religions adopt this if-you're-not-for-us-you're-against-us mentality. How about the third option? How about the people who just don't give a shit about your retarded fantasy? I don't mind the imbeciles that buy into this nonsense, I mind that as a society we give them such a wide berth. Every once in a while you'll come across a guy who is a Disney fanatic—the one who makes the weekly pilgrimage to the Magic Kingdom, has a denim jacket covered in Donald Duck pins, and says things like "I've ridden Pirates of the Caribbean over thirty thousand times." You immediately realize the guy is a kook and start making fun of him. But you sure as fuck don't respect him. What's the difference between this nut bag and the guy who dresses like an undertaker with a beard down to his waist and fucks his wife through a sheet? Or the guy who treats his flock of goats better than his flock of wives and can't make it fifteen minutes without falling to his knees and praying? And by the way, if I ran

Guantánamo Bay, not only would I double down on the waterboarding, I'd take that arrow they have out in the rec yard that points toward Mecca and spin it toward Vegas.

I'm certainly not a student of religion, but I am a student of psychology, and there's one thing I know: When you're secure in your beliefs, you don't need a bullhorn. Think of it as a game of twenty-one and you just got dealt blackjack. Why do you give a shit what the guys sitting on the stools to your left and right are doing with their cards? Just sit on your ace and king and wait for the payout. You show me a guy who never stops talking about what a badass he is, and I'll show you a guy who doesn't truly believe he's a badass. Randy Couture doesn't spend the better part of each day trying to convince his neighbors that he can kick their ass. I'll take it a step further: I believe if I took most people who said they had a personal relationship with Jesus Christ and knew there was a heaven and shot them up with Sodium Pentothal and a couple of roofies, I could get them to admit that there probably wasn't a heaven and that their relationship with Jesus Christ was about as good as Angelina Jolie's relationship with Jon Voight. And then I would have sex with them. Why waste the roofies?

None of these idiots really believe in God. Especially all the evangelicals and politicians who are banging male prostitutes or their nannies. They just want you to believe they believe so they can take your money, get reelected, or both. If Jesse Jackson really believed in the big man in the sky, would he have knocked up a woman on his Rainbow Coalition staff when he was married for thirty-five years? He says God speaks to him. I guess God never sent him the message about pulling out. And Jesse was the "spiritual counselor" to Bill Clinton after he got caught being blown by a chunky intern. Of course these self-righteous fucksticks don't believe it. If they did, they wouldn't engage in this behavior. Please permit me one last quick analogy. If you put me in a room, gave me a *Playboy*, pointed up at a camera mounted on the ceiling, and said there's a guy who controls your destiny in the next room watching a monitor and I believed it, I wouldn't beat off. But if I saw the camera was made of Styrofoam and there were no wires going to it, I'd have at myself. These guys know they have a fucking Styrofoam camera.

I hate that we have to pretend to respect all religions, especially the ones that are trying to blow up airplanes and pizza parlors or are actively involved with ethnic cleansing. Someone should just call them what they are, nut jobs. And don't give me that shit where "It's not all of them. It's only a small percentage." Sure, it's a small percentage, but it's enough to bring down the Twin Towers. I don't blame them, they're nuts. I blame us for not shouting, "You're fucking nuts. I don't respect your retarded beliefs. Now what are you going to do about it? Nothing, because your stupid religion has kept you in the Stone Age. What are you going to do, fly your fleet of Mach 3 jets over New York and bomb it? No. You're so backward technologically that you have to use *our* planes to bomb us." Here's my question to all people and all religions. It's the same thing I want to ask all the communists out there. How's it going? How's it working out for you? I watch the news and it doesn't look like it's going so well.

These people who tell you all religions should be respected are the same idiots with the COEXIST bumper sticker on their Prius. Who is this message for? You're pulling into the Whole Foods in West Hollywood and parking with nine other Priuses sporting COEXIST bumper stickers. It's preaching to the choir. Actually, the gay men's chorus. The people who need to get the all-religions-are-beautiful-and-can-work-in-harmony message aren't there. Do you think Ahmadinejad is pulling his armored SUV in behind you to pick up a nine-dollar organic avocado and a wheatgrass smoothie? This would be like going to a Beverly Hills private school to deliver an important message about staying out of gangs. Your stupid bumper sticker is falling on deaf eyes. The people who really should get the "coexist" message are literally on the other side of the world. The regions that need these stickers barely have cars to put them on. And again, they wouldn't heed this coexist idea anyway. They'd stone you to death for having the audacity to be driving as a woman.

If this is on your car, please drive into oncoming traffic.

So no matter how crazy the religion is, we need to respect it? What about cults? Cults are religions, but instead of churches they have compounds, and instead of priests they have bearded weirdos with acoustic guitars. Every cult starts out as peace, love, and folk music, but eventually gives way to "bring me all the thirteen-year-old girls." All cults are about fifty-year-old white guys nailing teenage runaways.

I was thinking about the Manson family. I'm not proud of it, but whenever they show that archival footage from 1971 I think, Hmm, not bad. Those chicks were nineteen and hot. Charlie essentially had a harem. Let me tell you something about these chicks: If Charlie could hand them a steak knife, tell them to go up the hill, break into a stranger's house, and brutally stab anyone who's inside of it and they say, "Fine," believe me, there's nothing they wouldn't do in the bedroom. Orgies and back-door lovin' are light lifting compared to breaking in through the back door of the LaBianca residence. Charlie was the messiah to them: There's nothing they wouldn't do with him, to him, or to each other while he watched. He had a good thing going. I'm betting at some point when Manson declared, "Okay, we're gonna take the harem of hot nineteen-year-olds, put them in the van, and tell them to stab random Los Angelenos," Tex Watson said, "You know what? Maybe just one more daylong orgy. Let's get the race riots started next weekend. I'll get some Boone's Farm, you get some weed, and let's just daisy-chain it. Just one more time before we send them off to prison for the rest of their lives." What was Manson thinking? You have some land, there's no such thing as

AIDS, you have a bunch of hot nineteen-year-old runaways, and you're gonna get them all thrown in the joint? Believe me, I would still be on that dirt patch in Chatsworth having sex if I were Charlie. That's how you know he was nuts—not the stabbing, but that he gave up the nineteen-year-old punanny. Makes me sick.

Every time you argue with a religious person, they pose this question: "If you were walking down a dark alley, would you rather encounter a group of Christians or a group of atheists?" Before I answer that, let me ask you a question, my religious-zealot friend. What percentage of inmates on death row are atheist or agnostic? Of course I'd rather deal with people who had their own internal moral compass rather than a group that could stab me and be absolved of their sins. And where is this alley, and what year is it? Not if the alley is in Jerusalem during the Crusades.

I wish we could adopt the same policy with religion that the army adopted some years ago in regards to chugging cock. "Don't ask, don't tell." I won't ask you who you're currently praying to, you shut the fuck up about your Santa in the sky, and, speaking of the army, if you get out of line, we send over the Predator drones. Thank you, and I'll see you in hell.

FOODS I HAVE
A BEEF WITH

I have a strange history with food. I'm part owner of an Italian restaurant, and the food at Kimmel's football Sunday is sometimes the
highlight of my week. But growing up, I was a crazed raccoon and
the world was my Dumpster. My parents didn't cook. If they did prepare anything, it was shitty seventies health food like that natural
peanut butter that doesn't spread and just rolls on top of the bread
picking up pieces of sprouted wheat. My mom was Chef Boyar-don't.
This is the woman who once gave out walnuts for Halloween. And
my dad cooked about as well as he snowboarded.

When I was a kid, I'd stare at the snack drawer at my friend's
house the way Travolta stared at whatever was in the suitcase in *Pulp
Fiction*. It would glow and I'd hear an angelic hum. My mom would
never let food like that in my house. Everything was macrobiotic and
tasted like gerbil pellets. In the seventies we were constantly bom-
barded with messages about how everything was bad for us. Don't sit
too close to the TV, microwave ovens will give you a brain tumor,
white flour is the white devil. Yet not one word about the sun and
skin cancer. We were constantly riding our bikes shirtless in the San
Fernando Valley in the middle of summer. We would go to the beach

armed only with a towel. Not one ounce of sunblock. My mom was part of the whole Age of Aquarius thing, and she took the "Let the Sun Shine" message literally. How could the sun be bad? The Incas worshipped it and, more important, there wasn't a white male behind it. It wasn't built by a defense contractor. That was the problem. Hot dogs and saltines were all the work of the Man, and anything an old white male produced was bad for you. White bread was the ace of spades in my mom's deck of terrorist cards. Why was that the one that had the target on its back? Because it started with the word *white* and was associated with this country. But she never had a beef with pumpernickel. As if there's any nutritional difference between pumpernickel and white. The difference was one piece looked like a slave owner and the other looked like LeVar Burton. I blame it on Richard Nixon. No one in my mom's generation trusted the Man after him. Thanks, Dick. You ruined my childhood.

L.A. RESTAURANTS

Since this is the food chapter, I'll start with something near and dear to my heart and my home: L.A. food, and how they've fucked it up.

Let me take you right through the menu. A guy who looks like a bi-curious waif model comes to your table and says, "Our soup of the day is pureed summer squash with a lemongrass reduction. There's no dairy, no animal protein, no trans fats." In other towns they tell you what's in the soup. L.A. is the only town that tells you what's *not* in the soup. It tastes like someone took baby food, put it in a sock, and dipped it in warm water.

If you went to Chicago and told them what's *not* in the soup, they'd beat the shit out of you. They've got chunks of beef, a head of cabbage, russet potatoes, and a cow's heart. I'm not vegan. I like the big chunks. That's the fun part, when you hit an iceberg of animal floating around in a sea of broth.

Now, on to the salad. Who's in the mood for lawn trimmings? If you hate beefsteak tomatoes or the crackle of iceberg lettuce between your teeth, then L.A. is the town for you. We have "greens," which are essentially a pile of leaves covered with salad dressing so light and thin it looks like dew on a ficus tree. It's "vinaigrette," which is basically douche with a little olive oil mixed in. Here's a quick tip when it comes to salad dressing: If light won't pass through it, it's good. Thousand Island, ranch, Roquefort. You could take a 120-watt lightbulb, dip it in Roquefort, screw it in, and finish developing your film. Salad in Los Angeles is more cud than salad. We all just sit there chewing like the cows we won't eat.

Now on to the main course. If you like goat cheese, L.A. is perfect for you. We put goat cheese on our pizza, on our entrees, and all over our salads. I don't know when this retarded vote went down but I wish I had been there to stand up and yell, "I hate goat cheese!" Have you ever had a slice of pizza and thought to yourself, "You know what's missing from this experience? The pungent smell of goat as I inhale to take a bite." Goat cheese smells like a goat. And the last time I checked, there were no goat-scented candles, air fresheners, or aftershave.

If you like Italian food, you've come to the wrong town. If you like gay Italian food, you'll be in hog heaven. All you do is take the pasta, remove the meatballs and the red sauce, add pine nuts and attitude, and you've got L.A. Italian, my *paisan.* If you like authentic Italian food you can go to New York because L.A. doesn't have a Little Italy. On the other hand, if you've got a hankering for some Ethiopian, we have a little one of them. How many other cities can boast they have a Little Ethiopia and no Little Italy? I don't know how the "Little" sanctioning body works, but shouldn't the big version of your "Little" have at least one building with a third story before you start franchising?

Who'd like a beverage? I don't know about you, but one of my favorites is iced tea. Lots of caffeine, no calories, and the refills are free. L.A. used to serve iced tea; now we have passion-fruit iced tea. Passion-fruit iced tea tastes like someone boiled potpourri and stirred it with a scented candle. It doesn't taste anything like iced tea. This is another vote I evidently missed in some sort of ill-conceived secret town-hall meeting L.A.'s been having. The insidious part of phasing out iced tea for passion-fruit tea is that regular iced tea is not even an option on the menu anymore.

I now make a point when ordering iced tea to ask if it's real, regular iced tea. My wife, who's typing this (Hi!!), will remember a trip to the Getty Museum for what was supposed to be a nice Sunday outing. We made reservations at the hilltop restaurant. As we were taking in the view of Los Angeles and I was pointing out the Crips' territory versus the Bloods' turf, the waiter asked if we wanted to order drinks. I ordered iced tea and then immediately asked if it was real iced tea. He assured me it was. Five minutes later I got a tumbler of something that tasted like a florist took a shit in it. I said to the waiter, "I thought you said you had real iced tea." He said, "That *is* real iced tea." It was at that moment I knew we'd turned the corner and lost the passion-fruit war.

Now I know a couple of you assholes are thinking, I like passion-fruit iced tea. That's not the point. The point is it doesn't taste like iced tea and I ordered iced tea. Iced tea is its own flavor, just like coffee is its own flavor. And if passion fruit is so great, how come there's nothing else on the planet that's passion-fruit flavored? Passion-fruit toothpaste? You ever see that on a store shelf? How about passion-fruit pie? How about passion-fruit yogurt? How about passion-fruit Jell-O? Obviously it sucks as a flavor if it couldn't crack the Jell-O starting lineup. I know I sound insane, but I'm passionate about my hatred for passion fruit.

One more quick restaurant story. I was sitting in a restaurant on Wilshire Boulevard next door to the La Brea Tar Pits (reason 128 not to live in Los Angeles: We have a hole filled with used transmission fluid and we treat it like it's fucking Mount Rushmore) and I was getting into my usual iced tea debate/argument with the waitress when she said, "You know, most people prefer the passion-fruit iced tea." At that very moment a woman at a neighboring table who must have been eavesdropping, although to be fair I could be heard outside the restaurant, said to the waitress, "Oh, is it passion-fruit iced tea? I'll cancel my order." It was the proudest moment of my life, second only to the birth of one of my twins.

Now on to dessert. I know you're wondering how L.A. can fuck up something as simple as dessert. I'll explain. L.A. is a melting pot with culinary representatives that span the globe. Thai, Japanese, Mexican, Korean, Chinese, et cetera. All nations that do great dinners followed by some of the shittiest desserts ever devised. Anyone for deep-fried green-tea ice cream? Or flan? Let's face it: The best dessert is American dessert. Warm apple pie with a scoop of vanilla ice cream on top. The problem is all these assholes have too much national pride to move over and let us handle the sweets. There's nothing worse than going out and having a satisfying Mexican meal only to have it end with a churro. Hey Mexico, what's up? You guys counting calories? Because I just ate a pillowcase of tortilla chips, two pitchers of margaritas, and a cow dipped in cheese. One of you dipshits can't go on a pie run?

Now that your dining experience is over, it's time to overtip your mattress (model/actress) and make sure you have some cash left over to tip the valet who undoubtedly moved your driver's seat up so far it was on the other side of the steering wheel and stole the change and your roach out of the ashtray. Bon appétit!

P.S. One more thing about iced tea. The goddamn passion-fruit iced tea also fucked up the Arnold Palmer.

WATER

Every nutritionist for the last fifteen years has been extolling the virtues of H_2O. You should drink at least eight full tumblers a day. That's the key to weight loss. I'd love to see a chart from 1979 with average water consumption on one side and average weight on the other. I know as the water consumption goes up, so will the weight. We drink more water than ever, yet we're fatter than ever. How can this be the key to nutrition and weight loss? And if another asshole gives me the speech about our bodies being 70 percent water, I'm going to make his face 100 percent fist. How much water do we really need to consume? I spent the better part of my youth running wind sprints on a football field in the San Fernando Valley during the dog days of summer in full gear with nary a bottle of water in sight. As a matter of fact, at that time they thought water was bad for you so they deprived us of it. And there wasn't one fat kid on that football team. Except Higginstaller, but I think that was a thyroid problem.

Obviously it's a multibillion-dollar-a-year industry that preys on our obsession with health, our children, and body image. And when did water become an expensive part of every dining experience? Nine dollars for a bottle of flat or carbonated water times two or three if you have enough people around the table? I'd love to build a time machine, go back to 1974, and explain to my dad that we just went out to dinner and spent thirty-two dollars on water. By the way, there's a handful of people I'm friendly with—Sarah Silverman comes to mind—who won't drink the carbonated water. I can't stand going to eat with those people because the notion of spending nine dollars for a bottle of water is mind-numbing enough, but when it tastes exactly the same as what came out of the hose bib in front of my mom's house, it's devastating. At least the carbonated stuff feels like I'm buying a beverage.

But here's where the conspiracy part comes in. I've been out to dinner a hundred times with a table of eight or more when the waiter has come by and said, "Would you like to get started with some spar-kling water, still, or just tap water?" And the person to my right says, "The regular flat water is fine." Five minutes later the guy returns with four blue perfume bottles filled with the world's most expensive flat water and starts pouring. I know he's conveniently misunder-stood the person's request for tap water. And nobody is cheap enough, or bold enough, to pour it back into the bottle and say, "Take it back." If the bar is where these restaurants make their money, isn't this just a logical extension of that? I've gotten into loud, semi-embarrassing arguments with my wife when somebody at the table we're out to dinner with says, "Flat water is fine," meaning "free water from the tap." But I see the dollar signs pop up in the eyes of the waiter, so as he begins to turn and head toward the kitchen, I say, "Excuse me, she was just asking for tap water. I know you think she ordered bottled water." This then garners the groan from my wife: "How do you know what she ordered? Leave him alone. Why do you have to be up in everyone's business?" Then I turn to the girl who ordered and say, "Did you mean still bottled water, or did you mean a glass of tap water?" That's when my wife reenters the fray. To me: "Leave her alone. She's not on trial." To her: "You don't have to answer that." Now it's on. I loudly announce this convenient misunderstanding is a multimillion-dollar industry. I know this is taking place in restau-rants around the world every second of every day. It's free versus more expensive than your average store-bought bottle of Merlot.

SPORTS DRINKS

At some point somebody realized kids were getting fat from drink-ing too much punch and soda. So we figured out another high-fructose-corn-syrup delivery system, which was sports drinks. Same calories, same coloring, same chemicals, but now everyone can suck them down with impunity because Michael Jordan and Derek Jeter drink them. This should be illegal. You shouldn't be able to call something Vita-water and have it be calorically on the same par as fudge. If we don't stop with all these health drinks, we're going to explode. All these kids are walking around with neon-purple Gatorade. These colors don't coordinate with anything in nature unless it's on the chest of a hummingbird. And every sports drink needs to be EXTREME!!!!! The names of the flavors don't even make sense. These are actual flavors of Gatorade: Glacier Freeze, Riptide Rush, and Arctic Rape. Okay, I made that last one up. What the fuck does a glacier or a riptide taste like anyway?

THE HOSPITAL

I went in to get hernia surgery a couple of years ago. It was the same procedure Dr. Drew underwent a couple of years before, and he promised me I would be in a lot of pain after the operation. I thought it would be physical pain—I didn't know he meant emotional anguish after I woke up in the recovery room when I was handed the pack of saltines and a fruit-punch box. Twenty grand's worth of surgery and you get forty cents' worth of snack at the end, and it isn't even good for you. I once heard a nutritionist say the worst food you could put into your body is a soda cracker. They're just shortening, sodium, sugar, and white flour. When I was bitching about this to Dr. Drew, he said the reason they do that is that many patients' stomachs are sensitive coming out of the anesthesia. I said, "I didn't suggest we go out for Indian food. How about a fucking Wheat Thin and some OJ?"

I know it would be against hospital protocol, but Christ, if there was ever a time a guy could use a beer, it's now. Plus, I'm sure a Sam Adams, from a purely nutritional standpoint, kicks the shit out of the grape punch and saltines. And I'm being driven home, so let's party.

HONEY

A tablespoon of honey is probably the work of two hundred thousand bees and the pollen of a million flowers. The work that goes into it is astounding. Given the process of making honey, it should be a lot better for you. It should be a magical elixir. You should never age and it should make your dick grow. And it should cost like seventy dollars an ounce. Instead it's just slightly better for you than sugar. If you replaced sugar with honey, instead of morbidly obese you would just be fat. And it should come in a squeeze bottle shaped like a bee, not a bear. We've decided bears love honey. But have you ever seen a bear eating honey? If bears could talk, they'd be pissed at this stereotype. There should be some sort of bear anti-defamation league.

SPECIAL K

Not too long ago, I realized that the *K* in Special K stood for "Kellogg." How is it that it took me until halfway into my forty-fifth year to figure this out? Special K isn't even really a cereal. It's more a base for cereal. It's a cereal substrate. You can't eat it without slicing a banana or capsizing the sugar bowl on it. Maybe that's what makes it special. Maybe they mean special like Special Olympics.

MOVIE-THEATER FOOD

The movie theater is brutal if you're on a diet. Whenever I'm trying to lose weight, it seems like I go to the theater with someone who's decided to pack on a few. My wife will get a Hebrew National hot dog, caramel corn, and some Goobers. How long can you sit next to a person, smelling their hot dog, hearing them suck on the Coke, and staring at their trash-can-sized tub of popcorn, without saying fuck it? Movie theaters should have an eating section and a dieting section. Also, a quick message to movie-theater owners—if you don't want me to keister a Snickers into the theater, lower the goddamn prices.

GOOBERS VS. RAISINETS

Speaking of movie food. Raisinets outsell Goobers ten to one, but any sane person knows chocolate-covered peanuts taste better than chocolate-covered raisins. I think it's the name. One is Raisinets, and the other is named after the semi-retarded mechanic from *The Andy Griffith Show*. This just goes to show you what Madison Avenue can do. They got behind an inferior product and manipulated everyone into thinking it was better. Also, I can't believe George Washington Carver came up with 256 things to do with peanuts but didn't think of Goobers.

MOUNDS VS. ALMOND JOY

Why would anyone get Mounds when there is Almond Joy? Could there be a worse name for a candy bar? Why not just call it Lumps or

Piles? One has the word *joy* in it, and the other is something termites live in. Plus it's confusing: Almond Joys have a *mound* of almond on top.

I'm not cheap but I have a poor person's mentality because I was born among super-downtrodden people. I can't turn something down if it is free. If I order a sandwich and the waitress says, "That comes with cat shit on it," I would say, "Put it on the side." It's not like the Mounds is twelve cents cheaper or you get 10 percent more coconut. Even if I were allergic to almonds, I would still get the Almond Joy, pry them off, and put it on eBay. Essentially you're offering the same product, minus the best part, and giving it an inferior name. This would be like offering a second Milky Way, without the nougat, and calling it Turds.

KETCHUP PACKETS

Life is a process of constant evolution. Just like computers, cars, and cell phones: By the time you get them home, the next model has already hit the showroom. Everything has evolved except the ketchup packet. Horseshoe crabs have evolved more than the ketchup packet. Someone signed off on them in 1956 and made the proclamation, "There'll never be a better way to transport ketchup than this tiny, filthy, plastic, unopenable condom packet." It's absolutely insane how long this horrible design has hung on.

There's no clear way to open it. No pull tab, no perforated stripe, no pop top. It's like trying to give a hamster a reach-around. You have no choice but to place it in your mouth and use your teeth like a bench vise while your hand tears the packet away. This creates a diagonal rip that goes further down than it does across. The end result is ketchup all over your shirt and a filthy corner of plastic in your mouth.

This brings me to a bigger point. Why is it in the germophobic, Purell society we've built, in which we cover our hands with our sleeves to open bathroom doors and the time-honored handshake has been replaced by the Howie Mandel fist bump (call me old-fashioned, but I remember when one gent fisted another, it wasn't up top), we happily shove these filthy packets, probably fresh off a container ship from China and dripping in melamine and roach feces, into our mouths?

The only thing that's got more shit on it than that ketchup packet is the cardboard burger box we milk the ketchup onto. The one the high school dropout with SARS handed us at the drive-through window fresh off a pallet from the back of a stake-bed truck that came over from Arkansas. Here's the bottom line. Not how many germs there are or how foolish we are. No. It's how none of this shit matters. If you were gonna get sick, it would have been from the two thousand ketchup packets you put in your mouth that were from God knows where.

The day the first McNugget was sold in 1980 should have spelled the end of the ketchup packet. If they can figure out a way to get forty-five different flavors of sauce into those convenient dipping containers, why not ketchup?

And don't get me started on soy sauce. That's an even bigger abortion. It comes in the same packet as the ketchup, but soy sauce lacks the viscosity of ketchup, so when it tears open it goes airborne and quickly becomes weaponized. Nothing ruins a white dress shirt faster than a paintball shot of black soy sauce. What's up? Do we not have other containers? Couldn't it come in one of those little plastic airplane booze bottles or the keychain-sized Tabasco containers? How about you put the fucking soy sauce in that? Nope, we cannot improve it. I just spent eighty-seven dollars on take-out sushi, couldn't you spend three cents on a functional container to hold the soy sauce?

One last complaint about the ketchup. Everything has been super-sized except the ketchup packet. You've got eighty pounds of fries and a thimbleful of ketchup. Somewhere during your ninth packet, you've managed to moisten four fries.

JEWISH FOOD

As a people, Jews are not exactly stuntmen. Danger is not their middle name, it's Neil. You won't find them jumping the fountain at Caesar's Palace, riding in dune buggies, or on the vert ramp at the X Games. But when it comes to food, they suddenly turn into Johnny Knoxville. Cow tongue, gefilte fish, pickled herring. They're the only people who think cold gelatinized mackerel sounds good. And have you ever had a chicken-liver omelet? Of course you haven't, you're sane. When these guys pull up to the dinner table they should be wearing leather red-white-and-blue jumpsuits and be sponsored by Red Bull.

RAVIOLI

I never order ravioli at a restaurant because they only give you six of them. Canned ravioli is a disaster, but the flash-frozen stuff that comes in a sheet and you toss into the pot is usually decent. I've never had a bad outing with that ravioli. The great thing about ravioli is that there's nothing you can put in it that's bad. "What is this?" "It's beef." "Awesome." "What is this?" "It's cheese." "Awesome." "What is this?" "It's pumpkin." "Great." "What is this?" "This is BBs from a shotgun shell." "All right, I'll try it." "What's this?" "It's one of your mom's spent tampons." "All right, I'll give it a shot."

PIZZA

Pizza is a controversial topic. People will argue that the thick-crust deep-dish is the best kind. I have no problem with deep-dish. But to me the best deep-dish pizza from the best deep-dish place in Chicago doesn't stack up against a slice of average New York–style thin crust. I'm talking about the kind you can fold like a taco and funnel the grease directly into your mouth. For most guys, pizza's in about the same category as blow jobs. Some are better than others, but even a mediocre one is good. Unfortunately, there are those that are hell-bent on fucking up a simple food that is universally loved. Here's how you fuck up a pizza. There's a highfalutin way to fuck up a pizza and a NASCAR white-trash way to fuck it up.

Let's start with the top-shelf pizzas. I've never had a mushroom pizza or a black olive pizza or a sausage-and-onion pizza and announced, "Something's missing. I know what it is, it's poached salmon." I could eat pizza three meals a day, seven days a week, and would never grow tired of the seven or eight traditional pizza toppings and the two thousand possible variations you can create from those. What is it with our endless obsession with changing things that shouldn't be messed with? There's nothing less broken on this planet than pizza. Megan Fox should get a nose job and a tummy tuck before we start considering altering pizza. If you don't like a good sausage-and-onion or Canadian-bacon-and-olive pizza, then you don't fucking like pizza and you should get the fuck away from *my* pizza. You homos should spend your extra culinary effort fixing the salads you fucked up eight years ago. I would rather stand in the orchestra pit for two thousand straight showings of *Puppetry of the Penis* than eat a pizza with goat cheese.

Now for my blue-collar friends who enjoy inexpensive delivery pizza—Domino's, Papa John's, et cetera. Let's deconstruct these shitty pizzas like it's a gastronomic crime scene and get to the truth about why they suck. Let's start at the top and work our way down. The toppings. I'm ashamed to say that I can't tell the difference between Domino's pepperoni and a high-end trattoria pepperoni. The mushrooms are essentially the same, the onions are the same, the black olives are the same. So it's not the toppings. On to the next suspect: the cheese. I bet if I shaved you a sliver each of Mario Batali's mozzarella and Little Caesar's, you wouldn't know the difference. So let's continue our ridiculous investigation. Now we get to the sauce. I know there's such a thing as great pizza sauce, but it still comes down to crushed-up tomato, basil, and a little garlic. Not that Pizza Hut hasn't found a way to fuck up this amazingly simple task, but I still claim it's not the real culprit. If this were a robbery, the sauce would merely be the wheel man who will be found shot in the van near the alley where they switched cars. Who is the Keyser Söze of this culinary crime? The dough. The crust is the kingpin. It's bad and there's too much of it. It's like a band you hate coming out with a double album. It has the consistency, flavor, and girth of carpet padding. If they made their crust thinner, not only would it save them money, it would make them money because we would eat more of their pizza.

Here's my analogy. You either want to be on the beach with the thin crust or out past the breakers with the Chicago-style thick crust. It's in between where you get pummeled. Think about it. Who likes doughy crust? Kids. And what are kids? Tiny, dumb adults. Therefore if you are into that chewy, spongy dough, you are mentally deficient. Also, I'm no dietician, but everyone knows carbs are the worst thing you can eat. And the pizza with three times the crust is going to have three times the carbs. Domino's thin crust is fine; if they were smart, they'd only make that. But of course they refuse to learn this lesson and come out with stuffed crust. Again, this is for morons. The point of the crust is to have a dough handle for the rest of the pie. There's already cheese *on* the pizza, it doesn't need to be *in* the pizza. If you want a tube of melted cheese, order the goddamn mozzarella sticks. This is also a declaration that you make a horrible pizza. It's the culinary equivalent of pleading insanity: You know you're not winning the case, you're just hoping to avoid the chair. And Domino's, Pizza Hut, and other chains, please stop trying to kill us with your dessert attempts. Two slices of your stuffed-crust Philly-cheesesteak pizza is equivalent to eating a gingerbread house. Do we really need to cram in another two thousand fudge-flavored calories?

I hate the people who love the vegetable lover's pizza. Nobody who loves pizza wants the horn of plenty dumped onto their pie. This always gets ordered for the handful of vegetarian assholes who have to destroy everyone else's dining experience. Someone should just order a dinner salad for those douchebags and let them eat it in the car. Or better yet, just order them a goddamn mushroom pizza. It's not that vegetarians love vegetables, it's that they love cows. Oh, and hate people.

Now that I've said my piece on pizza, let's get into how to order it. Here's how not to order it: "There's thirty guys showing up for the Super Bowl party. Give me ten cheese and ten pepperoni." I find pepperoni is tolerated but never loved. Like a chick with a pretty face and a fat ass. Guys will have sex with her, but they'd rather be with the Victoria's Secret model. Or in this case, the sausage-and-onion or the meatball. Now that's a pizza I'd like to have sex with. I claim the "give me ten cheese and ten pepperoni" is a vestige of our childhood when you'd go to some kid's house for a birthday or slumber party and Mama knew that the eight-year-olds would eat anything with salt and grease she slid in front of them. This mentality gets dragged into adulthood and eventually the office place when it comes time to order pizza for the Christmas party. Here's my ten-pizza, please-everyone ordering combo: two cheese, two pepperoni, two sausage-and-onion, two meatball, one black olive, and one mushroom. There. All bases covered, everyone's happy, and I guarantee you the two meatballs will be gone before one of the pepperoni pies expires.

BLUEBERRY, CHOCOLATE, AND JALAPEÑO BAGELS

Another food that's often ordered at the workplace is bagels. When it comes to ordering bagels, I'm going to need you to take everything I just taught you about pizza and throw it out the window. In the world of bagels, less is more. I feel qualified to speak about bagels because even though I'm not a Jew I do possess many Jewish qualities, such as a huge cock and an incredible vertical leap. We started off with two or three varieties of bagels and worked our way up to 175. This is why when the peon from the office returns from the bagel run you can look forward to the blueberry bagel, the jalapeño bagel, the cranberry bagel, and the chocolate bagel. By the way, we've had chocolate bagels for two hundred years—they're called fucking donuts. So instead of enough plain, onion, and egg bagels to go around, he gets a United Nations chub pack of bagels nobody wants. But here's the problem. Eventually, because it's free and somehow free food at the workplace turns everyone into a bear at Yellowstone Park, the cranapple and strawberry-yogurt-flavored bagels get consumed, and this sends the message to the lackey, "Nice work. Next time order the exact same thing."

TRAIL MIX

Another office-food abortion is the trail mix. Is there anything sadder than the trail mix after it's been sifted through? Once the raccoons in the office have picked out the M&Ms, peanuts, and smoked almonds, there's nothing left but a busted banana chip and a couple of raw sunflower seeds. This is what you should do when you start a new business. Buy a tub of trail mix and put it out. Let all your employees sift through it. Whatever's left at the bottom, don't buy any more of that crap. We don't like it. Why not just buy a thing of smoked almonds, a thing of honey-roasted peanuts, and a thing of M&Ms? Isn't that what people want anyway? Have you ever heard somebody say, "I could really go for some of those weird round date-pellet things with the white powder on the outside"?

The other problem with trail mix is that it has the illusion of being healthy. But if you ever read the back of the bag, you'll see a handful of this shit has more calories than a pack of Twinkies. Much like the Raisinets, I'm convinced the reason for its popularity is the name. If it were called by its real name, "I Hate 75 Percent of What's in This Mix Mix," they'd never sell a bag of it.

VARIETY PACKS

They talk about variety being the spice of life. Variety is not that great, especially variety packs. They sound good at first, but it's the same as trail mix. Some stuff you like and a bunch of crap you don't. Me and my wife were watching TV not too long ago and she was eating a lime Popsicle. I said, "Give me a hit off that." I tasted it and thought, This tastes like ass. Lime Popsicles suck. So I asked, "Why do you like lime Popsicles? How did I marry someone who likes lime Popsicles? I hate lime Popsicles." She replied, "I don't like them either." So I said, "Why are you eating a lime Popsicle if you don't like them?" Then she said, "Well, I wanted a Popsicle and we were at the end of the variety pack." We'd gone through all the cherry ones, all the orange ones, all the ones we like, and were left with four lime ones. So my wife was eating a Popsicle she didn't want to eat because it came in a variety pack.

And who buys the cereal variety pack? Why not just get one regular-sized box of cereal you like instead of twelve key-chain-sized boxes, nine of which suck?

CAKE VS. PIE

Cake probably outsells pie by a margin of fifteen to one, yet pie is a superior dessert. So how does one explain this anomaly? I will explain in painstaking detail, but let's first just set some ground rules. When I say pie is better than cake, I mean your average pie versus your average cake, because I know what many of you are thinking right now: "There's a German bakery on the east side of town that makes a seven-layer dark chocolate with a raspberry center that is out of this world." That cake is sixty-three dollars and requires a two-week lead time. Here's my simple experiment. If I said, "Pie lover, I'll give you nine dollars to purchase the pie of your choice, and cake hole, you also have nine dollars to purchase the cake of your choice," and I put them both out at an office party, which would get eaten first? Obviously it would be the pie. Because down the street from me, as we speak, there's a Marie Callender's that has a huge banner that says ANY PIE, $7.99, and a smaller sign beneath it that says NEGROES EAT AT THE COUNTER. I'm assuming that's older. Or you could take that eight dollars to the nearest supermarket and pick up a lard-frosted sheet cake, which, if you say it fast and with an Israeli accent, gives you a more apt description.

So why the disparity in sales? I believe it's because the cake makes a better platform for candles, messages like HAPPY 25TH ANNIVERSARY, soccer fields, and SpongeBob. You can't put a goalpost on an apple pie. How fucking retarded are we that we pick an inferior-tasting dessert based on its ability to deliver a message? Can you imagine making that argument for any other food? "Sure, the lobster tastes great, but I'm going with the SPAM because I can set an army man on it." Why do cakes even need themes? We know it's the kids' fucking birthday, and the cake is the last thing that comes out—we've already seen the pile of presents and the pointy hats. It's not as if they brought out a birthday pie we'd all get confused and start singing "Happy Kristallnacht." And just like my stuffed-crust argument, when you bring out a dessert that has a detailed re-creation of the *Avatar* rain forest, you're basically admitting your food sucks. And don't get me started on this new Photoshop frosting technology. Am I the only one who thinks it's a little bit weird to take a knife and put it across the neck of an exact representation of your seven-year-old in a Dodger uniform? (By the way, if you had one of those machines in the seventeenth century, you would rule the land. "He hath placed my image on a confection. What sorcery is this? Dismiss Michelangelo and give this man a thousand gold pieces to frost the ceiling of our greatest chapel.")

Let's examine the wisdom of the time-honored birthday candle. I'm no Howard Hughes, but somewhere around the third attempt to blow out the candles, the one in which the five-year-old is joined by his sister and heavyset uncle, I'm out. Once there's more spittle than frosting, I magically become diabetic. And as long as we're on this archaic practice, let's talk about the novelty candle, the candle that goes out and then reignites, forcing Grandpa to dig deep and blow a hot wind of Polident and tuberculosis over the cake for yet another round. And then the same guy who washed his hands thirteen times that day immediately grabs a wedge and digs in. Would anybody do this if instead of cake, Grandpa was blowing on a pan of lasagna? Every motherfucking person in that room would be like, "Hey, Grandpa. We're going to the Olive Garden."

And speaking of unsanitary, how about the practice of removing all the army men and football players from their frosting foundation and licking the base? Do you think those plastic figures with the lead-based paint were transported like an organ and placed on top of the cake in the OR? Or did a fat junior-college dropout just grab them from a shoebox she keeps open under the counter and stick them on the cake in between nose rubs?

So let's review. The reason the inferior form of dessert outsells the far superior form fifteen to one is because you can stick plastic shit on it. Goddamn, are we dumb. My final and perhaps most compelling argument for why you should serve pie at your next party instead of cake is simple. When you put out pie at a party, it attracts a crowd. You have to tell people, "We're not going to cut into it until after dinner has been served." With cake, there's never a line. Some poor bitch gets put in charge of distributing it to guests around the party. Here's how that interaction works. Someone who looks like one of your mom's friends shows up where you're sitting holding a small paper plate with a wedge of cake on it. "Would you like some cake?" "What kind is it?" "I think it's vanilla." "I'm cool." "Are you sure? How about I just set it down on the arm of the sofa. You might change your mind." Later on that night, that wedge of cake will be found with one finger of frosting removed and a cigarette put out in it. That has never happened with a wedge of pumpkin pie.

But a note of caution to all of my pie-toting friends. Don't think you can head to the supermarket and get a decent pie. I don't know if it's the mass production or the fluorescent lighting or the MSG, but whatever it is, those pies suck. And they're still $7.50. For another buck nineteen, you could go to a pie shop and get a real pie. And don't get cute with the flavors. Pineapple is not a pie filling, and chocolate pie is nothing more than pudding in a pie tin. If you're going strawberry or peach, make sure it's in season. Now go out there and eat like champions.

THIS CHAPTER IS NOT A HATE CRIME

Racism is a topic we never get tired of discussing in this country. Here's my semi-offensive take on racism.

First of all, we have to admit that there's a certain amount of cultural pride that is inherent in all human beings. If you turn on the television and there's a boxing match on, you will usually root for the guy who looks most like you. But if you find out that the guy who looks less like you is from your hometown, you may start rooting for him. Or if the guy who isn't your ethnicity was pronounced dead after an incident at a public pool when he was only nine and has beaten the odds to vie for the welterweight championship. For me it doesn't take much. If the guy who looks like Wesley Snipes is the underdog and the guy who looks like Greg Brady is unbeaten (I know that's never going to happen), I'll be rooting for the black guy. Because I always root for the underdog. All things being equal, every bit of history aside, people are going to root for the person who looks most like them. I don't think I'm different from anyone else who's being honest. I don't know if that's good or bad, I'm just saying it's built into all of us and we should just accept it.

OUR "RACIST" CULTURE

The left would like us to believe we're living in a racist culture. Well, the highest-paid person on TV, Oprah, is black and possibly even female. The highest-paid movie star is Will Smith. The highest-paid singer is Beyoncé. The highest-paid athlete, pre-divorce, is Tiger Woods. And of course the guy who leads the country these people all live in is black. Permit me to go Dr. Seuss on your asses for just one moment. What if there was a planet where 90 percent of the population were white Sneetches and 10 percent of the planet were black Sneetches. But the highest-paid performers and athletes (and I don't just mean for what they do on the field, I'm also talking about endorsements) and the leader of all the Sneetches, as voted on by the entire Sneetch population, were black Sneetches. And what if I went on to tell you how racist the white Sneetches were. Wouldn't you stop and say that doesn't make sense? How racist could they be?

For every real racist, there are twenty-five guilty white guys trying to undo what that guy and his grandfather did and actually be nicer. If a white guy cuts me off, I shout, "Fuck you, motherfucker!" But if a black guy cuts me off, I don't say anything, A) because he's packing, and B) because I don't want him to think I'm doing it just because he's black.

RACIST OR ASSHOLE?

I have a theory that's going to sound convenient because I'm a white male, but if the brothers who stole this book will hear me out (see, that's a racial joke), I will attempt to explain why it feels like there are so many racists in this society. You're confusing assholes for racists.

First, let's talk about "driving while black" and the LAPD. The

LAPD are basically assholes to everyone they pull over. And I've been pulled over for everything from not having a front license plate to flicking a cigarette ash out the window. Not throwing a cigarette *butt* out the window, but flicking an *ash* out the window. And *not* in Malibu during fire season, in Hollywood in November. I had a cop pull me over on my motorcycle and tow it when I begged him to let me just push it and park it on a side street and leave it there. He said, "Tough shit," and while I was hitchhiking home I saw my motorcycle pass me on the back of a tow truck. I once got a jaywalking ticket in a crosswalk because the cop said I began walking after the light started blinking "Don't Walk." I arrived on the other side so far in advance of the light changing that the asshole motorcycle cop had time to cross the intersection behind me and the light had still yet to change.

You think the LAPD picks and chooses who they pull over and who they're assholes to based on the color of their skin. Now, I've never tried to outrun a cop in my car and been caught, but I'm sure if I tried and was caught, they'd beat the shit out of me. The same way they beat the shit out of the brothers. I'm not saying there are no racists on the LAPD—what I'm saying is, there's an army of assholes on the LAPD that you think are racist because you're black. If I was black, I could draw no other conclusion than that the cop who wrote me the jaywalking ticket was a racist.

Let's move from cops to fellow citizens. In almost every home I've lived in, I've had a run-in with an unreasonable neighbor: calling the cops every time I had a party, accusing me of things I didn't do—I won't bore you with all the details, but let's just call it general douche-baggery. But here is one specific example.

I have a home now that when I bought it was a dilapidated, rat-infested mess. I dumped almost a million dollars and a ton of sweat equity into it, and I turned it from an eyesore into a palace. I have an old man who lives next to me. An old white guy. There is a hedge between our two homes. It's not growing into the sewer pipes, it's not obstructing his view; it's not doing anything except offering a little privacy. But he called the Department of Building and Safety on me. He didn't come and talk to me; he called Building and Safety, who sent over a letter and then an inspector. The neighbor even checked the box that said "unsanitary living conditions" despite the fact that my house is pristine. So I said to the guy, "Why do you have an issue with this hedge?" And he screamed, "It's above regulation height." I replied, "So is every hedge on this hill. Most people like it that way. Next time, instead of getting the city involved, ring my buzzer, tell my gardener, or just leave a note saying, 'Hey, the hedge is a little high. Please have your guy cut it.'" Four months later, I got another summons from the Department of Building and Safety for a court appearance. And it hasn't stopped. I just got another super-shitty letter from him the other day threatening me about the hedge.

Fortunately, I have the great privilege of being white, and thus the knowledge that this guy is just an old fuck and not a racist. If I was black, Hispanic, Asian, or even Jewish, I would have no choice but to assume he was a racist, and I don't think any reasonable person would disagree.

Here's my final synopsis. Again, I'm not saying there are no racists, I'm just saying you're inflating the numbers by mistaking a lot of assholes for racists. These shitty neighbors/cops/nine-dollar-an-hour dickheads behind counters/rude garage attendants aren't racist, they're assholes. I wish they were racists; as a rich white guy, that would make my life easier.

People need to understand the difference between passively racist people and actively racist people. Every guy I know loves a race joke, will use derogatory terms to get a laugh, and probably has thoughts that range everywhere from "I hope there's not a bunch of Middle Eastern guys on my flight" to "I'd rather a Japanese family bought the house next door than an Israeli family." Our society would love to label them bigots and racists. But my point is, unless they've ever acted on any of these thoughts, who gives a shit? If you call a fat guy fat when he's not in the room and never say a thing to his face and you don't have any policies against hiring fat people, then what the fuck's wrong with a fat joke as long as fat Marty isn't within earshot? I believe this country is filled with people of all ethnicities who like to toss around racially insensitive jokes and racial epithets but would never do anything to harm, degrade, or deny employment to anyone because of their race. I'm sure many of the people reading this book, at some point in their life, wished that someone was dead. But that doesn't make you a murderer. Killing somebody makes you a murderer. Making a Polack joke doesn't make you a racist. Not hiring a Polack makes you a racist. And writing a book where you say *Polack* doesn't make you a racist either.

I'd argue that the guilty white liberals in this country are actually more racist. Take the example of drugs coming in from Mexico. The left is basically apologizing to Mexico and explaining that it's our consumption of these drugs that's creating the market and funding their corrupt government, police, and army. It's not the drug dealers' fault; it's our fault for consuming the drugs. Then why are these same people coming down on the tobacco industry? They just manufacture the product; we create the market. If nobody smoked, they'd be out of business. And what about gun manufacturers? The lefties don't like them very much either, yet all they do is make a product. So why does Mexico get a pass while Philip Morris and Smith & Wesson don't? Race is the answer. Two of them are rich and white, one of them is poor and brown. And it's always Whitey's fault. While constantly complaining about racism, they engage in the ultimate racism. They treat Mexico as if they are inferior and incapable of governing themselves. If these drugs were coming out of Canada, they wouldn't be blaming the U.S. They would insist that Canada fix the problem and fucking fast. It's belittling and far more racist. Just like when the news reported about what was going on in the Superdome after Katrina. Every rich Manhattan honky I knew was shouting, "There are three-year-olds being gang-raped! Why isn't Bush doing anything?" If the Superdome had been filled with white people, your question wouldn't be "Why isn't Bush doing anything?"—it'd be "What the fuck is wrong with those people?"

And why are the charges of racism only directed at white people? Not too long ago, Miley Cyrus got in trouble for a picture where she pulled her eyes back to do the Asian squinty-eyes thing. But what about Japanese anime, where all the white people have enormous round eyes? Sure, we do an exaggerated version of what we think Asian eyes look like, but they draw ours in a caricature too. Our eyes are rounder than theirs, but they don't look like dinner plates. Each one is an exaggeration, so why was Miley Cyrus raked over the coals while Speed Racer got a free pass? Because we don't give a shit. We don't have a chip on our shoulder. Us roundeyes have a sense of humor, which perhaps we should export.

DIVERSITY SEMINARS

Not only does every employee of every corporation have to sit through a bullshit sexual-harassment seminar, they are also mandated to have three hours of their lives stolen for a diversity and racial-sensitivity seminar. I had to sit through these when I was working for CBS radio. They always do a question-and-answer thing at the end of this garbage, and I declared to my lackeys that no one could ask any questions or I would fire their ass. The more questions asked, the longer we were going to be stuck in that room. Ironically, I then ended up dragging the thing out because I eventually reached the tipping point and couldn't handle the bullshit being piled on.

The woman conducting the seminar, who looked like Maya Angelou with the giant amber beads and muumuu, posed this retarded question: "A Hispanic male robs a liquor store. The only information the news has is that he is Hispanic and male. Should they mention his ethnicity?" At this point you, like me and every other rational person, are thinking, "Of course. Whatever is necessary to get the word out and catch this guy." But I kept my mouth shut. Florida from *Good Times* declared no, his ethnicity should not be mentioned because there are too many Hispanic males in Los Angeles (twenty thousand more slipped in while you were reading that sentence). To say that fact would draw suspicion on every Hispanic male in the population. At that moment I hit my saturation point with Aretha Franklin's less talented sister and asked, "Then why are you bringing up that he's male? I'm male—I don't want to get lumped in with liquor-store robbers." Her response was as stupid as her original point: "But he was a male." I shot back, "He's Mexican too. Why do we have to ignore that fact but not the fact that he's he's got a dick and balls?" Take that, Cinco De Maya Angelou.

EVERYONE EARNS IT

So let's drop the act and just face the fact that as a race, you earn your stereotype. We're supposed to celebrate our differences, but as soon as somebody points out that some of those differences are negative, that person gets called a racist.

It's an all-or-nothing attitude that causes the problem. Ironically, the Berkeley-educated white folk who attack me and say, "Not *all* black men are in prison" and "Not *all* Muslim men are terrorists" are the first ones to get the petition going to have a peanut-free school because *one* kid has an allergy. Not *all* the kids have a peanut allergy, so why should *all* of them suffer? I'm not saying "all" of this group or "all" these people, but "some" of this group and "enough" of these people.

As I stated earlier, whether you are a car company or a race, you earn your reputation. Don't believe me? Take a look at this chart of ethnic stereotypes.

STEREOTYPE	ETHNICITY
Big Noses / Run Hollywood and the Banks	Mexicans
Large Penises / Great Athletes	Asians
Excel at Math	Native Americans
No Sense of Humor / Love Hasselhoff	Blacks
Make Good Prize Fighters / Gardeners	Indians
Love Rap / Teenage Pregnancy	Canadians
Make Great Doctors / Computer Techs	The Irish
Uptight / Have Bad Teeth	Brazilians
Terrible Drivers	Germans
Treat Women Like Property / Are Religious Zealots	Swedes
Own Convenience/Liquor Stores	The British
Constantly Drunk / Love Casinos	Jews
Constantly Drunk / Love the Celtics	Arabs

If you believe there's no truth to stereotypes, then nothing in that chart seemed odd. But admit it, you fucking hypocrite, you laughed.

My "everybody earns it" theory extends to the gays, who technically aren't a race but, fuck it, it's close enough. They have anti-defamation leagues, their own parts of cities, and parades. That's enough to qualify as a race. Plus gay is its own race because that's the number-one attribute that gets made fun of. So if you're busting the chopsticks of a fat Chinese gay guy, the first insult is about his sexuality. Then eventually you work your way down to fat and Chinese.

Before you call GLAAD, let me say this. I have no problem with gay people. I'm open-minded, but closed-behinded. I love the gays. All they do is pay taxes for schools they don't use, for prisons they don't inhabit, and to repair potholes their peach-colored MINI Cooper convertibles don't create. Meanwhile, they rarely use government programs and they don't crap out more kids that use up resources. In fact, they gobble up all the world's unwanted kids. They recycle like hell, their cars always have a fresh coat of carnauba wax, and the lawns of their houses look like someone took tweezers and nasal-hair clippers and finely manicured them. Their homes look like country clubs. You don't see the gay guy with an El Camino up on blocks and a sofa rotting on the porch. Those are the Jews. (Oh, confused? I thought you didn't buy into stereotypes.)

The gays take care of their homes and their community. As a group they care about the environment, they are very civically minded, and nonviolent. You don't need to worry about a gay guy putting a knife in your back at the ATM. Plus they leave all the chicks for me. (Hold this page up and high-five it.) You want to live in the gay part of town. If you live in L.A., all you need to know about the gays versus other groups can be determined by a drive down Santa Monica Boulevard. Santa Monica Boulevard is a long, filthy, graffiti-covered stretch of asphalt that cuts through the heart of Los Angeles. Except for one two-mile stretch that has medians with green grass, spotless sidewalks, and happy couples strolling with laptops and lapdogs.

Al Gore is obsessed with big business and its carbon footprint. I'm obsessed with groups and their social footprint. And the gays have a small social footprint. This is a stereotype they've earned, and it's a good one. But another not-so-good one they've earned is on full display at the "pride" parades.

The juxtaposition of people at these parades demanding respect while dressed in assless chaps is funnier than anything that hack John Waters could ever shit out. Don't worry, gays, your respect is coming. It's just around the corner. Continue dragging your gimp partner down the street by his nipple clamps. You'll soon get that respect you so richly deserve. Society is *this* close to accepting you and your life partner with the handlebar mustache and the studded leather thong.

A quick pitch for the dictionary folks. In the next edition, I would like to include a new definition for the word *parade*—"any more than eight gays congregated together." That should be the term, like a flock of geese or a pod of whales: a parade of gays. Also, please add the term *behymen*, as in "a man who has never been with another man still has an intact beyhmen."

Allow me to make a controversial point to show that despite all the cries of how homophobic and intolerant our society is, we're actually very accepting: There's surprisingly little gay-bashing based on how repugnant we find the act of gay sex. To be clear, I'm not saying we should step up the gay-bashing: I'm just saying it's surprising there's not more.

Straight men have a visceral reaction to gay porn. I would rather witness a nun get lowered into a wood chipper than watch ten seconds of gay porn. And this isn't just me. Dr. Drew, one of the most open-minded, tolerant guys in the world, confirms this. When straight guys see two dudes tongue-kiss, they get nauseated. It's the way we're wired. When men are straight, we're straight. It's not like chicks, who can become a lesbian on any given weekend. Heterosexuality for men is a life sentence. For women, heterosexuality is like a club where they get their hand stamped but can come and go as they please. If you show a girl two dudes going at it, you'll get a light "Ew." Show a straight guy a clip of *Glory, Glory Hole-elujah,* and he'll be swept out of the room by the tidal wave of his own vomit. And it's not as if we have delicate sensibilities. The same guy who would rather poke his eyes out than watch five frames of cornholing is the same one who, if there's a clip of a fighter getting a compound fracture in the octagon, will forward it to all of his buddies under the subject line "You Gotta See This."

So the fact that this is something that is universally physically repugnant to straight guys and yet virtually none of them, not counting the religious nut jobs, ever raise a hand to gay men is a sign that we're evolved. Or super-lazy. We're not the backward homophobic nation that some people paint us to be. Don't get me wrong, there's still progress to be made in the marriage and "don't ask, don't tell" department, but look at other countries. Over there gays don't even have the right to *exist,* never mind adopt. The reason you don't ask and don't tell in Yemen is because they'll stone you to death or put a burning tire around you.

And it can't get more damning than this: Every straight woman would rather watch two chicks going at it than gay porn. In other words, women who love cock would rather watch a video with no cocks than one with two cocks.

Let me wrap up with this:

I love it when a black guy says something racist against white people and they call it "reverse racism." As if white people were the only group capable of being "real" racists. White people didn't invent racism, we just perfected it.

I WANT MY FUTURE BACK

According to the TV and movies of my youth, by this point we were all supposed to have flying cars, robot butlers, and a crystal that would power our house for a thousand years. We were supposed to be living a technological utopia. But that's not the case. I'm consistently disappointed by how the things we create to make our lives easier tend to fuck them up worse.

Growing up, we had a black-and-white Zenith TV in a metal case with fake wood grain that you could pound on. You could beat the shit out of it. It'd go vertical or horizontal or the stabilizer would go off. I'd be trying to watch *Maude* and it would be all over the place. So I'd come up behind it and do that Fonz move. *Boom*. And it would straighten out. To fix something back in the day, you didn't have to be a technician. You'd just slap it on the side or whack it on the top. Even with cars, you'd start to smack the dash and shout, "Come on, baby." There used to be radios you could hit, TVs you could whack, even toasters you could hit if they were mistreating the bread. I used to have an electric space heater with the coils in the metal sheath. I was living for a while in the garage of my dad's house. It didn't have heating or air-conditioning. During the winter it would be cold as shit, so I would sleep with a space heater next to my bed. And at some point in the night the thing would start making this weird harmonic buzz and vibrate. So I'd just whack it once and it would straighten out. It would be cool for about twenty minutes, and then it would start up with the buzzing and I'd smack it again. Nowadays, if your iPhone starts fucking up, you don't start mashing it. You're gonna fuck it up worse. If your Prius doesn't start, you don't drop an elbow on the dashboard.

We've fixed a lot of the problems with certain pieces of technology, but there are a lot of products that have stood still or even gone backward.

TOASTERS

Where's the toaster technology? Toasters haven't progressed since Lucy and Ricky were on TV, but now we've got an ankle monitor to make sure Lindsay Lohan hasn't taken a drink. Imagine traveling back in time to the forties and telling someone sitting around their kitchen, "In 2010 this toaster isn't gonna toast bread one second faster than it does now. Not one goddamn second. But there will be a thing the size of a pack of cigarettes you strap to your ankle that will contact a satellite if you've had a thimbleful of Kahlua." They'd slam your head into their Formica tabletop and bury you in the backyard.

And half the time the toast comes out burned. Why was it built with the ability to burn the toast anyway? Do we need the ruin-my-breakfast setting? There are degrees that people enjoy, from lightly toasted to dark brown. But nobody wants briquette. Jacuzzis go from warm to hot, but not enough to kill a human or poach a salmon. The heater in your car can get pretty warm, but it will never go up to blast furnace and melt your face. Why do I need to be able to smelt ore in my toaster? I bet the toaster manufacturers have some kind of unholy alliance with the bread companies. I picture a guy who looks like Karl Rove, wearing a gold Toaster Manufacturers of America blazer and smoking a cigar, saying, "What if I could guarantee that every seventh piece of bread ends up in the garbage? It would increase your sales by fifteen percent." Then we see the Pillsbury Doughboy laugh, slide a briefcase full of cash across the desk, and say, "I think this is the beginning of a beautiful friendship."

MICROWAVES

Microwaves haven't been around as long as toasters but are also desperately in need of an overhaul. If I want to make some tea, it takes as long to heat that cup of water as it would in a kettle. Then there are mugs that I can't touch after they come out of the microwave because they are hotter than lava while the water in the cup remains room temperature. And the man who invents a microwave that can handle foil is going to be a billionaire. Why hasn't this happened yet? We could keep dumping money into Africa, or we could put some R&D into a microwave that can deal with the little metal handle on Chinese takeout containers.

Takeout/doggy-bagged food comes in one of three containers: either the foil pan with the bendable lip and the clear plastic top that never fits back on once it comes off, the aforementioned cardboard container with the coat hanger, and the good old foil swan. None of which will work in a microwave. Either somebody has to create a microwave that tolerates metal or the fuckwads who are in charge of designing the takeout containers should do something that is nonmetallic. This doesn't feel like too tall an order to me. It's not 1943, and we're not in the army. Open your fridge. Is there any metal in the containers? The milk carton, the egg carton, the tub of margarine, the Sunny D bottle, the yogurt cup . . . stop me when one of these fucking things has a paper clip's worth of metal in it. But every fucking container choice on the market for the microwave contains some sort of metal.

Pardon me. I did forget a fourth option that doesn't contain metal. It's that white Styrofoam one that melts and becomes one with the half-eaten burger and fries you're attempting to reanimate. And for those of you who are asking, "What's the big deal? How about you just scrape the contents onto a plate and zap it that way?" you're missing the point. The best part of the fettuccine Alfredo or whatever you're reheating is trapped between the creases of that foil container and will never be set free by the futile scrapings of your cold fork. Thanks.

CELL PHONES

There are a couple of problems with cell phones. The biggest problem is that cell phones work like a dimmer when they should be more like a toggle switch. You should either get a full signal or it shouldn't work at all. It'll usually give you just enough signal to hear the person you're trying to talk to ask, "Are you there? Can you hear me?" There's enough signal to have it ring, but not enough for you to have the conversation.

Also, when my cell phone is running low on batteries, it will beep to let me know. And then eleven seconds later, it does it again. And then again and again and again. I got the message the twenty-ninth time the beep interrupted my call. You're burning what's left of my precious battery with your incessant chiming. And then I have to press the thing to acknowledge I know the battery is running low. You have a battery and it's low. I get it. Why do I have to press your belly button like the Poppin' Fresh guy? Remember four seconds ago when you told me? I heard you that time. Leave me alone. I'm on the phone. I think I could talk for an extra hour and a half if it didn't keep beeping.

The problem is I'm walking down a sidewalk in L.A. or driving my beater truck to Home Depot and my charger is in the other car. The fucks who designed this phone act like I'm standing at a Radio-Shack leaning against a wall of chargers, heard the first beep, ignored it, and decided to head out to the desert, drop peyote with Jim Morrison, and chase an imaginary Indian.

And it's unclear how long you have. You should get one heads-up when you have ten minutes of talk time left, and one more that comes in at the thirty-second mark so you know to wrap it up.

Recently I was sitting in a casting session. The poor girl who wasn't going to get the job was standing there acting her ass off, and right in the middle of it one of the producers' cell phones went off. It rang three times before the guy could corral it and shut it off. Why does the cell-phone ring need to repeat at paint-can-shaker speed? We heard the first one, and now we're frantically trying to pull it out of our coat pocket at the theater. Everyone in the room heard it ring and then ring again four tenths of a second later. Why can't it ring once and then give you a five-Mississippi to shut it off? Doc Holliday isn't quick enough to get that iPhone out of his holster before the second ring. And like the battery beep, do you think we're going to forget? As if the phone would ring and we'd announce, "Glad it got that out of its system. That will never happen again." After the initial ring, you should get a full ten seconds to answer it. After that it could go into its regular mode. No one in the theater wants to hear that cell phone ring a second time, least of all the guy who is desperately trying to pull it from his pocket. Why hasn't this happened? Who is against this?

And the aforementioned producer's phone was set on vibrate. Let me say this about the vibrate function. People treat vibrate as if it's a switch that means the phone doesn't exist. It says *vibrate*, not *invisible*, not *never manufactured*. You've got a block of brushed titanium rattling on a solid mahogany desk. This is actually louder than if it just rang. It sounds as if you attacked a cookie sheet with a dentist's drill. When I go into these casting sessions, I leave my phone in the car. Why do people insist on bringing their phones places they can't answer them? There's nothing so important that you'll take the call. Unless your wife is nine months pregnant and could go into labor at any moment, there's no reason for your phone to be on. It's not as if it will buzz and you'll shout, "It's Commissioner Gordon. To the Batmobile!" It's not President Obama, it's your mom telling you the *Ghost Whisperer* is going into syndication.

Plus people don't count cell phones as real phones. Here's what I mean. I can't tell you how many times I've been talking on my cell phone pumping gas or standing out on a sidewalk and someone's come up to me and said, "Hey *Man Show*. Can we get a picture? Where are the Juggies? Where's Dr. Drew?" If I was sitting down at a desk and talking on an old-style phone with a cord attached and that same guy walked into my office, he would have done the hands-up "my bad" and slowly backed out through the door. A conversation is a conversation whether you're using Bluetooth or a can with some yarn through it. Show some fucking respect.

And let's talk about the design. I got into an epic battle on my radio show with the sound-effects guy Bald Bryan regarding the design of the iPhone. Bryan is a very smart and very confident guy, which is good in a lot of respects, but it also means that when he is wrong he digs in his heels and won't give up. One day I was making the accurate point that there is a conspiracy element to the iPhone's design. It may not be a covert, secret, backroom conspiracy, but there are definitely problems that aren't being addressed because the company profits. I argued that the iPhone is intentionally designed to slip out of your hand so that you'll drop it and have to replace it. Think about it. I like my iPhone, but it's shaped like a bar of soap and has about the same grip. How much money does Apple make each year from people dropping these devices? If you could create a product that people buy once every few years or replace every few months, which direction are you going to go in? Imagine any business working this way. What if you just made self-propelled lawnmowers and the handle design was such that people would constantly lose control and ram them into trees? And then instead of paying to repair them, they just came in, apologized, and bought a new one? Wouldn't that be a nice windfall for your lawnmower business?

And let's not forget to factor in the accessory market. For every second iPod and iPhone bought, there is a twenty-five-dollar rubber case purchased so that you don't drop it again. At this point many of you hard-core Apple fans (get it? hard-*core*?) may be taking the side of Bald Bryan. Please permit me a few sentences to shut you all the fuck up. In a former life, I handled tools for a living. Every wrench, every belt sander, every cordless drill, every tool that fit into your hand felt like it belonged there. The shape, the materials used, the textures of those materials were all designed for one purpose and one purpose only: to not be dropped. If you design circular saws that slip out of people's hands, the consumers are going to be out of fingers and you'll be out of business. There's no fucking such thing as a screwdriver with a smooth, slick titanium handle, you ass-wipes. When you hold that iPhone up to your ear, does it feel as if it belongs in your hand? Because mine feels like I'm holding a trout. Apple's claim to fame is ergonomics. Simple, intuitive design. They're geniuses when it comes to everything inside the iPhone, but when it comes to the design of the outside, they magically turn into retards. I don't buy it.

And you don't think they're aware of the thousands, perhaps millions, of these devices that are replaced each year because they slid out of people's hands or fell out of people's sweatpants when they were getting out of their car? What if they lost a hundred dollars every time one slid out of someone's hand and hit the ground? You don't think the next generation of iPhone would have a thin rubber membrane around it or be knurled like the grip of a cop's nine-millimeter pistol? Of course it would. Could you imagine if these assholes designed steering wheels? Every third car would be in a drainage ditch.

189

THE SNOOZE BAR

Alarm clocks were around for 150 years before the snooze bar got worked into the equation. This is a horrible thing to design into an alarm clock. How many man-hours have been lost? How many flights have been missed because of the snooze bar? You think, "I've got to be at LAX at seven o'clock— I'm gonna set the alarm for five thirty." But you never factor in the hour you lose hitting the snooze bar eighteen times. The snooze bar should have a cutoff. Three strikes and you're up. You know what does have a cutoff but shouldn't? The cordless-phone locator. Have you ever gone looking for the phone around your house and you can't find it so you hit the locator button? It rings two times and then it stops. It goes *Brrrrng* so you take one step to the left and it goes *Brrrrng* again so you take one step to the right. Then silence. You're standing right there in front of the base where you started and you don't know if it's upstairs or in the basement.

Who decided that gets a cutoff, but the snooze bar is endless? It's like an all-you-can-eat buffet. I think I've figured out what people love about the snooze bar—it sounds cool. It sounds like a club Johnny Depp might have part ownership of. "Hey, Jack White's doing an acoustic set at the Snooze Bar." If it was called the "loser knob" or the "loaf plunger," you would be too ashamed to hit it. And should this option even be available? Cars all have chimes that go off when you don't fasten your seat belt, but there's no switch that makes the annoying buzzer stop, and the reason for that is because they want you to put your fucking seat belt on. The snooze bar is the way for you to drive fifty miles out of town without ever having to fasten your seat belt. It doesn't make sense. It's a device that lets you sleep attached to the top of a device whose sole purpose is waking you up.

SHOELACES

Every time I put on a pair of running shoes, I have to double- and triple-knot them and then stuff the excess into my sock so I don't trip because they give you an extra fourteen feet of lace. Who does this benefit? Does the shoe company profit by just giving away millions of linear feet of lace every year that no one wants? With every high-top basketball shoe I've ever owned, I eventually find myself clipping and then cauterizing the laces. I hang them over a flame and seal them up. And when I think about my dress shoes, I get livid because they give you no lace in those. No lace. I needed to hire a small Asian woman to tie my suit shoes. You shouldn't need tweezers and a magnifying glass to tie a pair of shoes. You can try to do that bow, but halfway through the wedding one of them always comes undone. It's the wrong kind of lace. It's stiff, plastic, and round. What's the deal? Are they fucking with us? There's way too much lace on the athletic shoe and not nearly enough on the dress shoe. Couldn't we meet somewhere in the middle, shoemaking people? Cobblers of the world unite! You're driving me insane.

ROAD FLARES

I can't say enough about what a terrible idea this is. After the orange reflective triangle was invented, shouldn't these have gone the way of the dodo? If you walked up to the scene of an accident smoking a cigarette, six highway-patrol guys would tackle you to the ground. When they were done zip-tying you and putting you in the back of a cruiser, they'd continue their work throwing burning flares around the flipped-over SUV. "Hey chief, we've got a jackknifed big rig blocking four lanes on the 101—what should we do?" "Start diverting traffic and I'll get those rolling fire sticks."

If you walk around a store, you'll notice that everything has stickers now. Fuck that, just walk around my house.

They make everything uglier. Like the sun visor of my wife's Jaguar. This is a fifty-five-thousand-dollar car. It's got Connolly leather seats, an Alcantara headliner, and burled walnut in the dash, but it also has the giant ugly yellow sticker you'd find in a beat-up Hyundai permanently welded to the visor. Would this have happened in the fifties? Could you imagine the designers back then being told they needed to add a fluorescent warning sticker to their artwork? They'd strangle you with a seat belt. (Which at that time were optional but are now mandatory and have a stupid yellow sticker for idiots who don't know how to operate them.)

It wouldn't be so bad if you could remove these bullshit stickers. Who decided that adhesives needed to permanently bond stickers to whatever they're attached to? If there was a nuclear holocaust, two things would survive: cockroaches and these goddamn stickers. Whether it's my floor jacks, my hammer, or my picture frames, I end up going at it with lighter fluid and a razor blade. Usually I end up with a bunch of sticky bits of paper still connected to my stuff. If I really give it some time and elbow grease, I can get them off, but I still have a sticker ghost that collects dirt and dog hair. I love the sticker attached to the glass of a picture frame. As if you can get that off without leaving a glue mark that will eventually collect dirt and make it look like your kid has a Hitler mustache.

So now not only are they fucking up the aesthetics of what they're hot-glued to, they're destroying the functioning. I have a set of putty knives with yet more stickers. The label with the brand name is right on the blade, and you couldn't get it off with a team of Clydesdales and a blowtorch. So now in an attempt to get these off, I have scratched and bent what are supposed to be flat, smooth surfaces for evenly spreading spackle or joint compound. And since I can't get the sticker remnants off the blades, I end up mixing them into the joint compound and leaving chunks on my wall. Great job. Mission not accomplished. Or my hammer. This thing is supposed to have a grip so it won't slip out of your hand and kill someone. "Hey, let's put a supersmooth, nonremovable safety sticker on there." Are you fucking kidding me? Do you have no sense of irony?

They're also on every piece of fruit in the produce section. Have you taken a look at a tomato lately? They look like the side of a fucking NASCAR. It takes two hours to make a salad now. The first hour and forty-five minutes are spent peeling stickers. Whenever I complain about this, there's always some asshole who says you can eat the stickers. Great. Thirty years from now I'm going to shit out a fourteen-pound ball of stickers. I'm sure when you're done smoking a cigarette you could swallow the filter and it wouldn't kill you, but why the fuck should we have to do it?

Even underpants come with a sticker. "Inspected by." This should prove to be especially helpful when I craft my thank-you letter.

Dear Inspector 4427-49,

Without brave Americans like yourself, with your eagle eye and your cat like reflexes, my chub pack of Hanes may have been a grave disappointment. Please accept this ripe sticker as a small token of my gratitude.

Your biggest fan,
Adam

P.S. If you see Inspector 6248-21, please tell him this is the third subpar V-neck tee I've received with his sticker on it, and that when it comes to inspecting he couldn't hold your jock. Which, by the way, falls under the jurisdiction of Inspector 7846-39.

HOSPITAL GOWNS

I don't understand the hospital gown. First off, we should take the word *gown* out of it. What other gown do you wear that has your ass hanging out? (Though that would make ballroom dancing more interesting.) I have personal experience with the pain in the exposed ass that is the hospital gown.

In 1999, after many years of holding the focus pads as a boxing trainer, I had developed a large cyst on the palm of my left hand that needed to be surgically removed. It was a simple outpatient procedure, in and out that day. But they still made me do the hospital gown.

Before the surgery, they came in to get me prepped. They gave me the gown and told me they needed my underwear. Keep in mind, for this operation I would be laid out like Jesus on the cross. They were going to take my arm, strap it down and out 90 degrees, and operate on my palm. Granted, my palm and my junk are usually fast friends, but this was one occasion where they were far apart. I said to the nurse, "How much farther away from my crotch can you get?" They insisted I hand over the Hanes. So I said, "You give me one goddamn good reason I need to take my underwear off." He replied, "Certain underpants are made of a cotton-Lyrca blend that could ignite."

I have not encountered this phenomenon of underpants spontaneously bursting into flames. Does this happen? A guy is jogging and the friction causes them to combust? Has anyone ever said, "My grandfather went that way"? I think maybe they were just trying to screw with me. I imagine them in the doctors' lounge before the surgery: "I wonder if we can get this dipshit to give up his underpants." "Tell him they might catch on fire while he's asleep." "Twenty bucks says he won't go for it." "You're on."

So I, like any person with an intact brain, responded with skepticism. The guy said, "You'll be hooked up to some electrical equipment—it could spark and cause a fire." I said, "Please give me the form that will release you from any liability. Give me the under-pants waiver. I'll happily give it my John Hancock so that you can work on my hand without staring at my cock. If I wake up and my balls are on fire, you will not be held responsible." Everyone's worried about getting sued for everything. They need you to hand over your underpants, need you to close the overhead bin with nothing in it, need you to agree not to bring peanuts into the school, need to put a warning sticker on everything, need you to leave the beer inside the pool hall when you go out to smoke, blah, blah, blah. What about a waiver? How about a dignity waiver? A universal waiver I can sign that says I get to keep my goddamn underpants and carry an alco-holic beverage outside of the bowling alley to blow a butt. If I chuck the bottle at a cop or perform a hate crime with it, don't worry, I signed the dignity waiver. You've got immunity. If, God forbid, my underpants go up in an inferno and I wake up with a smoldering patch where my pubes used to be, I can't sue the hospital. I've signed my dignity waiver.

I'm not uptight or homophobic, but when a group of strangers wants to drug you and the last request before you go under is to give up your underpants, you can't help but feel vulnerable. But I lost the battle and ended up relinquishing my boxer briefs. So I wake up from the surgery, I'm groggy, my arm's in a cast, and my ass is hang-ing out of the gown. And there's nothing I can do about it. Because the goddamn thing closes in the back. It's impossible to reach even if I don't have my arm in a sling. This is your design? A garment that lets your ass hang out, and if you try to cover your butt cheeks, you end up going in circles like a dog chasing its tail? And never mind the ass. Even though it's open in the back, it somehow finds a way to expose your balls, too. If you want to see some old-man back sack, head on down to the hospital. And no place has more cold metal sur-faces than a hospital. You need a wool sweater for your ass, not an open-backed sheet with sleeves sewn onto it. I want a bathrobe and I want my underpants.

TAMPON STRINGS

This idea is for the ladies, although I guess it would prevent many men from getting grossed out. There is nothing more embarrassing than that string popping out of the bathing suit at the pool or beach. They should be flesh-colored so they blend up against the skin. We could make different skin tones for the women of color (or the white chicks with the horrible orange spray tans). It's not like you couldn't find them if they weren't white.

Or even better, my million-dollar idea: novelty tampon strings. If you're going to have that thing hanging out, you might as well have some fun with it. You could have a lawnmower rip cord, a dynamite fuse, or a luggage tag. Or how about one of those chain pulls to turn on the light fixture? They could be personalized, like a concert lanyard for groupies, or peyos for the Jewish girls.

And you could make them for special events, like a graduation tassel, or for Halloween, a rat tail. Imagine if you were drunk, the chick you hooked up with at the Halloween party got naked, and you just saw a rat's tail hanging out. How freaked would you be? I'm just saying women are always striving for individuality and a signature look; this is how they can do it.

And for you hard-core chicks out there who are into barbed-wire tattoos and aggressive piercings, nothing says "I like rough trade" like a hangman's noose dangling from your labia.

PACKAGING

The packaging on kids' toys has gotten insane. Everything is wired down, vacuum sealed, spot welded, riveted, and duct taped. It's a Barbie, not gold bullion. You need a microhead screwdriver, a blowtorch, a diamond-blade saw, lineman dykes, and a team of forty mules to open it. I have to start opening my daughter's Christmas presents a year in advance. "Sorry, sweetie, I know you want this Dora the Explorer now, but I'll have it open by the time you lose your virginity." I understand securing a product for shipping, but anyone who's attempted to remove Barbie's ten-speed and realized it was impossible because they didn't have a microhead Phillips screwdriver will tell you this is excessive. So why spend all the extra time, resources, and energy for this exercise in frustration? I think I know. Most of this stuff is manufactured in China. They're not allowed to celebrate Christmas there, and this is how they exact their revenge. "Good luck getting Thomas the Tank Engine out of his cardboard bear trap. I'll see you in hell, roundeye."

BACK-UP BEEPERS

Let me hit you with a jag about back-up beepers. These are in every garbage truck, cement truck, and almost anything with wheels. They are way too powerful. If it's trash day in Sacramento, I can hear it all the way down in L.A. How many decibels does this sound need to be? Why does the thing that only needs to alert people eight feet behind it have a fifty-six-block range? You're waking me up on the second floor of my house that's a mile away from where you're crawling in reverse. What are the chances of you backing over me in my bed? How many hours of sleep have been ruined versus how many lives saved? Seriously, think about how many of those beeps you've heard in your life and compare it to how many times you've needed to get out of the way.

And have these beepers prevented one kid from being crushed by a FedEx truck? And even if they did, who cares? So what if a couple of kids get run over each year? It's a small price to pay. That's just Darwin driving the truck, taking out the trash. If your kid thinks it's a good idea to play with his Legos behind a steamroller, we don't need him and you don't either. He's just gonna end up crashing on your couch, eating your crap, and flunking out of junior college.

BLENDERS

We could have stopped with the blender in 1951. The blender they mixed daiquiris in to celebrate Eisenhower's election was adequate. The same guy who told me I needed to drink fourteen gallons of water a day also told me I needed a commercial-style blender to make protein drinks. A trip to the kitchen-supply store and $275 later, I returned with a thirty-pound, five-horsepower superblender. I'm sure it would do a great job of mixing whatever was in the hopper if whatever was in the hopper wasn't on the kitchen curtain or your face a millisecond after you flipped it on. If you put it on low, liquefied fruit will shoot out all over your shirt. If you put it on high, the ice for your margarita will actually penetrate your sternum and get lodged in the cabinet behind you. It has two speeds—Explosion and Eruption. And it has a rubber top that never stays in place and for some stupid reason has slots in it so you have to lean on it with a dishrag. The best blender that money can buy, and it still makes you look like you are in a fruit bukkake video.

CAR TECHNOLOGY

This is another thing that has gotten too powerful. Cars now have back-up cameras, cruise control that senses traffic, and some can even parallel park themselves. It's like you barely have to drive. Cars are turning into spas. I was driving my wife's car recently and she has massaging, heated seats. I've never been more comfortable in my life. Halfway through the drive I felt like I was going to crap myself and take a nap. Next they're going to add a device that comes out of the steering wheel and gives you a hand job. I think that's why they have airbags, so that when you nod off and drive into a phone pole you can just stay asleep on that pillow until the cops show up.

The modern automobile is jam-packed with gimmicks and features that none of us give a shit about, such as rain-sensing wipers. When's the last time you were driving, it began to rain, and you thought to yourself, "I'm just not physically up to turning on the wipers. Maybe I can park under an overpass or stop at a dairy until the storm blows over. But I'm definitely not moving my hand laterally four and a half inches and flipping a switch a quarter turn"? Or how about the three-way seat memory? You can program in a setting for you, your wife, and Shaquille O'Neal. This is important so that when the valet moves your seat, with the touch of a button it will go back to its original location. The reason this is ridiculous is that with the touch of another button that is right below that button, you can move the fucking seat back yourself. Or there's the air-conditioned glove box for your beverages, which is awesome if you're homeless but you own a 2011 Infiniti.

This stuff is nothing more than car manufacturers jacking off on a brochure. It sounds great, but it doesn't amount to a hill of shit. However, there are few things that all modern cars should have, yet almost none do. First and foremost: a system that is responsible for keeping the inside of the car below "center of the sun" in the temperature department when it's parked out in the middle of a shadeless expanse of blacktop for three hours at a Costco in August. How insane is it that you could climb into your eighty-thousand-dollar luxury automobile with every appointment known to man, yet have the skin on the back of your thighs blister when it touches the piping-hot black leather seats? It's a very simple equation. The car needs a second battery to run an air-conditioning pump and a fan without turning the engine on when the internal temperature of the car gets above ninety degrees. It could all be controlled by computer; it could shut itself off if the battery got too low. Believe me, if they can do the steering-column paddle shifters and the individual tire-pressure sensors, they can do this. Why they're not fucking doing it is driving me to distraction. If you take a black car with a black interior and park it in the sun, the temperature inside the car will be hovering around 125 degrees when you get inside. That's why pets, small children, and midgets die if you leave them for more than an hour. Why should I climb into something that would kill a schnauzer? Now, I realize some of you fucksticks are saying, "Why don't you just turn on the air conditioner?" Okay, why don't you take a red-hot horseshoe that a blacksmith is working on, dunk it in a pail of water, and then place it between your ass cheeks? The point is the fucking thing is still hot. Ironically, by the time the air-conditioning does its job and the temperature inside is low enough to sustain life, I will have completed the four-mile drive back to my home. I recently went to almost every high-end car dealer and asked them if their flagship even had the fan that recirculates the air to at least keep it under 115 degrees inside the car. None of them offered that option. Yet it is available on a twenty-six-thousand-dollar Prius.

The next thing we need is to be able to operate the power windows at least a minute after the key has been removed from the ignition. There's nothing worse than shutting off your car, removing the key, putting it in your pocket, and realizing one of the kids rolled the back window down halfway. I know I sound like the world's ugliest American when I say what a pain in the ass it is to have to reinsert the key and turn it to the on position just to get the window back up. The reason this particular one chaps my hide more than others is I remember reading an article in one of my car magazines about a Mitsubishi Starion that had this feature. That was in 1987. My 2007 fifty-thousand-dollar Audi does not have this feature. And that pisses me off to no end.

Last one: a seat-gutter system so that the wallets, the change, the ChapStick, the cell phones, et cetera that inevitably fall between the side of the seat and the transmission hump end up in the trunk in one of those trays you put your watch and keys into at the airport-security conveyor belt.

And please get the Internet in cars so my podcast can start making money.

HOTEL PILLOWS

This is another example of progress run amok. Every time I travel, I find myself at a hotel with a bed that has a bunch of those huge pillows on it. There's not a medium one in the batch. They range from large to humongous to ginormous. These pillows are the size of an air mattress that stuntmen jump into. You can't toss one goddamn waif pillow in the mix? How about one regular-sized pillow so normal people can sleep the way they do at home? I sleep on my belly so it feels like my head's propped up on a parking block.

Some stuff doesn't need improvement. Hotel pillows were fine before someone decided they needed to go on creatine. But allow me another hotel-related complaint to get into the topic of standardization and uniformity.

SHOWER KNOBS IN HOTELS

Some have the one you pull out and turn, others have the one that looks like a stick shift, some have the dial that goes clockwise to get hotter, others have the dial that goes counterclockwise. Some even have the old-school two knobs, one for hot and one for cold, that you have to mix. No matter what form it takes, it's never what you have at home or what was in the last hotel you stayed in.

How many millions of gallons of water are wasted each year by scared travelers who are afraid to step into the shower because they don't understand the knobs and don't know if it's going to be colder than liquid nitrogen or boil them alive like a lobster? Like the airport, the hotel is a well-regulated zone. Every three-hundred-pound fire door on every room has a pneumatic closer attached to it, as required by law. Couldn't we add just one more code about using the same shower knob that's at Adam's house?

POWER BUTTONS

I have a hundred remote controls for all the electronic devices in my house. And between these hundred remotes there are a hundred different locations for the power button. The power button used to just be a big red button in the upper left-hand corner. It was the most important button and therefore got the prime spot. Now they're spread out all over the remote like Al Qaeda sleeper cells. There is no consistency. TiVo banished the power button to the middle of the remote and shrank it down to the size of a blackhead. Thank God our forefathers only had one television set so they didn't have to deal with this.

I had to put nail polish on the power button of my digital camera because it's chrome on a strip of chrome. And right next to it is an indistinguishable button that does God knows what but has a little lightning-bolt symbol, which could easily mean power. But hey, it's a Kodak. They're new to the photography game. They'll figure it out eventually.

The point is that we need some goddamn uniformity. Every time

I travel, I spend the first twenty minutes in my hotel room staring at the remote with drool dripping out of my mouth like Kim Kardashian looking at a chessboard. There are certain things we've agreed on in society that have made everything easier. All side-by-side refrigerators have the freezer on the left, doorknobs all turn toward the hinges to open, we all drive on the right side of the road. How many more head-on collisions would there be if it were like, "Well, I have a Ford, so I drive on the left"?

SOFA-BOTTOM HEIGHT

We need to standardize sofa height as well. I have a couple of sofas in my house and underneath every one is a graveyard for tennis balls and Hot Wheels. Anybody who has a dog, a child, or, like me, both, knows the pain and the knee ache of mashing his face against the filthy floor and stretching in vain for a Hot Wheel that is just out of reach. There is a code if you build railings that the pickets can't be more than four inches apart because a child's head could go through them and get stuck. Why not apply this same simple logic to sofas? Whether you have to lower them down to the ground or surround them with a heavy-duty dust ruffle, they should all have to pass this simple test: If Andre Agassi's dad can fire a tennis ball underneath it using that device he ruined his kid's childhood with, it can't be sold in the United States. And what the fuck is with sofa-bottom heights anyway? I'm staring at one as I write this that's three and a half inches off the ground. Tall enough to accommodate doggie toys, cell phones, and TV remotes, but not tall enough to get a vacuum or your arm under. Isn't this the worst of all possible worlds?

BEER BOTTLES AND CANS

As you should know by now, I like myself a beer. In my long and storied boozing career, I've gotten drunk out of every type of bottle and can.

I like a twist-off on my beer bottle. Once we perfected the twist top in the late sixties, that should have been that. The twist-off cap has existed for the Bible's definition of a generation, but some beers still have the pop-top. And there's no designation to let you know which kind of top you've got. Every Budweiser bottle is a twister except the stupid aluminum bottle, which you don't find out about until you scrape all the skin off your thumb and begin to question your masculinity trying to open it.

Beer is much better out of a bottle than a can. I think we can all agree on that. But a can will do in a pinch. I don't really have a problem with the beer can, but it does fit into the same category as the ketchup packet. All the people constantly sanitizing their hands are putting their lips directly onto a piece of aluminum that has gone from a factory in Atlanta into the back of a dirty truck to the regional distribution center, then sat in that warehouse collecting a nice layer of dust and forklift-exhaust particles until it ended up in the storeroom of the gas station where you bought it. For the month before the Indian guy ended up stocking it in that fridge, cockroaches were having drag races on it. And worse than just putting your lips on the can, you crack that little tab and push it into the drink. This filthy patch of metal is now dipped into your beer. Every sip you take has to flow across this dam of disease.

But the worst beer-delivery system is the plastic bottle at the stadium that's shaped like the glass bottle. I understand that one too many people got clocked in the head by a shit-faced shithead Raiders fan, but the idea that we had to get the good people at Hasbro involved because we can't stop throwing them onto the field is sad. That cold glass bottle feels great; it's pathetic to be sitting in the bleachers drinking your Miller High Life from a sippy cup.

And I'm not one of those cancer hysterics, but after it's been sitting in the sun you can smell the BPA emanating from the plastic bottle. I'm sure when that bottle gets warm plastic particles are breaking off, getting into the beer and thus into your body. In fifty years when we all have colon cancer from this, we'll be wishing we had stuck with the glass bottles and lived with the couple of downed referees.

Also, the plastic bottle does you no good in a bar fight. Do you know how ridiculous it looks to take an unbreakable plastic bottle, bounce it off a mahogany bar top, and say, "Come get some!"

PUSH/PULL

This is something we need to improve and get on the same page about. The PUSH and PULL labels on the door should be PUSH and YANK. I'm not Evelyn Wood, but when I'm walking and talking on a cell phone I just see the PU- and end up smashing into the door. How many people have crashed into that aluminum diner door and been embarrassed? *Push* and *pull* are too close. *Entrance* and *exit* shouldn't start with the same letter, either. And I'm this close to going off about *on* and *off*.

Contractions fuck everything up: *could* and *couldn't*, *has* and *hasn't*, et cetera. Take *does* and *doesn't*. They have exactly the opposite meaning, yet if your cell phone has a spotty connection, you could end up thinking that someone *doesn't* love you and *does* have cancer. We constantly make things harder on ourselves.

We also do this with confusing street names. This happens everywhere, but I feel it's particularly bad in Los Angeles. We have a Santa

Monica Boulevard, and underneath it there is a street called Little Santa Monica. Here's the easy way to tell them apart. Santa Monica Boulevard connects with Beverly Glen, Beverly Drive, and Beverly Boulevard. Little Santa Monica only connects to Beverly Drive. And that all takes place in a ten-block radius. What could go wrong?

Why do they always put these streets right next to each other? My buddy Jack grew up in a part of town called the Doñas. Every street in this square-mile section is named Doña Pequita, Doña Marta, Doña Emelia, et cetera. What the fuck?

Dear functionally illiterate developers or evil/maniacal city officials: The very essence of naming things is to distinguish one from another. If you put Bluebird Way next to Bluebird Circle, which is above Bluebird Drive, that flies in the face of this goal. My fantasy is that I one day find one of these motherfuckers, break into his house, wrangle his entire family at machete point into the living room, and ask, "What's your son's name?" "Lance." "Okay, good. From now on your wife, your daughter, and your dog are all going to answer to the name Lance. Now enjoy the rest of your tortured, confusing life."

Whether it's hospital gowns, hotel pillows, snooze bars, or street names, the question remains: Why do we insist on fucking with ourselves?

ADAM CAROLLA

DO YOURSELF A FAVOR

I have so much to give to my kids. Not monetarily or emotionally—I won't get off the couch. But I will yell so many things at them that will enrich their lives. I hope that if you've learned anything in the course of reading this book, it's that I'm a genius. I have a lot of wisdom to impart. Please read these tips and incorporate them into your life. Not only for you but for me, so I don't have to deal with you.

HOUSEHOLD TIPS

MICROWAVE COOKING TIMES The next time you're putting something in the microwave, instead of tossing it in for a minute, put it in for fifty-five seconds or a minute and eleven seconds. Gain back the time you spend moving your finger from the 1 to the 0 and just hit 5 twice or 1 three times. What's the difference between thirty seconds and thirty-three seconds to your cup of coffee? It's not like that extra three seconds is going to burn your tongue off. The same

207

rule applies all the way up. Two and a half minutes becomes 2:22, three and a half or four minutes becomes 3:33. Five minutes becomes 4:44. There is no 5:55. You shouldn't be eating anything that takes six minutes to microwave. Anything that takes that long should be boiled, baked, or fried. It may seem silly, but when you're on your deathbed and you remember all the wonderful things you did in the extra forty-nine seconds you accumulated over the course of your life using this technique, you'll thank me.

One more quick microwave-related tip. Toss your breakfast/ protein bar into the microwave and give it a five-second shot just to soften it up.

HOME SECURITY You should get yourself a barrel bolt lock for your bedroom door. It's literally a three-dollar item that anybody with a Phillips-head screwdriver could install.

It's not going to stop the shoulder of an ATF agent when they storm your house. But if you're a teenage boy, it will stop Stepmom from interrupting a spirited solo session, or if you're a teenage girl, you can avoid the uncomfortable silence that comes after waking up to discover Stepdad standing at the foot of your bed with a beer in his hand and his sweatpants around his ankles. Amorous couples with young children can also benefit greatly from this three-dollar investment. And you can avoid the scariest story on the news: "I woke up to see the crack addict standing over my bed holding rusty hedge clippers." If you want to go whole hog, you can install a dead bolt in your bedroom door, and that will give you time to get your gun.

I'm into gun safety as much as the next white supremacist. But I don't understand having something in your house for protection, keeping that device empty on the upper shelf of your closet, and the thing that makes the device effective—namely, the bullets—in a lockbox in the garage. I know it's safe, but the main people it's protecting are intruders. What if I said, "You should keep this Taser on your nightstand for safety but bury the battery for it in a mason jar in the backyard"? Would that make sense to anybody?

Here's my best-of-all-worlds home-protection plan. Get a shotgun. Not a Jed Clampett double-barreled type, and not a long skeet-shooting type. A shorter-barreled, lighter, law-enforcement-style shotgun. They're not terribly expensive, they hold eight rounds, and some even have a flashlight built into the barrel. The sound of the pump alone is enough to drive off the highest of intruders. But if that doesn't work, you don't have to be a marksman. Here's where the tip kicks into overdrive. Make the first round a blank. That way if the neighbor kid comes back drunk at three A.M. and crawls through the wrong window, all he'll get is sobering backfire instead of his head blown off. If the pump and the warning shot don't stop you, the next round is rock salt. If you get past that you're hell-bent on hurting me and my family, that's why the next six rounds are live. Trigger-squeeze number three is a full round into your chest. (That sound you just heard was Ted Nugent jizzing in his pants.)

But, as I've always said, the best form of home security is a Confederate flag. The Stars and Bars on the flagpole in front of the house lets everyone know not only do you have guns, but you're probably cleaning them right now. If you, as a white male in your thirties (I've seen the ADT ads), are casing a neighborhood and deciding which house is your home-invasion target, which are you going to hit, the house with the Confederate flag or the one with the hummingbird feeder and the cat-count sticker for the firefighters? If that feels slightly too racist for you, then the next best thing is the Don't Tread on Me flag. It's the same connotation—this is the home of a proud NRA member who is ready, willing, and able to fill your ass with buckshot if you so much as step on the lawn.

AVOID SLIPPERS WITH HARD BOTTOMS Don't get me wrong, by all means get a nice pair of slippers. Especially if you have tile floors. But the ones with the rubber soles eventually turn into shoes. Each time you step out of the house in those, you get a little bit farther from home and a little bit closer to homeless. It starts innocently enough: "I'm just grabbing the mail." Then it's "I'm hitting the drive-through—it's not like I'm getting out of the car." Soon enough it becomes "I'm just going to the liquor store—what do those losers care?" Eventually you show up at the office: "Hey, it's casual Friday, these look like Top-Siders." And finally: "So what if I'm going to the Oscars. It's shabby chic." I'm telling you, it's a slipper-y slope. (Good stuff, Ace man.)

BRIGHT-COLORED WALLET Avoid black wallets. Many cars, including my own, have black leather seats and black carpet. At night when the black wallet falls out of the sweatpants and gets lodged between the black seat and the black carpet on the transmission hump, it becomes undetectable by the human eye. Now you've got no cash and an irate hooker. I actually went to the length of spray-painting my wallet red. This is an endless source of amusement for everyone in my life, but that was five years ago and I'm still going strong with the same wallet. So suck it, naysayers.

The way to avoid this problem altogether is tip number 255: Only purchase sweatpants with zippers on the pockets.

DIGITAL TIMER Get a digital kitchen timer and put it on your nightstand. It's great as a backup if you have an important engagement. Let's say you absolutely need to wake up at six A.M. to get ready for a job interview or court date. You'll go to bed at midnight and set the alarm. Then also do some quick math and set the timer for six hours: That way if there's a power outage, or if in a haze you slap the snooze bar, you're covered.

That's just one use for the digital timer. It's also great for naps. Oftentimes when people take a nap they're afraid of going too long and fucking up their sleep cycle or missing the kid's recital. So they end up sleeping with one eye open, which defeats the purpose of the nap. Rather than resetting the alarm clock, just set the timer for however long you want to nap. And of course be sure to add an extra three minutes for beating off.

I may not be like most people, but I don't get up at the same time every day. Instead of setting an alarm to different times every night, I just use the digital timer. It's also good for travel if you want to take that nap and can't figure out the hotel clock.

PUT YOUR PHONE NUMBER ON STUFF Whether it's your iPhone, wallet, or laptop, put a nice sticky label with your phone number on it so if it gets lost you at least have the chance of getting it back.

I have my phone number written on the inside of my wallet with IF FOUND PLEASE CALL . . . . We did an experiment on my radio show where we left wallets in various parts of Los Angeles. There was no identification and no credit cards, just one hundred dollars cash and a phone number written in them. People found the wallets and called the show. They didn't know it was a radio stunt—they just found a wallet and wanted to get it back to the rightful owner. You have to realize that nine out of ten times, a lost wallet is not going to be found by a criminal. Criminals don't go looking for stuff on the ground. Usually it's going to be found by some hardworking, God-fearing busboy taking the subway to work. Despite what you may think, people are fundamentally decent and will do the right thing if given the opportunity.

LABELS If you're living in a home that has more than one portable phone—kitchen, den, bedroom, et cetera—put a label on each one so you won't mix them up and they'll find their way back to their correct cradle. You can go the extra mile and make a nice label with the Brother P-touch (which sounds like a monk who molests kids).

Also, while we're on phones. Shut the ringer off on the bedroom phone. You'll hear the ring from the one that's in the office and never be startled by the one that's two feet from your head.

SIXTY-DOLLAR AIR COMPRESSOR FROM HOME DEPOT
You don't have to be a contractor to get use out of these things. Invest in one of these and you won't have to go to the gas station to inflate your car or bike tires. You won't blow out a lung inflating pool toys

and air mattresses. You can use it to dry your laptop after you dump a cup of coffee on the keyboard. I'm not even going to get into the sexual possibilities.

MULTIPLES When you go to the store to buy nail clippers, screwdrivers, scissors, or other little items that you use every day, buy a couple and spread them around your house. Put some in your car and your office, too. Have a pair of scissors in every room. These things literally cost pennies and are easily lost. So have backups. The eighty-five cents you invest in a second pair of toenail clippers is more than worth it when you don't have to run around the house looking for them. In general this tip is more about time versus money. People are constantly kicking their own ass to save a nickel. How much is your time worth? Spend a little bit extra and get those precious minutes back to enjoy your loved ones—in my case, my cars.

PARENTING TIPS

FIND OUT IF YOUR KID IS A GOOD DRUNK OR BAD DRUNK

Let's face it. Your kid's going to have some relationship with alcohol. You should find out early on if it's a good one or a bad one. We all remember those friends from back in the day who turned into different people when they got drunk. I had friends who were the nicest, most rational guys in the world when they were sober and turned into belligerent, confrontational date rapists after nine beers. I've also had girlfriends who after a few too many Jack and Tabs would go up to my boss at the Christmas party and let him know what I really thought of him.

So it's important to find out early what kind of drunks your kids are gonna be. On my twins' sixteenth birthday, I'm going to take them to the park with a twelve-pack of Mickey's and get to the bottom of it. If, God willing, they just say, "Let's go to Tommy's and get chili burgers. You drive, we're too drunk," then it's time to toss them the keys to the liquor cabinet and get the party started. But I'll know they can't handle their booze if my son says, "You think you're hot shit, old man? Come over here and get some," and my daughter looks at me and says, "Someone's been working out."

SHOW YOUR SON YOUR DICK Before you start calling Child Protective Services, I'm not saying you should sit him down in the living room when he's fifteen and drop your drawers. Just at some point when he's old enough to have a fuzzy memory of it, step out of the shower drying your hair with the towel and give him a glimpse. Of course I don't mean in an aroused state. Maybe get a little blood circulating and just the right amount of baby oil to catch the light. Just once, and then never let him see it again. He'll think you're huge. This is an investment in your dick's future, a 401(cock), if you will. Because down the road he will definitely tell his friends, "My old man's got a huge honker. I saw it once." Then word will get around town that you're packing. You can look forward to some day when he's in high school and he brings his friends around and they look at you like a god. They'll be like, "Hey Mr. C," and give you a high five and a knowing glance. What he won't figure out until he's in his thirties is that you are just average but looked huge to his waist-high eyes.

TRAVEL/AUTO

TRAVEL KIT Get yourself a small bag and stuff it with an extra T-shirt, shorts and towel, and a toiletry kit with the travel-sized toothbrush, deodorant, et cetera, and keep it in your car. That way you're prepared with a change of clothes and can clean yourself up in case an impromptu hoops game starts up, someone tosses you into the pool, or you wake up in a strange hotel room with a hangover and a floozy.

FIX-A-FLAT Nothing is more pathetic and a greater sign that you are a loser than the space-saver spare tire on your car. (Unless of course that space-saver spare has a Denver boot on it, in which case you should just take the tire iron and beat yourself to death with it.) No matter where you live, but especially here in L.A. with all the shit littering our roads, you're eventually going to get a nail in your tire. Get a can of Fix-A-Flat and keep it in your trunk. Just hook it up and spray it in there. Then take your car to a place that can repair the tire. And you won't have to look like a pussy in front of your lady when you can't manage to get the lug nuts loose.

SUNGLASSES First, the multiple-scissors and multiple-nail-clippers rule applies here too. Keep an extra pair of sunglasses in the glove box so that when you leave the first pair in the house you're not squinting your whole commute. Also, if you ever go to a pool party, barbecue, or any event that starts while the sun is up and ends after the streetlights come on, don't set your sunglasses down. You'll miss them on the way out because it's dark. Put them in your breast pocket or hang them on your shirt—anything but set them down. But for Christ's sake, don't put them backward on your neck or on top of the bill of your ball cap. You're trying to get laid, not win a bass tournament.

BATHROOM/HYGIENE TIPS

PEEING IN THE SINK I've been a proud sink pee–er for over fifteen years now. Why waste water flushing the toilet when there is a perfectly good, crotch-height receptacle with a drain in every bathroom?

Pee in the sink and give it a quick spritz of water from the faucet. Many years ago Dr. Drew made the fatal error of telling me that urine was sterile. Since then it's been game on. Here's a challenge for you Pee-ya Hatas: You try to shave or brush your teeth while emptying your bladder into your beloved toilet and tell me, how much of it ends up in the potpourri dish?

ZITS A lot of people squeeze their zits. I have a better technique. Take a hot shower to loosen up the skin and open the pore. Then drop a pin into the pore. You'll know you hit the right one when it feels like puncturing the skin of a grape. A little resistance at first, and then it will drop in. Then you can pull the skin apart and drain it that way. Finish it off with a dollop of flesh-colored Oxy 10 and you're ready for your date. That way you don't squeeze the zit and inflame or irritate your face or ass. (Getting hot, ladies?)

SPACE HEATER FOR THE BATHROOM The only thing worse than the alarm rousing you out of bed at an ungodly hour is stepping into a frosty-cold bathroom moments later. The bathroom is often the coldest place in the house, and to compound things, you're either naked or in a towel. You could blast the heat all night while you're under a comforter and the bathroom would be toasty, but that means you'd be baking in your bed and throwing money out the window. Here's a cheap and simple solution: space heater. "But Adam," you ask, "you want me to leave the space heater on all night? Won't that waste electricity?" No. "But if I turn it on after I wake up it won't be warm until I'm driving to work." That's right, it needs to turn on twenty minutes before you walk in. "But Adam, they don't make space heaters with timers." This is why they call me Ace. For six dollars you can purchase a wall-outlet timer, the one you use to turn your Christmas lights on and off. Set it to heat up the bathroom fifteen minutes before you wake up. That way when you step into the room in your bare feet and boxers to brush your teeth in the morning, it's not like you're dropping the puck at a Penguins game.

SHAMPOOING The reality is you should probably shampoo once a week. There have got to be oils and essences that are meant to accumulate in your hair that you're not supposed to strip away. Think about it. What do you do right after you shampoo? You use conditioner. Why? To put back all the good stuff you just took out. Here's an even better example. I have never seen a bald bum. Have you? The average fifty-five-year-old CEO is balding. The average fifty-five-year-old bum has a head of hair like Phil Spector. What's the difference? The CEO has a marble shower with twenty different massaging heads that he uses twice a day. The homeless guy showers once a year at the beach.

ONE LAST BATHROOM TIP If you get ingrown hairs on your neck or bikini line, use a little Oxy 10 after you shave and they will diminish considerably. P.S.: If you're getting ingrown hairs on your neck *and* bikini line, please stay at home when I come to your town for the book signing.

LIFE TIPS

ARRIVAL TIME As a society we heap a lot of praise on those who are punctual and even more on those who are early. "The early bird catches the worm," "This guy is the first one in the office every day," et cetera. This next tip is a case for being late.

If we're meeting at a restaurant or the movies, be on time. But if you're going to someone's house, it's better to be late than early. People are never ready when you show up before the agreed-upon time. If you're coming over for brunch and you're twenty minutes early, the person is just going to be stepping out of the shower. If you're coming to a barbecue that starts at three o'clock, don't get there at two twenty-eight. The hosts will still be hosing down the patio and set-ting up tiki torches. Then you'll have to do that awkward thing where you say, "Pretend I'm not here," but then annoy them five minutes later looking for the bottle opener. And usually the couple throwing the party is having one of their biggest, stupidest fights of the year. "What kind of idiot doesn't know the difference between Sunkist and Orangina? You're a monster. This marriage is over."

That kind of early is horrific. But this tip is not just for your host's benefit. It's for you. Why throw away precious minutes of your life? They add up. Let's face it: Work begins the second you leave the house. You are on the clock as soon as you walk out the front door.

When I was doing *Loveline*, I was always exactly on time. I was late maybe four times in ten years. I saw no sense in showing up a half hour early to do nothing. *Loveline* was a two-hour show. Take that half hour, multiply it by five days, and it would add up to more than an extra show. Over the course of a month, it's like doing an extra week of shows. Moreover, if you multiply that half hour of sipping coffee with the flunkies from the station by five days and then multiply that by ten years, I would have lost fifty-four days of my life. God knows how old I'd be by now.

This all may be well and good for barbecues and radio shows. But I know a lot of you are going to draw the line when you hear about my next tardy destination—the airport. There's a reason why there's an endless line at the Cinnabon and the Chili's is filled to the point where people are having to eat standing up: stooges showing up too early for their flights. In order to fully absorb this next tip, first you're going to have to get over your fear of not flying. Missing your flight is not the end of the world. You're not on top of the U.S. embassy in Hanoi in 1975. You're in an international airport. There's hundreds of flights leaving each day, and I'll bet you at least twenty of them are going where you're supposed to be. So if you miss your flight, you can still get to your destination, just a couple of hours later and maybe eighty dollars lighter in the wallet.

Now let's do the same math I did with *Loveline*. Imagine you show up at the airport an hour earlier than you need to be there. Not an hour before the flight: an hour before the time you need to get through check-in and security. If you do that for three flights, you've lost the time it would take to fly from L.A. to Chicago. If you did it two more times, you could fly from L.A. to New York.

HAVE A "FUCK OFF" CHAMBERED AND READY TO GO

You're going to encounter dicks in your life—it's inevitable. One time during the first few weeks of my morning radio show, I was in the parking lot of Canter's Deli on my way to go get some postshow pastrami. Someone walking by recognized me and shouted, "Howard Stern was better." Without missing a beat I shouted back, "Fuck off." It caught the guy by surprise. He started explaining that he was "a producer," but before he could finish the pathetic excuse for his behavior, I hit him with a second round: "Go fuck yourself." Then I walked into the deli and enjoyed my lunch. Life is too short to deal with dickheads. These people need to be shamed publicly. If you're uptight about cursing, then having a "Beat it" in the breach is good, too.

FAKING IT This tip is for the gals. Personally I don't care if my many, many ladies fake orgasms. Either I gave you a real one or you think enough of me to avoid hurting my feelings. It's like ass kissing. Genuine or not, it's a compliment either way. But if you're with someone who can't get you over the hump, no pun intended, and you have to fake orgasms, hold back every eighth one. Just say, "Sorry, Oprah had on that woman whose face was ripped off by the monkey. It just wasn't in me tonight." The guy will think the rest of them were legit and you'll never get accused of faking.

TIPPING The tipping system is all screwed up. The people who really deserve the tips don't get them. For example, the wife will get the hour (actually fifty minutes) of massage and aromatherapy at Burke Williams for $125 and still have to tip the bitch out. Why isn't this included? Why do you have to give the masseuse another thirty bucks on top of the $125? What a scam.

And while we're in the area of massages, let me say this. If you can afford a massage, you don't need a massage. You know who needs a massage? The guy working on your roof while you're out getting a massage.

I also don't like the bullshit where you go out for dinner with a group of more than six people and the restaurant does the "gratuity included" on the bill. Let's look at the definition of the word *gratuity*— "something given voluntarily or beyond obligation, usually for some service." *Voluntarily*. If it's included it isn't a gratuity, it's a tariff. They don't give you the option. Eighteen percent (sometimes 20 percent if they're real assholes) is built in. What if the service sucks? You're still forced to give the "gratuity." In fact, this system makes sure the service sucks, because it's taken away the financial incentive to bring the food quick and keep the water glasses full.

And shouldn't the chefs be getting the tips instead of the waitstaff? Why should the cost of the food influence the tip? It all weighs the same. It takes as much time and effort to deliver a Morton's prime rib as a Denny's Grand Slam. But that Morton's waiter is going to get a big fat tip while the Denny's waitress is going to get screwed by the old cheap fucks who are busting out the abacus to figure out what 14 percent of $6.95 is and then leaving it in lint-covered pennies.

Whether it's an expensive restaurant waiter or masseuse, the "this is how they make their money" argument is a load of shit. They should be paid by the business. I wish when I was a contractor I could have done the job and then told the homeowner to tip the laborers. "Sorry, I don't pay them. Eighteen percent would be fair."

By the end of my carpentry career, I was really skilled. I could read plans, do the layout for framing, tell you the difference between a glulam beam and a Parallam beam, and I was driving a truck with three grand worth of them in the back. But I was making fifteen bucks an hour. Why does the hot twenty-one-year-old waitress who's banging the rich producer need to average forty dollars an hour?

Why does she deserve to make what an optometrist makes and not have to claim it in taxes?

So here's the tip about the tip. Why not tip the laborers and minimum wagers? Like the Home Depot guy. He's going to get a hernia or die trying to pull the tankless water heater from the top of the aisle rack. Next time you're at the Taco Bell, if the kid taking your order is nice, tell him to keep the change. You just got nine tacos and a large Pepsi for $3.89. Give him a five and walk away. He'll feel great because it's unexpected, and you'll feel good too.

TRUST YOUR GUT Here's a little story to illustrate my next tip about trusting your instincts.

The year was 1995 and I was teaching more boxing and doing less carpentry, and thus it was time to do what all young men wearing blue collars yearn to do: get out from behind the wheel of my piece-of-shit pickup truck and get behind the wheel of a piece-of-shit car. I probably should have purchased a used Sentra or Tercel, but I was swinging for the fences. I wanted a Toyota Supra. The problem was my twenty-seven hundred dollars could have bought me a Civic with one owner and seventy-two thousand miles, but if I wanted a Supra it was going to have to be five owners, none of them German, and 151,000 miles. Here's the tip within a tip: Right now you could go on eBay and find a Jaguar from the eighties for fifty-five hundred dollars. But you'd be much better off spending that fifty-five hundred on a Nissan from this century. It's hard to turn down a Jag, a Mercedes, or a BMW for the same price as a Honda or a Toyota, but after you pay for a valve job and new transmission on that Jag, I think you'll see things my way.

Now back to our story. I scoured the *PennySaver* outside of the ninety-nine-cent store until I found a Supra for under three thousand dollars. I showed up at the guy's apartment building to check it out. (Mini-tip within a tip: If you ask a guy to pop the hood and he reaches for a mop handle to hold it up, he's probably not a loving owner.) Anyway, I was so excited to finally be in a bucket seat instead of a bench seat, I still bought it. I ended up replacing the shocks, tires, brakes, engine, and transmission—essentially every part but the dome light—over the next year. But there was still one component left to fix. The air conditioner. Now to you the air conditioner may just be another knob on your dash, but to me it was very symbolic. It stood for much more than cold air that was being pushed through a vent on a hot day: It meant success and prosperity. I grew up in the oppressively hot San Fernando Valley in houses that had sun-bleached driveways and no garages or carports. This meant whatever pile of shit happened to be in that driveway during any given summer was thirty degrees hotter inside than the 108-degree ambient temperature. And nobody ever had air-conditioning. I kept this sad legacy alive as an adult by living in a string of bad apartment buildings with only street parking and driving beat-up pickup trucks long past their prime. This was the first vehicle I'd ever owned that actually had air-conditioning. It just didn't work.

Sometimes on a hot summer day I would press that little blue button with the snowflake on it just to see it light up even if the air coming through the window and the vent were the same temperature. At this time in my life I was beginning my radio career, and even though I was only getting paid fifty dollars a bit, there was light at the end of the tunnel. So I decided it was time to conquer this hot-air demon. Even though I was starting to make some money, out of habit I decided to do the job myself. So I bought a rebuilt air-conditioning pump and the component called a receiver dryer. I rolled up my sleeves and got to work in the driveway of my rented La Crescenta home. Some hours later, I finished installing the components and it was time to go to the service station and have it filled with Freon. Now came the moment of truth. I started the car and pushed the blue button with the snowflake on it.

I could feel that air was coming through the vents, but I couldn't tell if it was getting colder or not. It didn't feel any different from the air outside but I just figured, ironically, that it would take the air conditioner some time to warm up. Ten minutes later it became apparent that it wasn't working and that the curse had not yet been broken. I'll spare you all the details of all the knuckle busting and all the trips back and forth from the parts warehouse, but the summer had come and gone and I'd still not figured out a way to get the air working in my '85 Supra. In my vain attempt to beat the heat I sadly, and ironically, spent an entire summer lying on a hot driveway underneath a black car on jack stands or standing in a parts warehouse in Van Nuys with nary a swamp cooler to be found.

The good news was the radio career had picked up enough that six months later I decided to break down and let the experts handle it. I brought the car to a place that specialized in air-conditioning repair. I told the guy behind the counter I didn't care what it took: This car needed air-conditioning, and it needed it now. He told me, "You come back here at five P.M. and this baby will be blowing cold arctic air." I jumped into Jimmy's car and we went out for a celebratory lunch. Before I knew it, it was four thirty and time to make my way back to the shop. Jimmy dropped me off and headed home. I confidently strolled into the office. The mood was somber. The manager opened with, "I've been calling you over and over again." I said I was out. I asked if the car was ready. He said, "No." I asked, "Well, how far into it are you?" He said, "We haven't even started." I asked, "Why not?" He said, "You took the keys. That's why I'd been calling. "

This, of course, was pre–cell phone. To be fair, it was not pre–cell phone for normal people, sort of like the Carollas huddled around a black-and-white TV in 1978 was not pre–color TV for normal people. I was crestfallen. Since I didn't have a way home, I told him I'd have to have someone follow me over the next morning to drop it off. I started out to the parking lot where the car was parked. He chased after me. "Oh, one more thing . . . while you were gone, somebody backed into it and pushed in the rear right quarter panel."

It was at this point I starting flirting with the notion of giving up. Maybe it wasn't meant to be. I decided to soldier forward. I dropped the car off the following morning, and when I returned that afternoon the air was still not working. A part needed to be ordered or something. Either way, eight months, thousands of dollars, and hundreds of man-hours into this endeavor, the air passing through the vents of my Supra was the same temperature as one of Suge Knight's farts.

Sometime the following week I got the call all parents of cars with no air-conditioning dream of. The manager from the shop said, "It's working. Come pick it up." This time it was my father's turn to give me a ride. My dad and I don't have a lot in common, so between his lack of knowledge/interest in building, boxing, or radio and my lack of knowledge/interest in jazz trumpet, jazz trumpet, or jazz trumpet, we don't spend hours on the phone talking each other's ears off. But one thing we do share is a passion for psychology. I told my father on the journey to pick up my Supra—a journey that was only three miles door-to-door but in actuality spanned hundreds of miles and thousands of tears—that I didn't think this car was meant to have air-conditioning. It just wasn't meant to be; I knew it in my gut. I predicted that the car would either be stolen or totaled.

A short time later I had flown from New York back to L.A. to audition for *Loveline* the TV show. I was on the balcony of my apartment on the phone talking to Jimmy, who was still in New York with *Kevin and Bean*. It was midnight.

As we were talking, a Ford F-250 pickup, going fifty down a residential street, without touching the brakes slammed right into the back of my car. It was an explosion of metal and glass. My car went careening into the street and the truck jumped the curb and onto the lawn of my apartment building. The balcony I was standing on was on the first floor, so I was staring down at the whole thing eight feet away from me. My car looked like an accordion. It was totaled. The guy threw his crippled truck into reverse and tried to drag it off the lawn. He was going to get the fuck out of Dodge in his Ford.

The point is that instincts matter. Whether it's on the job or in a relationship, you should trust your gut. Unless your gut is full of Mountain Dew and Slim Jims, in which case you're a cretin and should do the exact opposite of whatever your cholesterol-clogged heart is saying.

MOTIVATION No one came from a lazier, more apathetic family than me. If there was a laziness competition, my folks would take the gold, but it would have to be mailed to them.

So given this upbringing, it's no surprise that I had to break the cycle and teach myself how to make something of my life. I was like a bear that was raised in captivity and then was ill equipped to go out into the wild. So I started challenging myself. If you're thinking about something, don't procrastinate—do it, whatever it is. For me it was the coffee mug. I would be going off to my construction job in the morning and I'd have my coffee mug with me. After I finished it, I would toss it on the floor of the passenger side and it would roll around all day until I got home to my shitty rented apartment. I'd be getting out of the truck and the coffee mug would be out of arm's reach and I'd stare at it for a second and think, I should bring that in and rinse it out. But then another voice would come into my head and say, "Fuck it, I'll just get a new one tomorrow morning." The argument in my head would go on. "But then you'll have two mugs clinking around on the floor mat and one will get chipped." "Eh, just put it on the seat and that way they won't bump together." It was like a retarded version of those cartoons where an angel and devil would appear on Daffy Duck's shoulders and argue. After losing twenty minutes of my life wrestling with myself over whether to take the coffee mug in, I decided, "Do it this time. And from now on when you see that coffee mug, you pounce on it. Eventually it won't even be a thought anymore." Everything seems overwhelming when you stand back and look at the totality of it. I build a lot of stuff and it would all seem impossible if I didn't break it down piece by piece, stage by stage.

The best gift you can give yourself is some drive—that thing inside of you that gets you out the door to the gym, job interviews, and dates. The believe-in-yourself adage is grossly overrated. I don't trust people who believe in themselves. Your job in life is to fool other people into believing in you, not to fool yourself. If you take a look at my Social Security statement from 1980 to 1994, you'll see that I had no reason to believe in myself.

Your Earnings Record at a Glance

Years You Worked	Your Taxed Social Security Earnings	Your Taxed Medicare Earnings
1980	$ 232	$ 232
1981	746	746
1982	1,093	1,093
1983	2,289	2,289
1984	9,367	9,367
1985	0	0
1986	17,672	17,672
1987	2,553	2,553
1988	0	0
1989	22,543	22,543
1990	6,312	6,312
1991	0	0
1992	3,521	3,521
1993	3,984	3,984
1994	6,442	6,442
1995	36,221	36,221
1996	62,700	316,424
1997	65,400	354,661
1998	68,400	543,453
1999	72,600	1,237,903
2000	76,200	1,014,340
2001	80,400	1,085,165
2002	84,900	2,085,601
2003	87,000	2,005,179
2004	Not yet recorded	

The bad news is I no longer make what I made in '03.
The good news is if I did I never would have written this stupid book.

So focus more on motivating yourself and moving forward, and less on self-belief.

YOU CAN BE POOR BUT NOT STUPID Just because you're poor doesn't mean you have to be stupid. People are constantly wasting money and short-changing themselves on the good things in life because they don't understand cost versus value. Like the dunces who drive eight miles out of the way to the gas station where unleaded is five cents cheaper. Dummy, the amount of gas it took you to drive your '85 Aerostar van over there cost more than what you're supposedly saving. And is your time not worth sixty cents? How low is your self-esteem?

People do this with food constantly. We've all heard the semi-annoying five-dollar-foot-long Subway ads. Sounds like a good deal, right? But look at what you're getting: a pillowcase-full of shredded lettuce, a couple of presliced composite meat products, and some half

225

slices of processed, prepackaged cheese. For a buck more you can go to Giamela's (a fantastic sandwich place in Burbank, but you could replace it with any good local sub shop from any town in America). For under six bucks you get a six-pound masterpiece of meat, fresh onions, pickles, and tomatoes in good Italian bread. If you're going with the meatball sandwich at Subway, you'll get four of them that are the size of a golf ball in some watery Ragú. At a place like Giamela's, the meatballs are the size of a softball and need to be cut in half to fit in the roll. Then they get covered with a rich, hearty sauce. What's the better buy? The one from the chain sub shop that leaves you hungry an hour later, or the one that weighs as much as a Duraflame log that is so much you save half and eat it for dinner?

Another thing that falls under this poor-versus-stupid category is the bed. Let me give you a little bed background from the Carollas. I didn't know until I was into my mid-thirties that you could buy new furniture. I grew up in a house with four people sleeping on four separate beds and zero box springs. We were 0 for 4 in the box-spring department.

My mom had just a mattress on the floor. I always had only a very thin, cotlike mattress with no box spring. That in a room this big (see page 227). My childhood room is literally a closet now.

Every bed in the Carolla home was a half step up from a prison bunk. My stepdad slept on one of those square late-sixties, early-seventies sofa things that they had in the *Brady Bunch* den. Essentially you would take this long triangular pillow, throw it onto the ground, and it became a bed. It had the bad, scratchy, burnt-orange seventies slipcover and it was on those gold rolling casters.

Eventually I started buying mattresses from the Salvation Army that had been reconditioned, which means some ex-con flipped it over, beat it with a broomstick out in the alley, sprayed it with Lysol, put it in a Hefty bag, and sold it to me.

So given the long, pathetic history of the Carollas and beds, I'm going to give you, the reader, the same advice I plan on giving my kids:

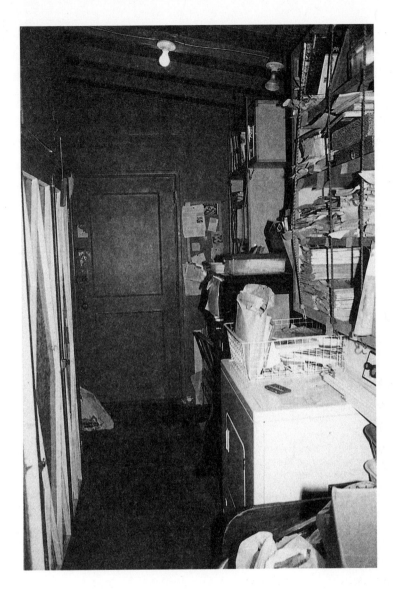

This is the room as it looks today. My bed was shoehorned into the corner, to the right of the door. The water heater and the electric meter were in the closet on the left.

Buy a good bed. It's not like you're gonna sleep every other week, or only Mondays, Wednesdays, and Fridays. You're not gonna be on the road with your band half the year. I'll be conservative and say 350 days a year you're gonna spend seven to eight hours, eleven to fifteen if you're a Carolla, in your bed. It's the most important investment you'll ever make. You always hear that thing where they say every cigarette takes a minute off your life. Every horrible night's sleep probably takes four days off your life. You're stressed out, your back hurts, you don't feel right, and you're not productive at work. Please buy a decent bed.

And get yourself a nice bathrobe. Even if you're not Bill Gates, a couple times a year you'll go out and drop seventy-five dollars on a decent meal for an anniversary or birthday. Why not spend that same cash on something you'll use every day? The pleasure of that filet mignon lasts about a half hour. A nice plush bathrobe will last you a couple of years and you'll wear it morning and night and, if you're like me, all weekend. Again, delayed gratification and value. I compare it to the baseball mitt. Instead of getting one made of vinyl that you have to replace, get a nice cowhide one for a little bit more and keep it your whole life. With the bathrobe, which makes more sense: spending ninety dollars every decade to have something that feels like you're wrapped in a warm cloud, or thirty dollars every other year for one that's shitty, itchy, and paper-thin?

Not to get too deep, but a lot of this is psychology. When you're poor, you feel beat-down and shamed. You don't feel like you deserve nice things. But saving a nickel by getting the generic pair of shoes at the grocery store isn't going to turn you into Richard Branson. So treat yourself well, which will boost your self-esteem and actually help get you into that next tax bracket.

DOES IT MAKE YOU MONEY OR MAKE YOU HAPPY? Ask yourself that quick, simple question before embarking on or sticking with anything, whether it be a job, a home-improvement project, or a relationship. If it doesn't fulfill one of those two requirements, then move on and let it go. Now, I agree that money doesn't necessarily buy happiness, but it sure as shit doesn't hurt. If whatever you're doing doesn't make you happy or at least provide you the money to go to a therapist or a liquor store to take care of that unhappiness, then it's time to blow that taco stand. Life is too short for anything else.

CHANGE On that note, I'll leave you with this last tip, and cue the inspirational music while you're reading it. This is roughly the speech I gave on my final morning radio show in 2009. Since then I've had two TV pilots, a successful podcast, several appearances on Leno, *Dancing with the Stars*, Howard Stern, et cetera, and sold out many live shows across the country. The end of that radio show wasn't the end of the world. In fact, I would have never written this book if I were still doing my morning show.

Change feels bad at the beginning. "I just got dumped by my girlfriend. This is horrible." "I'm moving. This is horrible." "I'm going to a new school. This is horrible." "I'm starting a new job. This is horrible." Change always feels scary. Why? Because it's unknown. And we're scared of the unknown. That's what freaks us out. We build our world around the known—this is my wife, these are my kids, this is my house, this is my car, this is my office. When that gets interrupted, it scares the shit out of us. But it's usually for the best. When you think about the lives where there is no change, they are the most unlived. Like the guy who's been a postal carrier for sixty-one years and lives in the house he grew up in. That's the opposite of change. Lots of change makes for a very rich, vivid, and colorful life.

Here's the problem. A lot of times you don't get to be the captain of your own change ship—other people make those decisions. When you make the call, it usually feels good. "I want to break up with that guy"; "I have a higher-paying job I'd like to move on to"; "The Bay Area is a much nicer place to live and I'm moving there." But when someone else decides, then your ass is freaked the fuck out and you don't know what to do.

But think about all the change that's happened in your life. Is it ever bad? Change is growth. That's how you measure growth. It's the rings in your tree. Sure, it can be bad temporarily: You're out of a job, you're out of your apartment, you're out of your relationship. But six months or a year down the road, you don't think, "I wish I still had that job," or "I wish I still lived there," or "I wish I was still with her." Anyone who's past the age of twenty-five has had several significant changes happen in their lives. They're always met with resistance. But if you have a rearview mirror, you'll look back and realize you are happier and better for that experience.

My Pop Warner team decided to wait until the championship game to make the CHANGE from undefeated. Now that's the look of growth.

TIME TO
CALL IT
A LIFE

I've always said, "Life is just the time between crapping yourself." (I'm planning on trademarking that phrase and putting it on a series of inspirational posters.) I have a lot of thoughts about the beginning and the end of our time on this mortal coil.

I recently did a live show and invited my old partner Dr. Drew and my old roommate, Ralph Garman, now star of the *Kevin and Bean* morning show, to join us onstage. Ralph's wife was pregnant at the time, Drew's triplets were all grown up, and my twins were three and a half. But the one thing we all had in common was infertility. For some reason the gainfully employed non–drug abusers who look at marriage as a lifetime commitment, or at least until the youngest hits junior college, couldn't figure out a way to shit out a kid without twenty trips to the fertility specialist. But if two dimwits hump in the back of a van in a Walmart parking lot, they can easily add a tenth to their brood of future addicts and welfare recipients. It seems that the higher the education level and tax bracket, the lower the sperm count. Whether you're a fan of God or Darwin, what the fuck is the plan?

The couple that has to make sure their mullets don't get tangled while they're literally knocking boots can have a kid for the cost of a six-pack of Stroh's. My kids cost me fifty grand. There were pills and injections for my wife, and I had to beat off into containers at facilities. Talk about killing something I love—it took all the majesty and romance out of having at myself while my wife was asleep in the next room.

You don't realize that your balls have their own schedule until a doctor is telling you when to have sex and where to jack off. I would ask my wife, "Can't I just beat off into Tupperware in the comfort of my own bathroom and then rush it to the place?" But the clinic was twenty-five minutes away and I guess the sperm is only good for twenty. (There are tube socks in my hamper that would beg to differ.) So I had to go to the clinic where they put you in that room with the hollow-core door that's been undercut because they used to have shag carpet. You can hear the nurses clomping around outside and clucking like chickens. A tile floor, a hollow-core door, and an inch and a quarter of daylight underneath it actually act as an amplifier. It's a good thing I had a lot of roommates and learned how to rub one out while they were twelve feet away fucking around making noise. They could be in the next room stabbing each other with fireplace pokers and I could still finish off. I'm a ninja when it comes to masturbating. I'm like a safecracker. I work quickly and I work alone.

At the clinic they offer you porn, and at first you have to pretend to be confused. "Hmm, *pornography,* you say. Don't believe I know that word. It's pictures of nude people? I was unaware of this innovation. Well, if you say so. I'll try anything once. You're the expert." And it's always the poorest selection. That basket of porn is like the kids' plastic pumpkin a week after Halloween. The Reese's, Snickers, and Almond Joy have been pilfered, and all that's left are a few scattered Necco Wafers and a dog-eared *Hustler* with Seka on the cover. You end up beating off to chicks from the eighties with Nagel paintings behind them who died of a drug overdose ten years ago. My cock was insulted. The pocket in the seat in front of you on the Southwest flight has more jackable material in it than the porn basket at the fertility clinic.

We did a *Man Show* bit once where Jimmy and I went to one of these clinics. We were going to compare our sperm to see whose count was higher, but we also decided to race and see who could produce it the fastest. So we stood in the hallway, one of the producers, Beth Einhorn, hit a stopwatch, and we sprinted into our rooms. By the way, this was Beth's first day, so it must have been bizarre to explain to her loved ones when they asked, "How was your first day on the new job?" "Oh, I timed two guys while they spunked into cups." So it was essentially the cock against the clock. I came bursting out of the room three seconds before Jimmy, but that was only because he had the dignity to pull his pants up before exiting. We accounted for that and realized we were on exactly the same jizz clock. Its like when women work together for long enough and their cycles sync up.

So years later, when my wife and I were trying to get pregnant, I'm at this fertility clinic and I know I can wrap this up pretty quickly. But I don't want the nurse to watch me walk into the room, tie her shoe, and then see me walking out with a bucket of jizz. So I did that casual jack move, the one you see the guys from the gangbang porn doing. It's the masturbation equivalent of the runner at the stoplight jogging in place to keep the heart rate up, or a Golden Gloves boxer whose fight isn't for another hour shadowboxing. Cutting to the chase, my sperm were fine, my wife's eggs were fine, and there was no reason we couldn't get pregnant. A couple of months and some in vitro fertilization later, Lynette did eventually get pregnant with my twins, the boy and what's-her-name.

This seems like the best place to recall a horrible yet hilarious moment in my life. It was my first night on *Dancing with the Stars*, and everyone was a bundle of nerves. Marissa Jaret Winokur, the chubby chick from *Hairspray* on Broadway, was one of the contestants, and she was especially anxious. She was taking the competition very seriously and she was due to dance last. The only thing more nerve-racking than dancing in front of twenty million people is pacing around for an hour and forty-five minutes waiting to do it. People were giving her stupid advice like "Have fun out there" and other shit that isn't constructive: A) That's not advice, and B) nobody has ever had fun because somebody yelled at them to have fun. After my dance, I left the stage and ran into a pacing, on-the-verge-of-throwing-up Marissa.

I could tell she was all up in her head, so I pulled her aside and thought I would offer some sagely advice that would calm her nerves. I said, "You're not going to have fun out there. You're going to have an experience out there. Don't run from it, or try to mask it with a shot of Patrón, embrace it. It's a crazy rush." Then I continued, "It's like giving birth. It's painful, it's scary, but it's life affirming. You don't want to be passed-out and not experience the miracle of child-birth." Then, like a moment out of an episode of *Curb Your Enthusiasm*, she immediately replied, "I had cervical cancer and both my ovaries removed. We have a surrogate that's pregnant right now." Another contestant, Penn Jillette, started laughing maniacally at what had just gone down. Visually it was surreal because she's five foot one in heels and Penn Jillette with his dance shoes on is knocking on the door of seven feet. Plus he's a comedian and a magician, so I thought they were screwing with me. I persisted, "No, seriously, are you sterile? Did you have your parts removed? No fallopian tubing at all?" She said yes, she was barren, it was like an ashtray down there. I had put my Capezio right in my mouth. I thought the whole child-birth thing was a great analogy, but I sent Marissa out to her first dance thinking about her long-lost ovaries instead of her paso doble.

I'm sure it would be little comfort to her, but being pregnant and giving birth is as big a pain in the ass as it is a pain in the vagina. The first thing that happens when you get pregnant is every dick-head tells you how it's going to change your life. It's not that big a deal. What is it with the worrywarts who want to talk you into being scared of shit? What do they get out of it? They'll be like, "What about college? Better start saving now." Let's get the kid out of the uterus before we start trying to get him into Harvard. Or especially the guys who will say, "Forget your sex life. It's gone. You might as well just rip your dick off and stab yourself in the eye with it."

Then when it comes time to give birth, you'll get a lot of idiots talking to you about "natural birth." People will say, "You know, you don't need to have a physician." I understand I might not need one, but we do have them. These are the same jag-offs who say, "We can do dentistry without numbing." Yeah, but you do have something called Novocain, right? Go get it. We're not on a Civil War battlefield. Why are some kinds of progress good but other kinds bad? Tomorrow I'm leaving for New York to do a television show and meet the woman who's editing this book and it's going to take me five hours in the air, but according to a handful of nut jobs, I should take a covered wagon and eat my own leg on the Donner Pass. These natural birthers are right up there with the restore-your-foreskin people, who are just wackos who don't give a fuck about restoring foreskin—they're trying to restore a hole in their childhood by filling it with a cause. Getting so wrapped up in something that falls under the heading of Who Gives a Shit? means there are deep underlying psychological issues. Whether it's natural birth, restoring foreskin, or toxin flushing through colonics, stop talking to me about it and start talking to a therapist.

Another aspect of our relentless androgynous culture is getting men involved in the whole birthing process. This happened to me. First they were like, "Hey, we have the sonogram. Here's a picture of the kids. Keep it. They'll get a kick out of it when they're older." I replied, "I don't think they'll care." The woman said, "How could it hurt?" I shot back, "How could it help?" Did she think someday my son would be showing this to his high school football buddies? They looked like two hamsters in formaldehyde.

Why are men talked into being in the room during the birth? I would have preferred not to be in the room. First, it's not a big room. It's not a gymnasium or a blimp hanger. It's small and cluttered with people and equipment. Do you need another jack-off standing around who doesn't know what the fuck is going on? We have that policy across the board in life. You can't mosey behind the counter of a McDonald's and start making your own Big Mac. So why here? All they do in hospitals is tell you, "Excuse me, sir, you need to wait," "You can't go in there," et cetera. Yet with that room, it's "Come on down." They might as well put western doors on that fucking room with a guy who looks like Jed Clampett saying, "Come on in, pull up a stool, sit a spell."

Before you go into the OR for the C-section, they put you in a holding room where you nervously wait for go time. This was a medium-sized room with two beds and one bathroom. We were the only couple occupying it. As I was leaving the bathroom, I ran into the nurse, who told me in a rude tone, "Sir, that bathroom's only for patients. Your bathroom's down the hall." I answered her the way I answer all shitheads with a pointless agenda: with a vacant stare and subtle "So what are you going to do?" Later on, she overheard me talking on the cell phone and calling her a bitch and had to swing by to make sure I knew she heard me. After the kids were born, some nervous coworkers came up and basically apologized for her, saying she did that with everyone, she's not a nice person, and they don't know what to do about her. I told them I had a novel idea—perhaps they should fire her ass. This was the most stressful day of my life, not counting the Rams' first Super Bowl appearance, and I gotta have Fuckface Nightingale up my ass engaging in one of my least favorite behaviors—the lecture about the thing that has already happened and will never happen again. Hey cunt, I just emptied my bladder and we're going down to the OR in the next twenty minutes, so unless I funnel a twelve-pack of Milwaukee's Best, I doubt I'll be heading back into the commode. And it's not like I'm going to be back the following week with a new set of twins. I, with the help of my insurance, just gave your establishment thousands of dollars. Perhaps you could holster the stink-eye and get back to your first love . . . mercy killing. I've said it before and I'll say it again, it is up to all of us to verbally abuse these douchenozzles. The more they're humored, the more empowered they become and the worse society gets.

And then there's cutting the cord. This story is a metaphor for my life. It's another example of somebody trying to get me interested in something I'm not interested in and not taking no for an answer. "Would you like to cut the umbilical cord?" "No thanks, I'm cool." "You'll regret it if you don't." "I'll take my chances." "It's a real impor-

ADAM CAROLLA

236

tant experience." "Is the guy who normally cuts the umbilical cord not available? If so, tell me. If not, please shut the fuck up." I've wasted at least a third of my life telling people no for the fifth time. I understand why they think it might be an important experience for me; what I don't understand is what's in it for them to convey that to me for the fifth time. And when did everyone buy into this notion that we had to start bonding with our kids at zygote? Here's how you bond with your kids and imprint positive parental imagery: You be a good fucking parent. You take an interest in what your kids are interested in, you encourage them, you communicate with them, and you see if you can keep the beatings and the molestation to every other weekend. If cutting the cord created some kind of magical bond, then how come none of us have that with the doctor who cut our cords? Does anyone even know the name of the guy who cut their cord or where they are now? No. Why? Because we don't give a shit. And do you think Bill Gates or Winston Churchill or Evel Knievel's dads cut their cords? Fuck no. And they turned out pretty good.

Anyway, I told anyone who'd listen that not only did I not want to cut the cord, I didn't even want to be in the building. I thought I'd be out in the parking lot handing out cigars. But the next thing you know, somebody handed me a pair of shears and said, "Start cutting." I said, "But they already cut the umbilical cord." We were standing six feet away over a clear plastic table. The guy said, "Oh, you don't cut it when it's attached. It's just symbolic." Now I was confused and pissed. The entire time assholes were telling me how important it was to cut the cord and I was saying I don't want to be performing surgery on my wife, they neglected to mention the part where I was cutting a half inch off the cord after it had already been cut. I attempted to put the right-hand cutting shears into my left hand and almost dropped them onto my daughter's eyeball in the process. I was, in the end, forced to cut my kids' cords, and I can guarantee you that any of the unspoken good vibes that were created with my kids because of this act are far outweighed by the deep-seated resentment I have toward them for forcing me into it.

And in our effort to give every kid a gender-identity disorder, the first thing we do is put them in the pink-and-blue-striped beanies.

Not pink *or* blue. Pink *and* blue. Are we trying to turn every child into a David Bowie circa *Ziggy Stardust* he-she? And once they go into the nursery, there's thirty kids spread out. They're all swaddled up in these Tupperware bins, and one of the ways you can recognize your kid, or at least narrow down the field, is by gender. If they showed me two kids—one with a blue beanie and the other with a pink beanie—next to each other, I'd go, "There are the Carolla twins." Now when you get hold of them, especially when you have twins, you can't tell them apart. I still can't tell them apart. The brainiac who had the idea of a confusing, ambiguous, light-blue-and-light-pink-striped beanie should be shot. Have any other great ideas? How about instead of red for stop and green for go we mix them and have one big brown light? Fucking retard. And is the fifty-fifty version any cheaper than a solid powder-blue or pink beanie? No. It's probably more expensive. Just buy a thousand pink units and a thousand blue units and stop the gender bending.

Giving birth is tough, but let's not treat it like it's anything more than it is. I can't stand the mommy bloggers, the women who have kids and then decide to go online and write about the dos and don'ts. You know, hard-hitting topics like "Sack Lunch. Friend or Foe?" It's all the same forty-year-old white chicks. They act as if they're the first women on the planet to give birth. It's so narcissistic. Meanwhile the Nicaraguan woman who is actually taking care of their kids has four of her own in high school. Actually three dropped out, but the point is that she crapped out four kids when she was nineteen through twenty-one and they're all fine. The whole world crapped out kids before these bitches and obviously they were crapped out, too. You're forty-one and all of a sudden after you have a kid you must write a children's book and a blog to explain to other people how to do it. You're telling us stuff we've all known for a billion years. It would be as if I discovered beating off at age forty and had to tell all my friends. "Attention fellas, there's a way to have an orgasm without hiring a prostitute. You grab your cock, and you just pull it. It feels awesome. Are you listening? Why aren't you writing this down?"

Moving on to the end of life. Aging sucks. Here's how, as a guy, you know there's no God: The only parts of a man's body that keep growing are your balls, your ears, and your nose, the three parts of your body you wish got smaller. Not your biceps and your cock. Those wither away. The shit you wish would grow gets smaller and the stuff you don't want to grow sags. It's no picnic for the ladies, either. At least as men get older they get better-looking. The hair gets gray and they get dignified. Dr. Drew gets sexier as he gets older. There's not one guy who's said, "Liz Taylor. I wouldn't have hit that at nineteen, but now that she's seventy-five I want to nail her. I'll break that other hip."

You also know you're starting to get old when you go into the swimming pool wearing a hat and sunglasses. When you're young you're frolicking, doing cannonballs, and playing Marco Polo. The more you wear going into the pool, the older you are. I'm only forty-five and I go into the pool with a shirt, hat, and sunglasses, which means I'm this close to going in with a three-piece suit, spats, a pocket watch, and a monocle.

We insist on making fun of old people in this society. Lots of jokes about Grandpa and his Depends, how slow Grandma drives, et cetera. Considering we all hope to live to a ripe old age, this seems horribly ill conceived. Making fun of a group you pray to one day be part of would be like joining the Klan right before you made the transformation that Robert Downey Jr. did in *Tropic Thunder*. Why would we make fun of something that, God willing, we're going to become? I suggest we get back to basics—making fun of Polacks and Puerto Ricans.

I love when the news shows people, usually from another country, who just hit their one hundredth birthday. They inevitably ask them the stupid and predictable question about what they did to live so long. The answer is never from eating fruit and exercising every day. They tell you that they get up, have a shot of brandy, smoke a pack of Lucky Strikes, eat a Twinkie wrapped in Canadian bacon, go to work at the asbestos factory where they have a hearty lunch of Styrofoam peanuts, then come home for six tumblers of grain alcohol. By the way, these people probably drank tap water every day of their hundred years, loved peanuts, and never touched a drop of Purell.

Then, after we get the noninformation from the unwrapped mummy on the news, we get to hear the anchors laugh and say, "He's one hundred years young." I hate that cliché. Even worse is "He died of a broken heart." People always say that when a person's spouse dies and then he dies a couple days later. It's dumb. Technically, everyone dies of a broken heart. It stops beating. And the other stupid death-related cliché is "You can sleep when you're dead." I don't think that's been confirmed. You may be able to sleep when you're dead, but what if you can't? What if it's like flying coach when you're up against the bulkhead and your seat won't recline? I don't know about you guys, but I'm not taking any chances. I'm gonna take a nap.

After you die of a broken heart, your poor relatives are going to have to cough up for a funeral. This is another time when dickheads try to extract money from you with guilt. We do from the cradle to the grave. When you have kids, they'll try talking you into the expensive pre-preschool by saying things like "Don't you want your kid to have a head start? Don't you want this for your child?" No, he's two, he's eating a Lego and shitting himself right now. I don't need to spend the equivalent of a down payment on a house so he can play with finger paints. I've already regaled you with the tale of my son and the corrective helmet. They play on your guilt. That's from ages zero to ten. Then at some point you die, and it becomes "I think your uncle Ted would want the Ambassador casket." Ted's dead. He's not part of the conversation. I know you're trying to guilt me into the velvet-lined coffin with gold trim, but I'm pretty sure his corpse is indifferent to which box it decays in.

Though I do think I could make a lot of money with my idea for a big-and-tall funeral parlor. Everyone is getting bigger nowadays, so I'm sure the coffins and grave plots have had to kick it up a notch, too. Why not a big-and-tall funeral parlor? I'd call it Larger Than Life.

I could even sell the funeral suits for the deceased at my big-and-tall men's shop, Big Sir.

I don't like to tell people about deaths in my family. It's not because I'm narcissistic or too wrapped up in my own shit, it's because it puts people in an uncomfortable position. There's that weird awkward pause. Then that person feels compelled to offer up some loss in their life, and it's never a direct comparison. "Oh, my cat just died, so I know what you're going through." This is usually followed by the "If there's anything I can do. . . ." As if you're going to take them up on it. "You know, a fresh coat of wax on the car would really take the sting out of Grandpa's demise."

I went to a funeral once where the rabbi mispronounced the name of the deceased no fewer than twenty-eight times. There should be a policy where if the person speaking says, "Although I didn't know Gabe . . ." you should be able to shout, "Then get the fuck offstage!" The Sandman from *Showtime at the Apollo* should come out and sweep you off. Sit down and let someone who knew Gabe up there. At my funeral I don't want some guy saying, "I didn't have the pleasure of meeting Alan Carelli. . . ." This is one drawback to the Jews doing their funerals the next day. They could use a little extra prep time to get off-prompter.

I want a big turnout at my funeral. Not for me, but for the people I leave behind. I want them to be surrounded by others. I want people around my widow and my many trophy widows. Plus, open pews at a funeral is like a restaurant where there's only one other couple eating there. It's sad.

And I want it abundantly clear that I wouldn't want you to go on working after I die. People say, "That's what he would have wanted." No, I want you to drop everything. Clear your calendar. I want a national day, nay, a national week of mourning with flags at half staff across the country. I want the flags on the greens of golf courses at half staff.

And I want wailing and crying. I need a big black woman to throw herself on the casket and say, "Take *me*." I want the entire cast of

Precious screaming like banshees and trying to jump into the open grave. I'd never get that kind of emotion out of my own family. It would be like having Marcel Marceau there. And they're so cheap, they'd probably try to make me bring the champagne to my own wake.

When my grandfather Lazlo died, the Carollas went with the most pathetic postmortem option possible: the Neptune Society. This is the group that cremates your loved one and scatters the ashes in the ocean. Sounds classy, right? Think again. You just call them up, "Hey, Grandpa's dead," and they say, "All right, Bert will swing by in about forty-five minutes. He'll probably drop by Arby's, get a little dinner first." In my grandfather's case, the guy just showed up at four A.M. in a station wagon. Not a hearse, a regular station wagon. He filled out a couple of forms and tossed Grandpa in the back of the wagon. I'm surprised he didn't put the corpse in the passenger seat so he could use the diamond lane on the way to the crematorium. We never saw the body again. I don't even know if they cremated him. There were no oceanside speeches, no golden urns, no rose petals floating in the bay. That would cost an additional fifty bucks. Just some dude and a fake-wood-paneled station wagon. It cost something like $280. My grandfather's funeral cost less than my blender.

The only less dignified option would be to leave him out at the curb on trash day. Here in L.A. the black bin is for trash, blue is for recycling, and brown is for dead relatives.

Over the years I have prepared a list of things I want to do before I die:

- Have my hands registered as weapons.
- Get kicked out of a casino for winning.
- Jump into a body of water with a knife between my teeth.
- Have a cape removed onstage.
- Have a sports jersey pulled over a nice suit.
- Be killed by the person I told to kill me if I started to become a zombie.
- Wipe down a gun.

- Silently communicate/point to my watch underwater.
- Punch out my undercover partner who is about to say something he shouldn't and blow our cover.
- Play bass in an all-black band, be the only white guy, and whisper something onstage to the conga player and then laugh.
- Put my hand over the mouth of a beautiful woman to stop her from screaming and alerting the bad guys.
- Get shot at and brush it off, saying, "I ain't got time to bleed."
- Be able to say someone attempted suicide over me: "She threw herself on the train tracks."
- Catch a punch and twist the guy's hand until he goes down to his knees.
- Have a celebrity shorten my name in an interview. "Bobby De Niro says working with Ace was great."
- Be embroiled in a lawsuit that leads to a heroic story: "I broke the leg of a gangbanger robbing a liquor store, and now he's suing me."
- Stop a crime by throwing something. A guy steals a purse and starts running. I throw a can of corn football-style and knock him out.
- Track someone. I dismount my horse, then do that low squat where I pick up a clump of dirt and let it sift through my fingers.
- Hawk a championship belt or Super Bowl ring at a pawn-shop when I hit rock bottom.
- Shout, "Release the hounds!"
- Be lost in the Utah desert with a hot chick, then come across an old Indian guy and speak his language.
- Pull a fake mustache off someone and shout, "A-ha!"
- Have a hot towel on my face at a barbershop with a cigar sticking out.
- Dislocate my shoulder to get out of a straitjacket.

- Snap Larry King's suspenders and turn him into a pile of ashes.
- Shout "Not on my watch. . . ."
- Direct a movie called *Awesome* so that entertainment shows will have to refer to me as "*Awesome* director Adam Carolla." Then follow it up with the sequel *Hung Like a Rhino.*
- Drive a car off a pier onto a garbage barge.
- Be stripped of a crown.
- Tell my team to "synchronize watches."
- Dry-shave with a machete.
- Pull down a surgical mask and say, "There's nothing I could do," or beat someone on the chest and shout, "Live, damn you!"
- Box a kangaroo.
- Demand unmarked bills.
- Drape a suit jacket over handcuffs in the front like John Gotti.
- Fend off a Kodiak bear with a torch.
- Pop the locks on an attaché case full of money and slide it across a table.
- Be tied to a chair with a hot chick.
- Have to choose between cutting a red wire and a blue wire.
- Fight someone on top of a moving train.

My biggest regret is that I hear you fart a couple of times after you die and I won't be around to enjoy it and, appropriately enough, laugh my ass off.

CONCLUSION

Thank you for purchasing/borrowing/winning this book at the world's worst charity raffle. No matter how you got it, I appreciate you taking the time to read it. I know that this book covered a lot of ground, from politics to pizza toppings, flying first class to taking ceramics class, homophobia to home improvement. I have many, many more things to say about these and other topics. But that's for the next book. So until then, thank you and *mahalo*.

ACKNOWLEDGMENTS

This book would not be possible without the dedication, wit, and nimble fingers of Mike Lynch. This project would never have become a reality without his involvement. As a matter of fact he's typing this right now. And also my agent, James Babydoll Dixon, and my wife, Lynette, who encouraged me to write this book when I was hell-bent on a coffee table book entitled *Dade County Black Prom, 1977–1985*.

I should also thank my literary agent, Dan Strone, my editor, Suzanne O'Neill, and the whole team from Crown for letting a guy who's never read a book write one.